D0070073

The Marketer's Guide to Public Relations

WILEY SERIES ON BUSINESS STRATEGY
WILLIAM A. COHEN, Series Editor

The Marketer's Guide to Public Relations

How Today's Top Companies Are Using the New PR to Gain a Competitive Edge

THOMAS L. HARRIS

Foreword by Philip Kotler

DISCARDED BY TM

John Wiley & Sons, Inc.

New York • Chichester • Brisbane • Toronto • Singapore

TAYLOR MEMORIAL LRC
CENTENARY COLLEGE
HACKETTSTOWN, NJ 07840

073150

659.2
HAR

In recognition of the importance of preserving what has been
written, it is a policy of John Wiley & Sons, Inc., to have
books of enduring value published in the United States
printed on acid-free paper, and we exert our best efforts
to that end.

Copyright © 1991 by John Wiley & Sons, Inc.

All rights reserved. Published simultaneously in Canada.

Reproduction or translation of any part of this work
beyond that permitted by section 107 or 108 of the
1976 United States Copyright Act without the permission
of the copyright owner is unlawful. Requests for
permission or further information should be addressed to
the Permission Department, John Wiley & Sons, Inc.

This publication is designed to provide accurate and
authoritative information in regard to the subject
matter covered. It is sold with the understanding that
the publisher is not engaged in rendering legal, accounting,
or other professional services. If legal advice or other
expert assistance is required, the services of a competent
professional person should be sought. *From a Declaration
of Principles jointly adopted by a Committee of the
American Bar Association and a Committee of Publishers.*

Library of Congress Cataloging-in-Publication Data

Harris, Thomas L., 1931–
    The marketer's guide to public relations : how today's top
companies are using the new PR to gain a competitive edge / Thomas
L. Harris ; foreword by Philip Kotler.
        p.   cm. — (Wiley series on business strategy)
    Includes bibliographical references and index.
    ISBN 0-471-61885-3
    1. Public relations—Corporations.   2. Marketing—Management.
3. Corporate sponsorship.   I. Title.   II. Series.
    HD59.H276   1991
    659.2—dc20   90-41327

Printed in the United States of America

10 9 8 7 6 5 4 3 2 1

Foreword

The 1990s will mark an era of intense competition, both domestically and globally. Small companies, large companies, and megacorportaions will compete vigorously for the consumer's dollar. To win the consumer's dollar, these companies must first win a share of the consumer's mind and heart. They must know how to build strong consumer awareness and preference.

But in an overcommunicated society, consumers develop communication-avoidance routines. They don't notice print ads; they "tune out" commercial messages. They busy themselves watching videos, working at the computer, going to movies and sports events, walking, running, cooking. Message senders are finding it increasingly difficult to reach the minds and hearts of target customers.

As mass advertising and even target advertising lose some of their cost-effectiveness, message senders are driven to other media. They discover or rediscover the power of news, events, community programs, atmospheres, and other powerful communication modalities. Sooner or later they discover "Marketing Public Relations," the discipline that Tom Harris calls MPR for short.

Marketing public relations is a healthy offspring of its two parents: marketing and public relations. Marketing public relations represents an opportunity for companies to regain a share of voice in a message-satiated society. Marketing public relations not only delivers a strong share of voice to win share of mind and heart; it also delivers a better, more effective voice in many cases. Messages are more effective when they come across as news rather than advertising. Companies capture attention and respect when they sponsor cultural events and contribute money to worthwhile causes.

Tom Harris has written the first book covering the emerging discipline of marketing public relations. He not only shows why marketing public relations helps companies gain competitive advantage but also how it is done by its most sophisticated practitioners. The book is "must" reading for marketing practitioners in their search for new ways to win the minds and hearts of buyers. It is also "must" reading for public relations practitioners who need to understand the special opportunities and problems in becoming an active agent in the marketing mix.

First books on a subject usually leave a lot unanswered. Tom Harris may have not only written the first book on marketing public relations but the "classic."

PHILIP KOTLER
S. C. Johnson & Son Distinguished Professor of International Marketing

J. L. Kellogg Graduate School of Management, Northwestern University

Preface

Ten or so years ago, I prevailed upon some of my colleagues in public relations to contribute some of their success stories to a proposed book about the then emerging but unnamed subspecialty of public relations that supports the marketing of goods and services. The working title was *America's Misunderstood Marketing Medium*. Apparently, the publisher misunderstood not only the medium but the message, and the book was never published.

But the times they are a-changing. Today the subspecialty has a name, or at least a working title—marketing public relations. This book uses the shorthand MPR to label a practice that could hardly be described as misunderstood in the 1990s. The growth of public relations and its acceptance as a valuable, sometimes essential, marketing practice is practically universal. Companies assign public relations staff specialists to their product marketing teams and engage public relations firms to help them get maximum mileage from product introductions, to keep brands prominent throughout the product life cycle, and to defend products at risk.

MPR budgets are growing as marketers recognize that, in an increasingly complex marketplace, the answer to every marketing problem is not always a 15- or 30-second television commercial.

This book is the first to separate the practice of marketing public relations from the general practice of corporate public relations. I am suggesting that a schism is in the making, that marketing public relations will move closer to marketing, and that corporate public relations (CPR) will remain a management function concerned with the company's relationships with all of its publics. Those publics, now often referred to as stakeholders, importantly include consumers and since it is generally recognized that companies should speak with a single voice, MPR and CPR will remain closely allied. This is especially true in situations where markets are blocked by government or community opposition. Still, it is my contention that MPR is both a specialized and increasingly important function that requires full focus on the consumer and those who influence buying behavior.

This is not a how-to book but rather a how-they-do-it book, relating how today's top marketers use MPR. Because of its almost universal use, the choice of case examples is arbitrary and is based on thirty years of personal experience and observations of programs that work. From among dozens of possible examples, I have limited my parameters to MPR as it applies to consumer products. Another volume could have been filled with equally impressive examples of the use of MPR in marketing business-to-business products and services. MPR is also widely used in the growing sector of nonprofit marketing, which is not discussed here. I have limited the discussion to companies, not individuals, although in the instance of highly visible leaders, the two often become inextricably linked.

Some readers may question the inclusion of practice areas that are not specifically assigned to public relations departments or firms by all companies. Special events, sports marketing, and cause-related marketing may, in some companies, be the responsibility of specialized departments and outside production companies, promotion firms, and advertising agencies, but in every instance public relations plays an integral marketing-communications role.

I hope that this first book on the subject will be followed by others that build on the ideas exposed here, contributing to both the practice and the documentation of an exciting new marketing medium.

THOMAS L. HARRIS

Highland Park, Illinois
January 1991

Acknowledgments

Where to begin?

With the nation's news media, I suppose. Throughout this book, the reader will find numerous references to and quotes from newspapers and magazines. These references are given less to explain a particular story than to document the role the media plays in communicating legitimate news about companies and their products to consumers and marketers. The proliferation of television business programs and the vastly expanded coverage of product and marketing news in newspapers and news magazines are proof of the interest of viewers and readers in these subjects. In the introduction to *The Wall Street Journal on Marketing*, Ronald Alsop and Bill Abrams point out that *The Wall Street Journal* began publishing a weekly column about marketing in 1980, amid the growing recognition that marketing was the single biggest challenge facing almost any enterprise. Since that "best of" collection of columns was published in 1986, the *Journal's* coverage has expanded to a "Marketing & Media" page published daily.

The Wall Street Journal, together with those other "national" newspapers *The New York Times* and *USA TODAY*, is quoted frequently, as are a number of major metropolitan dailies. Since coverage in the newsweeklies is the sought-after prize of many an MPR program, quotes from *TIME* and *Newsweek* are intended to verify that a product won recognition on the national news agenda. *Business Week, Advertising Age, ADWEEK,* and *ADWEEK's Marketing Week* were particularly valuable to documenting marketing news and the role of MPR in marketing programs as was the public relations press, particularly *Jack O'Dwyer's Newsletter, O'Dwyer's PR Services Report, Public Relations News* (which has long documented marketing public relations successes in its case histories), *Relate, Public Relations Journal,* and *PR Reporter.*

My colleagues in corporate public relations departments and public relations firms generously provided me with materials and case studies, including their prize-winning entries in the PRSA (Public Relations Society of America) Silver Anvil Awards, IABC (International Association of Business Communicators) Awards, and regional awards such as the Publicity Club of Chicago Golden Trumpets. These companies include: Ford Motor Company, Chrysler Corporation, General Motors, Eastman Kodak, American Express, IBM, Philip Morris, Quaker Oats, General Mills, Pillsbury, Gillette, and NutraSweet.

I also had the benefit of first-hand knowledge from a number of Golin/Harris clients. You will find references throughout the book to such clients as McDonald's, Campbell Soup, DowBrands, Keebler, Pearle Vision Centers, Warner-Lambert, L'eggs, Levi Strauss, Allied Van Lines, Johnson Wax, Midas International, Waste Management, California Avocado Commission, Catfish Institute, and National Food Processors Association.

My thanks to Bill Cantor, author of *Experts in Action* (second edition, 1989) published by Longman, Inc., for permission to include portions of material from my chapter on marketing communications.

Among the public relations, advertising, and sales promotion firms that provided me with information are Ketchum Public Relations; Porter/Novelli; Fleishman-Hillard; Manning, Selvage & Lee; Cohn & Wolfe; Cone Communications; Dorf & Stanton; Creamer Dickson Basford; Rogers & Associates; Miller Communications; Lesnik Public Relations; Burrell Public Relations; FCB Leber Katz; and Einson Freeman.

I want to thank Dan Edelman for all that I learned from him over the years we worked together. His pioneering work through the years opened new vistas for marketing public relations.

I especially thank my partner for the past dozen years, Al Golin. More than any other person, Al proved that good public relations is good for business through his work for McDonald's over more than three decades. His Big Ideas set the pace for the company that has become the model for using public relations to build public trust.

I appreciate the time that Al allowed me to devote to this book. Profuse thanks are also due my colleague Kathy Rand, whose ideas about the theory and practice of marketing public relations pervade this book.

I want to express my appreciation to my secretaries, Noreen Tyson and Janis Martinson, for assembling my badly processed words and illegible scribbles into the coherent book you are about to read.

Thanks to Professor Raymond Ewing, director of the Master's program in corporate public relations at Northwestern University's Medill School of Journalism. Ray has given me the opportunity to teach the first course I know of anywhere in marketing public relations. My graduate students were first exposed to some of the ideas presented in this book.

Special thanks are due to Professor Kerri Acheson, my one-time colleague at Medill, whose keen interest in the subject of marketing public relations provided the impetus for this book.

I am particularly indebted to Professor Philip Kotler of the Kellogg School of Management, one of the world's leading authorities on marketing, whose interest in public relations has greatly influenced not only me but marketers everywhere.

Finally, I want to thank my family. My wife Joie hasn't seen much of me since I began devoting my nights and weekends to this endeavor. Her constant support and encouragement made possible not only this book but whatever success I've achieved in this business. My son Ted, who is writing his second-year graduate-school paper in philosophy at Harvard, graciously shared the Macintosh with me during his vacations at home. I've literally written this book for my son and daughter-in-law, Jim and Lynn, who hold marketing positions with Miller Brewing Company and Quaker Oats, respectively. I hope that young marketing executives like them will find that the book expands their understanding of the role that MPR can play in moving their merchandise.

T.L.H.

Contents

PART *I*

UNDERSTANDING MARKETING PUBLIC RELATIONS

1

The MPR Explosion

○ The Ford Motor Company achieved a 50 percent brand awareness level among consumers and had orders for 146,000 Taurus and Sable automobiles before they were advertised or released for sale, based solely on public relations.

○ Campbell Soup Company's National Soup Month public relations program caused a 36 percent sales increase, the greatest for a one-month period in the company's history.

○ The Cabbage Patch Kids phenomenon was the product not of advertising but of a sophisticated public relations effort that saw the dolls featured on every major TV station and in every newspaper and general-interest magazine in the United States.

○ NutraSweet's announcement of the new fat substitute, Simplesse, achieved 30 percent brand awareness overnight after the story ran on network news and the wire services. The day it was approved by the Food and Drug Administration for use in ice cream desserts, the company was swamped with orders from grocery chains nationwide.

○ Cuisinart annual sales were only a few hundred thousand dollars until a 1975 *Gourmet* article, "The Phenomenal Food Processor," launched a mass hysteria that created a new kitchen appliance category, a new generation of cooking classes, cookbooks, and columns, and more orders than the company could fill. By 1977, the company was selling 250,000 of the premium-priced appliances yearly.

○ Reese's Pieces candy sales increased by 65 percent in the first month following the release of the film *E.T.*, in which the lovable space alien was shown following a trail of the candies.

○ Pillsbury products used in winning Bake-Off recipes register instant sales jumps year after year when the publicity hits.

o Gillette's Sensor Razor sold out within weeks of its introduction because of heavy, worldwide, prelaunch publicity and a single Super Bowl commercial.

o McDonald's served 30,000 Russians on opening day when Moscovites read about "Beeg Mak" and smiling service, instantly making it the company's largest volume store.

The bottom line is that marketing public relations works. That is why so many companies have made major commitments to public relations during the past few years. They range from small companies who cannot afford the high cost of television to major advertisers who recognize the unique place of public relations in the marketing mix.

Herbert M. Baum, President of the North American Division of Campbell Soup Company, says:

> Campbell Soup is a firm believer in building brands. Long-term brand equity, brand-building type of advertising and marketing are absolutely necessary for sustaining the effectiveness of our brands. At the same time, sales promotion, getting the immediate sale, the short-term buck is necessary to stay in the game. The hidden weapon is PR. PR is probably more effective in changing consumer attitudes about products today than advertising. It is easier for consumers to believe a message if it's coming from an independent third party than if you're shouting it in an ad.[1]

His view is echoed by the chairman and CEO of H.J. Heinz Company, Dr. A. J. F. O'Reilly. At his company's 1989 Global Communications Conference, he placed special emphasis on the importance of creative public relations. He told Heinz worldwide executives that advertising "is suffering from the law of diminishing returns" and that "we must think of new unconventional ways of reaching our audiences," citing "our old friend PR" as one of the ways.

The explosive growth of marketing public relations in the 1980s was fueled by the simultaneous recognition of its intrinsic value by corporations and the ability of marketing public relations professionals to devise programs that precisely support marketing strategies.

Philip Kotler, Professor of Marketing at Northwestern University's Kellogg School of Management and author of *Marketing Management*, the world's most widely used marketing textbook, remarks, "Marketing public relations in the future can only go one way: up." He says that "PR is moving into an explosive growth stage because companies realize that mass advertising is no longer the answer" and that organizations are merging PR into marketing, ending a long-standing "love/hate relationship."

Kotler sees a number of current developments that presage a closer working relationship between marketing and public relations in the future.

> Marketing practitioners are very likely to increase their appreciation of PR's potential contributions to marketing the product because they are facing a real decline in the productivity of their other promotional tools. Advertising costs continue to rise while the advertising audience reached continues to decline. Furthermore, increasing advertising clutter reduces the impact of each ad. Sales promotion expenditures continue to climb and now exceed advertising expenditures two to one. Marketers spend money on sales promotion, not out of choice, but out of necessity; middlemen and consumers demand lower prices and deals. Salesforce costs continue to rise, in some cases costing companies over $300 a call. No wonder marketers are searching for more cost-effective promotional tools. . . . Here is where public relations techniques hold great promise. The creative use of news events, publications, social investments, community relations, and so on offers companies a way to distinguish themselves and their products from their competitors.[2]

MARKETERS AFFIRM PR'S EFFECTIVENESS

The increasing awareness and use of public relations are documented in two recent surveys of marketing executives: one was conducted by Tom Duncan, Professor of Marketing at Ball State University, for Golin/Harris Communications; the other, by the management consulting firm of Gilbert, Farlie, Inc., for Hill & Knowlton.

The H&K study polled senior marketing executives at 20 of the top 50 national advertisers.[3] The larger-scale Golin/Harris study surveyed a sample of 286 *Advertising Age* subscribers who hold marketing and advertising positions with client organizations.[4]

Executives of both studies indicated that they were using public relations more than they did five years ago and that they will use it more in the next five. A packaged-goods marketing executive interviewed in the H&K study said, "PR is becoming more and more important. In the next five years, it will become the most important element of the marketing mix."

Two H&K respondents said that PR-dollar increases came specifically from advertising budgets, four said funds were supplemental, and fourteen said the dollars came from overall marketing budgets. Seven of the respondents said that their criterion for determining whether their PR programs were successful was increased sales, five said it was increased awareness, and four said increased market share.

Finally, two-thirds of those surveyed found public relations to be "very cost-effective."

The Golin/Harris–Ball State study was similarly supportive of marketing public relations. Here are the key findings.

1. Marketing public relations was perceived as being effective in a variety of areas that are traditionally the responsibility of advertising.

   o Marketing public relations was thought to be especially effective in building brand awareness and brand knowledge.

   o Even in areas of "increasing category usage" and "increasing brand sales," marketing public relations was seen as potentially effective.

   o Importantly, there were no areas in which the majority of clients said marketing public relations would not be effective.

2. While a majority of respondents said marketing public relations should be a part of the marketing mix, nearly the same number admitted it was not happening.

   o There was strong agreement that advertising and marketing public relations should strategically work together.

   o Marketing public relations was perceived as being more difficult to evaluate than advertising.

   o The potential for marketing public relations was seen as unrealized.

   o In some cases marketing public relations was considered more cost-effective than advertising.

   o The importance of marketing public relations increased in the past five years and was expected to continue to increase. The main reasons given were that marketers are becoming more sophisticated and that marketing public relations:

     —is made cost-effective by increases in media costs;

     —breaks through clutter;

     —complements advertising (increases the credibility of messages);

     —is proving itself.

3. The two areas in which public relations was used most by the sample were "trade/industry" and "consumer/product promotion."

4. For those organizations using outside public relations services (74%), one-third had these services directed by their corporate public relations department and one-half by the advertising or marketing department.

5. Three out of every four companies in the sample used marketing public relations.

6. Those who used marketing public relations used it most for product introduction; the next most common usages were for "complementing advertising and sustaining established brands."

7. Other uses were to build credibility and save money.

8. An increase in the marketing public relations budget was seen as most likely coming from advertising (34%).

9. Budget was the main reason for not using more marketing public relations. The second most limiting factor was staffing/time. Other reasons were that management did not understand/support marketing public relations, that it was difficult to evaluate, and that it was already being used to its fullest extent.

THE MANY USES OF MPR

Beyond the general uses cited in the survey, marketers are discovering a multiplicity of benefits that add value to marketing programs. Among the ways it is used are the following:

- to position companies as leaders and experts
- to build consumer confidence and trust
- to introduce new products
- to revitalize, relaunch, and reposition mature products
- to communicate new benefits of old products
- to promote new uses for old products
- to involve people with products
- to build or maintain interest in a product category
- to cultivate new markets
- to reach secondary markets
- to reinforce weak markets
- to extend the reach of advertising
- to counteract consumer resistance to advertising
- to break through commercial clutter
- to make news before advertising
- to make advertising newsworthy
- to complement advertising by reinforcing messages and legitimizing claims

- to supplement advertising by communicating other product benefits
- to tell the product story in greater depth
- to gain exposure for products that cannot be advertised to consumers
- to gain television exposure for products that cannot be advertised on television
- to increase viewership of sponsored television programs
- to influence opinion leaders
- to gain awareness through other than advertising media
- to test marketing concepts
- to reinforce sales promotion campaigns
- to reach demographically defined markets
- to reach psychographically defined markets
- to identify companies and products with ethnic markets
- to tailor marketing programs to local audiences
- to raise brand awareness through title sponsorships
- to distinguish companies and their products from the competition
- to create new media and new ways to reach consumers
- to win consumer support by identifying companies and brands with causes they care about
- to interpret the impact of emerging issues on the marketplace
- to open communication channels between marketers and groups who could negatively impact achievement of marketing goals
- to communicate marketing decisions in the public interest
- to defend products at risk
- to gain distribution
- to build store traffic
- to generate sales inquiries
- to motivate the sales force
- to win retailer support.

MARKETING PUBLIC RELATIONS COMES OF AGE

There are many signs that marketing public relations has come of age.

1. *Public relations has become a big and profitable business.* Public relations is an $8 billion industry and is growing at an annual rate of around 20 percent. It is estimated that half of all PR expenditures are

billed through public relations firms. During the 1980s, six of the top ten firms were acquired by advertising agencies. Five of the ad agency owners are public companies; they acquired major PR firms not only to offer broader communications services to clients and gain greater access to client top management, but also because PR offers them greater proportionate profit potential. *PR News* says: "The proven power of PR and its cost effectiveness in contrast to advertising motivated the advertising industry to add PR departments to their operations in order to help alleviate its financial woes." Shandwick PLC, the first worldwide, publicly owned public relations company, has become the largest of all PR firms, with annual fee billings of $180 million.

2. *Marketing public relations is the largest and fastest growing segment of a fast growing industry.* A study of the world market for public relations services, conducted in 1989 by Shandwick, estimated that 20 percent of the fee income of public relations firms throughout the world is generated by public relations for consumer products.[5] If industrial (15%), high tech (15%), entertainment (10%), business-to-business (5%), and health/medical (5%) fees are added, 70 percent of the business handled by PR firms is marketing-related, with the remaining 30 percent distributed among corporate, governmental, environmental, and financial billings. However the categories of PR services are broken down, the resounding conclusion is that the preponderance of money spent by client companies with their public relations firms is over-whelmingly devoted to programs that help clients sell their goods and services.

3. *Companies have recognized the growing importance of marketing public relations with bigger budgets and fatter paychecks.* Robert Dilenschneider, president and CEO of Hill & Knowlton, one of the largest worldwide public relations agencies, says the "million-dollar worldwide program, almost unheard of ten years ago, is now experienced with increasing regularity."

Today, talented senior public relations professionals in corporations and public relations firms earn salaries well into six figures. In February 1990, *O'Dwyer's PR Services Report* stated: "More than a dozen PR jobs are open at present with salaries ranging upwards of half a million. It's definitely a seller's market out there today."

Marketing public relations now "leads all public relations disciplines with its rapidly increasing importance and PR marketing skills are in greater demand than ever before," reports a recent survey conducted by the Cantor Concern, a leading recruiting firm in the public relations field.

4. *Public relations is getting increasing interest in the marketing and business media.* A cover story in *Business Week* reported on the effectiveness of PR in "micro marketing." A *Wall Street Journal* lead article suggested an expanded role for PR as the power of network advertising

declines. *Inc.* magazine profiled a PR firm's success in selling bananas, pain relievers, floppy disks, and the Brooklyn Bridge. An article in United Airlines' in-flight magazine proclaimed the 1980s as "the Golden Age of Public Relations."

Perhaps most significant of all was the attention recently paid to public relations in important trade magazines read by marketing executives. On March 13, 1989, *Advertising Age* ran a forum titled "PR on the Offensive." *ADWEEK's Marketing Week*, in a January 16, 1989, cover story on "The New Public Relations," declared that "the new PR is used virtually everywhere," and advised its readers to "stir some PR in your communications mix."

> Public relations used to be advertising's poor relation. Today it's a booming and forward-looking field. . . . Managing the news and creating an ambient mood around a product has become a strategic imperative, not a marketing afterthought. The goal of PR these days is not to amass clips, but instead to win market share. . . . The central doctrine of the new PR is that news about, say, a beer or a drug or a game, can be molded to match a predetermined marketing strategy—just like an ad campaign.[6]

Marketing public relations, as a subset of marketing or as a subset of public relations (depending upon with whom you are speaking), has been predicted to be one of the fastest growing areas in both fields.

5. *The academic community is showing greater interest in public relations.* Universities are responding to the growing demand for business leaders trained in public relations and for public relations practitioners trained in business. Northwestern University broke new ground a few years ago when the Medill School of Journalism pioneered a new Master's program in Corporate Public Relations that combined what was essentially the core of an MBA program with very specialized public relations strategy coursework. There I am teaching what is probably the first graduate course devoted exclusively to the subject of marketing public relations. Northwestern's Kellogg School of Management, one of the nation's most prestigious graduate business schools, now offers a course called "The Corporation, the Media, the Environment." Other business schools are sure to follow this lead.

TOWARD A DEFINITION

The designation *marketing public relations* arose in the 1980s because of the need to distinguish the specialized application of public relations techniques that support marketing from the general practice of public relations.

Marketing public relations has grown rapidly and pragmatically to meet the opportunities of a changing marketplace. In the process, it has borrowed and amalgamated thinking from traditional public relations, marketing, advertising, and research.

The practice preceded a definition of the function. The matter of definition is complicated by the fact that there are as many definitions of both *marketing* and *public relations* as there are textbook authors and industry experts.

The definition of *public relations* has been so elusive that in 1975 the Foundation for Public Relations Research (now the Public Relations Institute) enlisted 65 public relations leaders to sift through 472 different definitions and write one of their own. Here is what they came up with.

> Public relations is a distinctive management function which helps establish and maintain mutual lines of communication, understanding, acceptance and cooperation between an organization and its publics; involves the management of problems or issues; helps management keep informed on and responsive to public opinion; defines and emphasizes the responsibility of management to serve the public interest; helps management keep abreast of and effectively utilize change, serving as an early warning system to help anticipate trends; and uses research and sound and ethical communications techniques as its principal tools.[7]

The sheer length and complexity of the definition reflect the difficulty of defining such a multifaceted field. James Dowling, an eminent public relations leader and president and CEO of Burson-Marsteller, one of the largest public relations agencies in the world, has given up trying to define *public relations* altogether. Rather, he says that "public relations is what public relations people do" and points out that "public relations is almost impossible to define to a nonpublic relations practitioner because it has no context of its own. It is only definable in its relevance to other things."[8]

Marketing public relations can be defined more precisely than the larger concept of public relations because of its relevance to marketing, specifically to helping an organization meet its marketing objectives.

Likewise, *marketing* has been variously defined. Philip Kotler's operational definition is:

> Marketing is the business task of: (1) selecting attractive target markets; (2) designing customer-oriented products and services; and (3) developing effective distribution and communication programs with the aim of producing high consumer purchase and satisfaction and high company attainment of its objectives.[9]

At the Public Relations Colloquium 1989, Kotler noted how public relations helps the company achieve its objectives by "serving as protector and promoter of the company's image among its various publics."

> In carrying out its work, the company will come in contact with numerous publics. Its operations will impact on these different publics. Not surprisingly, some of these publics will seek to place requirements or constraints on the company. These publics will form a view of the company's cooperativeness and civic responsibility. The views of these publics of the company's behavior will affect their behavior toward the company and, therefore, the company's success. Thus, a company's ability to attain its objectives will be affected by the quality of both its marketing work and its public relations work.[10]

In this way, the practice of "good public relations" by the corporation ultimately affects the marketing of its goods and services. A distinction should be drawn, however, between the roles of corporate public relations (CPR) and marketing public relations (MPR).

MARKETING PUBLIC RELATIONS DEFINED

Drawing upon the most frequently used definitions of *public relations* and *marketing* and personal experience, I suggest this working definition of *marketing public relations:*

> Marketing public relations is the process of planning, executing and evaluating programs that encourage purchase and consumer satisfaction through credible communication of information and impressions that identify companies and their products with the needs, wants, concerns and interests of consumers.

HISTORICAL HIGHLIGHTS OF MPR

Perhaps the biggest question raised by the explosion of MPR is "Why did it take so long?" Despite the employment of new tools, techniques, and technology tailored to the times, public relations has proven its marketing effectiveness over the years. On August 26, 1986, a *Wall Street Journal* article entitled "Back to Basics" described public relations as an age-old promotional technique to better reach market segments.

Bernays Brings Home the Bacon

Age-old it is. In the time between the World Wars, Edward Bernays, now 97 years old, the founding father of modern public relations, was responsible for some remarkably successful marketing public relations programs.

Long before the public was concerned with things like cholesterol, fats, and nitrates, he made bacon and eggs America's favorite breakfast. By promoting the health benefits of eating a large breakfast, his efforts greatly increased bacon consumption and his meat-packer client's sales. Bernays also helped United Fruit Company boost banana sales by publicizing a study that showed that eating fruit helps fight cystic fibrosis.

Before the surgeon general's warning that cigarette smoking is hazardous to health, Bernays made it socially acceptable for women to smoke in public by arranging for debutantes to smoke in New York's Easter Parade. (Decades later, when the health issue arose, he helped get cigarette advertising off television.)

Before the invention of paperback books and their mass distribution at newsstands and supermarkets, he convinced the country's builders to build bookshelves in new homes so that they could be filled with hardcover books. His client: America's booksellers.

Another Bernays brainchild put a bar of Ivory soap in the hands of American schoolchildren. For years, the fad of soap carving, which he created, moved bars of Ivory by the millions.

Bernays could arguably also be called "the father of event marketing." He pulled off the publicity coup of the century for his client, General Electric, in celebration of the fiftieth anniversary of the electric light bulb. He called it the "Golden Jubilee of Light" and described it as the greatest tribute ever paid to any living man. The man, of course, was Thomas Edison, and for this event, Bernays moved Edison's boyhood home from Menlo Park, New Jersey, to Henry Ford's Dearborn Village in Michigan and recreated the great moment in history. When an NBC radio announcer gave the signal, people all over the world switched on their electric lights, adding their personal tribute to those of President Herbert Hoover, Henry Ford, Orville Wright, Madame Curie, J. P. Morgan, and John D. Rockefeller, all of whom were assembled for this auspicious occasion.

Bread, Deluxe

Although he would have eschewed the description public relations counselor for press agent, Benjamin Sonnenberg represented some of the most important personalities and businesspeople of the mid-20th century. His corporate clients included Philip Morris, Texaco, and Lever Brothers.

How he also helped a friend and neighbor named Margaret Rudkin is described in his biography *Always Live Better Than Your Clients.*[11] It relates how Mrs. Rudkin began selling her homemade bread during the depths of the Great Depression, baking the loaves in an old relic of a stove. When she and her husband needed a new one, they called

Sonnenberg for help. He obliged, and in return for the stove and his help in publicizing the bread, the Rudkins insisted that Sonnenberg have a one-third interest in their company.

Among Sonnenberg's accomplishments was the placement of the article "Bread, de Luxe" in a 1939 *Reader's Digest.* It told how Mrs. Rudkin used only the finest ingredients in her old-fashioned, home-baked bread and kneaded the dough by hand, and how she had built a quarter-of-a-million-dollar business on word-of-mouth advertising.

At the time the article appeared, production was 25,000 loaves of bread a week; three months later, it had doubled. The increased volume caused the company to turn other buildings on the farm over to bread-baking and to double the number of employees.

Mrs. Rudkin said,

> The mail which resulted from the story seemed to me to be absolutely staggering. By the time a month had gone by, I had received 3,000 letters and had to employ two secretaries because each letter had to be answered individually due to the fact that most of them enclosed money or checks ordering bread to be sent to all sorts of addresses, not only in the United States, but actually in Turkey, South Africa, Canada, England, etc.

The name of her company was Pepperidge Farm, and when it was sold to Campbell Soup Company in 1961 for $28 million, Sonnenberg got one-third of it in cash and stock.

Carl Byoir Brings Back Florida

Carl Byoir, another PR pioneer, and founder of a public relations firm that was the country's largest for many years, could be viewed in today's terms as a founder of both destination and nonprofit marketing public relations.

In pre-Castro days, Byoir conceived the idea of promoting Cuba as a winter resort for Americans and is widely credited with bringing South Florida out of the Great Depression and putting the resort business in the black. Among his innovations was a winter-long program built around a super sports program, including open and amateur golf tournaments, tennis championships, a national horse show, a national dog show, and a national Olympic Stars Aquatic Meet. All of these then-unique events were designed to capture headlines in the national press—and they did, attracting droves of vacationers to Florida.

Byoir has been described as a genius of fund-raising public relations. He was called on by President Franklin D. Roosevelt to promote his favorite charity, the National Foundation for Infantile Paralysis. Byoir came up with the idea of using the President's birthday to run fund-raising birthday balls across the country. Over 6,000 events were organized in 1934, raising over $1 million for the fight against infantile paralysis. In subsequent years, the birthday balls continued to enjoy the success of the first one.

Public Relations Makes a Company

No less an authority than former Lorillard president Curtis Judge told me that his company was "made by public relations." It all started for Lorillard with a two-part series, "The Facts Behind Filter-Tip Cigarettes," which appeared in the July and August 1957 issues of *Reader's Digest.* The articles analyzed tar filtration for all leading brands of cigarettes and found that Kent's then-new "Micronite" filter provided the most effective filtration.

Kent had never made the big sales league until the stories ran, but that August *The Wall Street Journal* reported, "Kent sales have reportedly jumped 500 percent lately—in the wake of *Reader's Digest* articles commending its filter."

Management consultant Chet Burger explained the Kent experience this way:

> It was a strong endorsement that Kent cigarettes had less tar and nicotine content than other brands. It came at a time when the cancer scare was under widespread discussion. And it was the editors of the *Reader's Digest* who published the statement, not the manufacturer of the cigarette. Since similar product claims had been widely advertised previously, it is a fair conclusion that many of the public believed the editors of the *Reader's Digest* when they would not believe the manufacturer. The editors were an independent, respected source; the manufacturer had a self-interest.[12]

MPR Makes a Market

In 1963, the 3M Company formulated a marketing strategy that would put one of the company's overhead projectors in every classroom in America. 3M announced its Assistance Grant to Education program, which would award $3,000 worth of its visual communications equipment to each of 500 schools, selected on the basis of written proposals detailing plans for use of the equipment.

The response was astonishing: 150,000 schools, more than one out of every ten eligible schools in the United States, submitted proposals! 3M gave away $1.5 million worth of equipment, which the company later admitted exceeded the total sale of visual products for the previous year.

The grants program was an investment that paid stunning dividends. Supported by a skillful grassroots public relations strategy, the program reached hundreds of thousands of teachers, principals, and school board members and caused them to think about how they would use 3M overhead projectors in their classrooms. Five hundred schools received them free, but thousands of other schools now recognized their value as a teaching tool, and the orders rolled in.

When the company shifted its marketing focus to the business market, an equally innovative—and equally successful—marketing public relations program was created on the concept of how to run more effective business meetings. The program was introduced at a New York press event featuring Rudy Vallee and other members of the cast of the then-current hit musical, *How to Succeed in Business Without Really Trying*. 3M became positioned as the business-meeting expert and the 3M overhead projector as the indispensable ingredient for running effective meetings. The program is still going strong decades later.

I supervised the PR agency effort for Daniel J. Edelman, Inc., and the 3M experience, more than any other, convinced me of the limitless potential of marketing public relations.

2

Marketplace Forces Driving MPR in the 1990s

In the 1990s, marketers will have a formidable task not experienced by their counterparts in the glory days of marketing. The surefire marketing methods of the 1950s, 1960s, and 1970s began to break down in the 1980s. The world changed so rapidly and fundamentally that marketers have been forced to retrench and reevaluate. The tried simply may no longer be true.

The marketing job is much tougher now than ever before; executives responsible for developing marketing plans must find ways to break through a climate of consumer resistance, indifference, and clutter. They must deliver a more imaginative message with credibility and impact.

"The wise advertiser is looking for new ways of getting across his message, and one of them is public relations," says veteran public relations counselor Daniel J. Edelman.

The environment of the 1990s and beyond will bring to corporations new challenges that cannot be addressed with the same old rules. The new marketplace offers opportunities for public relations to play an ever larger role in determining how the business community deals with its publics, markets its products, and interacts with a more global culture.

Public relations and marketing are being driven into a closer relationship by the same change factors that have revolutionized the very nature of business in the United States and the world.

THE MASS MARKET SPLINTERS

The mass market, as it was once known, is becoming a distant memory. Many new buzzwords have surfaced as firms grapple with the new diversity: "demassified market," "splintered market," "fragmented market," "niche marketing," and "micromarketing" (the splintering of consumer markets into segments defined by geographics, demographics, and psychographics).

The population has changed, necessitating a change in marketing. With the demographic shifts have come attitudinal shifts. The conspicuous consumers who characterized the "Me" generation have diminished, and older, more sophisticated shoppers with a desire for quality and diversity have emerged. Consumers are infinitely less brand-loyal, perhaps because of time and energy constraints or because there are so many choices open to them. The sophistication level of consumers has grown to a point where they no longer receive, much less believe, everything that is in the ad message.

Because of its credibility, public relations is well positioned to address an ever increasingly diverse population, and it is ideally suited to reach a much more sophisticated consumer.

TECHNOLOGY AND THE INFORMATION EXPLOSION

In 1982, in the book *Megatrends,* John Naisbitt described the shift from an industrial society to an "information society" and predicted that innovations in communications and computer technology would accelerate the pace of change by collapsing the information float—the amount of time information spends in the communication channel between sender and receiver. The United States has become an information-based society and a service economy. The mass media have changed, with television outlets proliferating and a profusion of new media covering an endless array of special interests. The consequent clutter has raised concern about how much information can be assimilated by the average consumer.

Technology has not only made the job of public relations more important, it has also revolutionized the way that public relations is practiced and given it more significance in the day-to-day business of business.

The New York Times has called the 1980s the "Age of Speed."[1] The number of telephones, including cordless and cellular, doubled in 20 years. They are found almost everywhere, from in-flight airliners to the family car. Today there are 6 million fax machines in use, instantly transmitting documents anywhere in the world where there is a fax machine to receive them. Not only words, but computer-generated pictures are sent by ubiquitous personal computers. VCRs give television viewers control over what they watch and when they watch it. And cable TV delivers news 24 hours a day.

The new media channels have given public relations greater opportunity to reach target markets faster and with more impact. Just as it took television to boost the advertising industry beyond anything that could hardly have been imagined even 50 years ago, so has every new development in communications technology, from cable TV to satellite to personal-computer and fax transmissions, stimulated the growth of public relations.

INCREASED COMPETITION

Managing the new business environment is becoming a greater challenge. Increased competition, from both U.S. and international sources, has changed the way that marketers do business. Companies are able to create and imitate successful products, offering consumers more alternatives than ever before. To be profitable in the 1990s, a company must use all available weaponry, including public relations, in what has increasingly become marketing warfare.

Bob Dilenschneider of Hill & Knowlton characterizes the change in marketing strategy this way:

> Marketing is indeed warfare intended to win consumer awareness and commitment. When network TV could deliver more than 90% of the homes in prime time, it was the weapon of choice. We have now entered an era of *strategic* marketing, and the choices are different. Advertising remains an important, but no longer an overriding, element of the marketing mix . . . and public relations has sharply ascending importance to successful marketing.[2]

THE DECLINE OF NETWORK ADVERTISING

While still the most persuasive advertising medium available to marketers, television is experiencing a radical transformation. The three networks that have owned American audiences since the advent of commercial television no longer dominate the medium. The combined audience share of NBC, ABC, and CBS was less than 70 percent in 1988, and the decline shows no signs of abating. The concern of the Big Three and their new bottom-line-focused corporate parents was tellingly revealed when they disputed the audience figures of A. C. Nielsen Company, the long accepted source of TV audience information. When Nielsen reported a 6 to 7 percent drop in people watching network television during the first quarter of 1990, the networks declared their lack of faith in the Nielsen figures and announced that they would substitute their own audience measurement system.

The television universe is rapidly expanding. A new commercial network, the Fox network, is attracting viewers away from the Big Three—2 of its shows were among the top 20 in 1989–90. Independent television stations that offer popular reruns and other syndicated programming have won 18 percent of the prime-time audience. The greatest threat to the networks, however, is cable TV, which now reaches more than half of the country's homes or almost four times as many as it reached a decade ago. By 1989 it had captured 20 percent of the prime-time audience and its audience is increasing geometrically. Advertisers spent $2 billion on "cable" in 1989, a whopping 30 percent increase over the previous year.

The proliferation of channels not only offers consumers a wide spectrum of choices but also gives advertisers a wide array of alternative opportunities to reach defined market segments more efficiently. Cable channels devoted to news, sports, arts and entertainment, science and nature, music videos, humor, and movies enable advertisers to reach targeted demographic and psychographic audiences more efficiently. While reducing costs and avoiding the waste of mass television, the sheer variety of choices puts greater demands on marketers.

Some audiences, however,—those viewing pay-cable and public television channels—are still unavailable to advertisers altogether.

The remote control device now used by three-quarters of TV-set owners has altered viewer behavior and has led to "zapping" commercials and "zipping" from channel to channel to sample the spectrum of available programming and/or avoid commercials, a practice that has become known as "grazing." Recent studies showed that half the remote users are frequent channel switchers.

More has been learned in recent years about consumers' ability and readiness to psychologically, as well as physically, zap nonessential communications. The information was no surprise. Consumers are bombarded with an overwhelming clutter of commercial messages. Depending upon which study is being quoted, research estimates that consumers are exposed to an estimated 50,000 messages a year per household.

The total effect of this transformation is that network television, the old reliable of advertising, can no longer be regarded as the only way, the best way, or, in some cases, even the right way to reach consumers.

The Impact of the VCR

Share-of-time competition from a limitless choice of prerecorded video cassettes offering movies, music videos, and instructions on every subject from good sex to good golf to good soufflés has cut into commercial television viewing.

Today 64 percent of American homes have at least one VCR and home viewing of rented movies is estimated at more than one a week. This has caused a number of companies to adopt an "If you can't beat them, join them" attitude and to run their commercials on movie videos. Pepsi-Cola started it by sponsoring *Top Gun*; Chrysler followed with *Platoon*, complete with a patriotic message from Chairman Lee Iaccoca;

and Downy continued the trend with the 50th-anniversary video of *The Wizard of Oz.*

Commercials on video cassettes are not immune to zapping. A recent Nielsen Home Video Index poll indicated that about two-thirds of the nation's VCR owners usually zap through commercials placed on movie videos. In 1990, Mitsubishi Electric Corporation began marketing a video cassette recorder that automatically edits out commercials when it tapes most movies broadcast on television.

Rising Television Advertising Costs

The new uncertainty of network television is rising simultaneously with the cost of television time. The average cost of a 30-second commercial in a choice prime-time spot is now $185,000. Many advertisers have resorted to 15-second spots, which must necessarily foreshorten the product-benefit message and depend more on building brand image. Forty percent of all network spots are now only 15 seconds.

A decade ago, a $2 million television budget was considered minimal. Today, according to some advertising experts, the acceptable minimum, is closer to $8 million to $10 million. To start with, the cost of producing a nationally broadcast commercial has tripled in the past decade to an average of $196,000 in 1989.

The turmoil in television advertising has important implications and creates enormous opportunities for marketing public relations. *The New York Times* states:

> Madison Avenue grew and flourished by selling mass-produced goods to mass audiences through mass media. But the nation's consumer market is not what it once was and advertising agencies are adapting only fitfully to a profound change: the splintering of the market into hundreds of small markets and the development of new ways of communicating to them. To tell consumers about the hundreds of new brands of cereals and dozens of new toothpastes, America's largest companies are grasping for new ways to communicate with people who are paying far less attention than they once did to 30-second network-television commercials.[3]

Keith Reinhard, chairman of DDB Needham and one of the advertising industry's most innovative thinkers, believes that advertisers must become more responsive to consumers' patterns of receiving information. "The consumer is not a TV viewer or a radio listener or a magazine reader. She has her own network."

The high cost of television time has eliminated it as an option for many advertisers. Many of these companies have taken advantage of the persuasive power of television, choosing to reach television audiences through the use of public relations. A skillfully executed PR placement can communicate more product information than an abbreviated

15-second commercial. Not only can the message be lengthier, but because it is broadcast in the context of programming, it also has a credibility that the advertising message may lack.

The Shift in Promotional Spending

The high cost and reduced efficiency of television and other measured advertising traditionally used by marketers have caused a dramatic shift in promotional spending in recent years. Robert J. Coen, senior vice president of McCann-Erickson Worldwide and the most respected forecaster in the business, predicted late in 1989 that the single-digit growth experienced by television since 1984 would continue in the first year of the new decade and that advertising would grow only 6.2 percent in 1990. Sales promotion is growing at twice that rate, while public relations is experiencing double-digit growth.[4]

Today, only one-third of total spending is in measured media, that is, television, radio, newspapers, and magazines. The remaining two-thirds is channeled into promotional and nonmeasured media spending. Veronis, Suhler & Associates estimates that $103.5 billion was spent in a recent year on promotional spending, including point of purchase and display, meetings and conventions, premiums and incentives, trade shows and exhibits, promotional advertising, and coupon redemption. This compares to $73.5 billion in measured media and $44.8 billion in direct mail and other nonmeasured media.

Despite the switch to promotion, recent studies indicate that overuse of some techniques may be counterproductive. The glut of contests and sweepstakes is "more annoying than enticing to most consumers," according to an exclusive survey conducted by the Gallup Organization for *Advertising Age*. The poll found that most adults do not bother to enter these contests and two-thirds say there are simply too many.[5]

ADVERTISING UNDER ATTACK

Shrinking profit margins are causing companies to take a harder look at their marketing costs. John Philip Jones, chairman of the advertising department at the Newhouse School of Public Communications at Syracuse University and author of a recent, much-discussed book, *Does It Pay to Advertise?*, says that, for many companies, the best way to realize a future profit increase is to "try to use less advertising because any reduction of advertising goes straight to the bottom line."[6]

The effect of leveraged buyouts (LBOs) and mergers has also adversely affected marketing spending. Companies defending against LBOs have to operate lean and mean, while those that have been taken over must cut costs to reduce the debt incurred with the LBO. Almost immediately after being taken over by Kohlberg Kravis Roberts in the largest LBO in history, RJR Nabisco began to slash its advertising budgets for all of its brands, eliminating advertising for some altogether.

In their effort to reach target customers more efficiently and effectively, marketers are increasingly moving from mass marketing into micromarketing, using new and specialized media, reaching consumers in the store, working closely with retailers to develop special promotions, and using event sponsorship and other public relations techniques to reach specialized, local, or ethnic markets. The link between advertising and sales, once accepted as gospel, is now being questioned by researchers.

Consumers maintain a healthy skepticism about advertising. A recent Roper Organization report reveals that 74 percent of consumers say ads encourage unnecessary purchases; 69 percent believe advertising increases prices; and 69 percent say ads encourage people to use products that are bad for them. In a report to the Advertising Federation Convention in 1990, Alex Kroll, chairman and chief executive officer of Young & Rubicam Inc., said that only 16 percent of consumers think most television and magazine advertising is useful and informative and fewer than 27 percent find advertising in newspapers useful. He called for business to create advertising "that is more useful and helpful."

Advertising in the 1990s faces yet another threat—the threat of taxation and regulation. In recent years, legislation has been introduced in 28 states that would restrict or increase the cost of media advertising. In 1990, there were over 30 pending bills in Congress and almost 400 pieces of state legislation that would restrict advertising. Other bans and limitations sought by some consumer groups and legislators, including those on the content of beer, alcohol, and tobacco advertising, are very real threats to the advertising industry. Concern about these issues was reflected in a panel discussion sponsored by the Advertising Club of New York on the topic "Advertising: An Endangered Species?" in 1990. According to *The New York Times*, it was "the largest Ad Club function in recent memory."

TV Effectiveness Challenged

Marketers of the 1990s may be faced with a problem even more basic than the decline of network television: the challenge to the long-held article of faith that television advertising works.

The research of Gerard Tellis, a University of Iowa professor, has sent shock waves throughout the advertising community. Tellis uses a sophisticated statistical model to analyze data from store checkout scanners. His work tracks consumer purchases against exposure to advertising and promotion.

This new field of "single source" research is in its infancy and at the time of this writing has been used to measure only toilet paper and detergent purchases in Eau Claire, Wisconsin. Tellis's conclusion in both categories as reported in *The Wall Street Journal* was, "TV exposure has a minimal effect, which is difficult to find at all."

According to the *Journal:*

> His research is still in the early stages, but its impact—particularly if its conclusions are duplicated by other studies—could be devastating. TV advertising accounted for 22% of the $118.3 billion spent on U.S. advertising last year (1988). It is by far the most popular, and most expensive, advertising medium there is. It has also long been thought to be the most effective. Research showing otherwise could reshape the advertising industry.[7]

John O'Toole, president of the American Association of Advertising Agencies (4As), responds to the question "Does advertising really work?" by citing the necessity for "value added" if a product is to succeed in competitive categories or global markets.

> Then there is the empirical evidence all around us. Companies that believe in and invest in advertising own the brands that lead in their categories. Share of voice in these categories almost always corresponds to share-of-market. When it doesn't, the power of the advertising idea is what influences ranking.

O'Toole defends advertising, in answer to those who "would like to believe that promotions that move goods into stores are an inexpensive substitute for advertising that moves goods out."[8] The advertising industry is striking back at its critics by doing what it does best, running ads extolling the virtues of advertising. The ads cite a Strategic Planning Institute study that the 4As says proves that advertising doubles the advertiser's return on investment. Furthermore, the ads state that brands that advertise much more than their competitors average a return on investment of 32 percent, while brands that advertise much less than their competitors average only a 17 percent return on investment.

MPR in the Mix

Nevertheless, marketers must determine what combination of advertising and other promotional elements will move goods in and out, weighing short-term sales objectives against the longer-term brand-building considerations. Marketing public relations is a promotional option that rounds out the marketing mix and adds value to the advertising campaign. While it cannot substitute for advertising, it can make advertising work harder.

Steven H. Lesnik, CEO of Lesnik Public Relations, believes that while

> advertising and public relations have the same purposes, public relations is the more multi-dimensional, more sophisticated discipline. That's why in this increasingly complex, commercial, social and political world, heavily dominated by instantaneous communications and by simultaneous but segmented public and private decision making on an unprecedented scale, advertising is in decline and public relations is on the rise. I believe that during the coming decade, PR will eclipse advertising in usefulness in many areas where organizations formerly depended exclusively on advertising. . . . I also believe the subtlety of PR has often proven more persuasive in an educated and enlightened age than the debilitating directness of advertising.[9]

H&K's Bob Dilenschneider points out that product clutter, information clutter, life-style clutter, and new advertising fee structures have all shattered what he has labeled "the three great myths of advertising."

> The first myth is that advertising professionals are very adept at measuring advertising effectiveness in terms of shelf movement and sales. Ad industry leadership is on record saying that the industry just now hopes to get a true measure of advertising effectiveness.
> The second shattered myth is that advertisers have a single, dependable system for explaining how consumers behave. We know that consumers learn, feel and do; but no one seems quite sure in which order these things happen. How can you buy mass persuasion without a dependable behavioral model?
> The third myth is that advertising goals are stated in terms of shelf movement and bottom line. More and more, ad goals are couched in psychological terms like awareness, perception, attitude and intention.
> In sum, advertising is acting more and more like what marketing PR has been accused of being for decades.[10]

Procter & Gamble as Micromarketer

A cover story in *Business Week* noted, "Rather than wagering big bucks in hopes of producing one boffo TV ad that will quickly boost sales, micromarketers spread their bets on lots of different efforts, each of which may pay off in small increments."[11] The article cited Procter & Gamble (P&G), the longtime leader in packaged-goods marketing and an apostle of network advertising, which has not only become a major sponsor of cable and syndicated television and other measured media, but is also using a variety of other media including radio, movie video cassette sponsorship, and specialized magazines, including those distributed exclusively to doctors for their waiting rooms.

P&G is also employing public relations for a number of its brands. Pampers changes 80,000 diapers a year at mobile Baby Care Centers at state and county fairs across the country. Pepto-Bismol sponsors a chili cooking contest, Coast soap a sing-in-the-shower contest, and Crisco an American pie contest. All are designed to generate publicity and word-of-mouth advertising, as are sponsorships of a hydroplane by Jif peanut butter and Pringles potato chips and a race car by Tide. Fourteen P&G brands joined together to sponsor a variety of events and sample visitors to Carnaval Miami.

BACK TO PR BASICS

The Wall Street Journal pointed out in the title of a front-page story that advertisers are trying age-old promotions, switching to direct mail, coupons, "and PR ploys."[12]

The story related that B. F. Goodrich spends 40 percent of its marketing budget on events such as local auto shows—sponsoring racers, dispensing technical advice, and putting up prize money. AT&T tries to reach its corporate customers by sponsoring the sports they favor: golf (the AT&T Pebble Beach National Pro-Am Golf Tournament) and tennis (the AT&T Tennis Challenge).

The article also noted that Kraft is using PR to popularize bagels nationally and quoted Joel D. Weiner, then Kraft's executive vice president of marketing, on the reason for introducing Lender's Bagels at a press party at New York's "21" Club: "So that the press would begin to pick up stories about bagels moving from being an ethnic food to being an American food."

The *Journal* piece noted: "At its best, PR can work better than advertising," pointing to the now-classic Cabbage Patch Kids introduction.

The article remarked on the cost advantage of public relations: "A PR budget of $500,000 is considered huge, while an ad budget that size is considered tiny"—and predicted that PR "is expected to be used increasingly for consumer goods."

ADVERTISING AGENCIES ACQUIRE PUBLIC RELATIONS

While the dollars spent on public relations will likely continue to be dwarfed by advertising expenditures, PR's double-digit growth has certainly not been lost on advertising agencies, large and small. While small agencies attempt to offer full services, including public relations, to clients, the giants have transformed the public relations agency business by acquiring most of the largest PR firms.

The reasons for these acquisitions were:

1. The perceived need for a full array of services matching competitive agencies;
2. The desire to provide one-stop shopping to clients, capturing business that was going elsewhere;
3. A recognition of both the growth rate and profit potential of public relations; and
4. The desire to take the opportunity that public relations offers to get closer to client top management.

Hill & Knowlton and Ogilvy & Mather Public Relations are now both owned by WPP Group; Burson-Marsteller, by Young & Rubicam; The Rowland Company, by Saatchi & Saatchi; Porter/Novelli and Doremus Public Relations, by Omnicom; and Manning, Selvage & Lee, by D'Arcy Masius Benton & Bowles. Ketchum Public Relations has always been an integral part of Ketchum Communications.

Some of the advertising-agencies-turned-communications-conglomerates are reporting that "nontraditional" subsidiaries, that is, public relations, sales promotion, and direct marketing, now contribute from one-quarter to one-third of their total revenues and an even greater percentage of profit. That is why the mega agencies aggressively promote the total communications, or one-stop-shopping concept, to their clients. Under such labels as "The Whole Egg" by Young & Rubicam and "Orchestration" by Ogilvy & Mather, agencies are making every effort to cross-sell all of their services, traditional and nontraditional, by convincing clients that a communications supermarket provides added value through better integration.

EXPANDING MEDIA OPPORTUNITIES

The proliferation of media options has greatly complicated advertising decision making, but it offers tremendous opportunities for public relations. These opportunities could hardly have been imagined a few decades ago, when the mass-circulation general magazines that had dominated Americans' reading, like LIFE, Look, Collier's, and The Saturday Evening Post, found it impossible to compete with television and ceased to exist. Their extinction eliminated a major outlet for product publicity. Network television owned 90 to 95 percent of the television audience a decade ago. It was dominated by sitcoms and soap operas that offered few opportunities for product exposure. As a result, public relations activity was largely directed to daily newspapers.

Opportunities in Television

Contrast the television situation of 10 years ago with today's. Now the 650 network-affiliated stations attract 59 percent of the total television audience. Independent commercial stations, whose number about doubled to 379 from 1983 to 1988, account for 24 percent of total television viewing. Commanding another 11 percent are 54 advertiser-supported cable networks, while pay-cable accounts for 6 percent.

The fragmentation of the television audience has wide implications for marketing public relations. The options for exposure have been increased numerically, and the changing nature of television programming has led to greatly expanded opportunities. Independents and cable have all expanded time slots for reality-based programming, as have affiliates in nonnetwork time. Inexpensive-to-produce, nonscripted programs, particularly talk shows that command large audiences, are made to order for guests to discuss product-related subjects. The cable networks have opened major opportunities for marketing public relations. This is particularly true of CNN (Cable News Network) which created 24-hour news coverage, one of the most important developments in journalism of the 1980s. CNN and ESPN (Entertainment and Sports Network) are seen in virtually all 55 million cable households. Moreover, "CNN World Report" appears in 7 million households abroad and in rooms in 200,000 hotels outside of the United States. FNN (Financial News Network), the major business and money channel reaching 33 million households, and its new competitor CNBC (Consumer News and Business Channel) from NBC are important new outlets for product news.

Since advertising on local news programming is the major source of station income, news programming has been extended with noon news, afternoon news, and expanded early evening news. With more time available, stations are supplementing hard news coverage with more "lighter side of the news" interviews and features. A company-sponsored guest preparing a recipe on the noon news or a brand-sponsored event covered on the evening news is not unusual.

So pervasive are MPR product placements in television today that *Advertising Age* commissioned Northwestern University's Medill School of Journalism to find out how many "free plugs" occur during the average broadcast day. The magazine noted that TV programs are peppered with "mentions of products by talk show guests, corporate logos superimposed behind newscasters' heads to illustrate a news story, signage or labels visible during dramas."[13]

Students viewed tapes of consecutive 24-hour-broadcast days of each of the Big Three networks, recording every brand-mention they heard. In a single day of programming, they found 818 instances of a recognizable product or mention of a brand or corporate name. News programs accounted for 360 (44 percent) of the brand-name inclusions; variety shows had 199 mentions; and news features, 117. The study also showed that the greatest number of mentions of products and brands came during the early morning news programs, that is, NBC's "Today," ABC's "Good Morning America," and "CBS This Morning."

Opportunities in Radio

Changes in the radio industry are also benefiting marketing public relations. Once predominantly a national medium, radio is now very much a local medium. There were 10,244 licensed radio stations in the United States in 1988, according to the *Veronis, Suhler & Associates Television and Cable Fact Book;* 4,902 were AM stations and 5,342 were FM stations.

While there are opportunities on all stations, the trend has been for FM stations to program music because of its greater fidelity and availability of stereo. AM radio is increasingly becoming a news, sports, and talk medium, offering abundant opportunities for guests to deliver product-related messages. Radio interviews tend to be longer than television interviews and often incorporate listeners' call-in segments, which can extend both the guest's time and commercial opportunities. Radio also offers a unique opportunity for trade-for-mention contests and promotions, in which very commercial product messages can be traded for product giveaways and contest prizes.

While not available for advertising, public radio receives support not only from listeners but also from corporations who wish to reach upscale audiences by identifying with such quality programming as National Public Radio's news programs—"Morning Edition," "Weekend Edition," and "All Things Considered"—which reach 5 million listeners a week. These and other network and local public radio programs also offer opportunities for coverage of sponsored events and spokesperson interviews.

Opportunities in Print

Trends in newspaper publishing favor marketing public relations. Despite the much publicized decline in afternoon newspapers, the total number of daily and Sunday newspapers is increasing: 1,650 daily and 838 Sunday newspapers are now published in the United States. Sunday newspapers offer special opportunities to reach readers who have more time to read on weekends, as well as those who do not usually read daily newspapers.

Because they contain more advertising, Sunday papers have more editorial space to fill. The trend has been to include more feature material, opening up increased public relations placement opportunities.

Marketing consultants have influenced daily newspapers to include more shorter, lighter articles and to publish life-style sections. *USA Today,* heavily influenced by television news style, has become a *very* major outlet for public relations material, including new-product introductions, sponsored events, and surveys. The proliferation of weekly suburban, community, and special-interest newspapers increases the number of print-media options that figure in many a marketing public relations plan. Weeklies offer an additional benefit in that they stay in the house and are read throughout the week.

The Magazine Boom

Product exposure in consumer magazines is of immeasurable value to marketers. Many a product has been pulled through the distribution system by consumers who demand the product from their retailer because they read about it in a favorite magazine or heard about it from someone else who did.

In the past decade, some 2,800 new magazines were introduced in the United States, 584 in 1989 alone. The *Veronis, Suhler & Associates 1989 Communications Industry Forecast* attributed the high number of magazines to increased consumer demand for specialized editorial content: "Magazine titles have proliferated as a result of publishers targeting their product to niche audiences and special interests. The industry's ability to segment its market to reflect the changing trends and interests of society has facilitated the growth of consumer magazines."

The implications for public relations are vast. Opportunities to reach consumers in publications focused to their particular interests have exploded. Cosmetic and fashion marketers have long known the value of editorial exposure in the fashion books. Carmakers have aggressively sought the editorial endorsement of *Motor Trend* and *Car and Driver.* Travel-destination marketers now have a half-dozen monthly publications, including *Travel & Leisure* and *Condé Nast Traveler,* available to portray their destinations in words and four-color pictures to well-heeled travelers.

The advent of the computer has given rise to a major new category of consumer magazine. The typical airport newsstand offers more than a dozen titles like *PC World, PC Magazine,* and *PC Resource* to computer buffs. Users of Apple's Macintosh computer even have their own magazines, *MacWorld* and *MacUser.* Like the carmakers, high-tech hardware and software companies value, and eagerly seek, the editorial endorsement of these publications for their products.

The list goes on and on, niche by niche, providing news, features, pictures, and product reviews to eager readers and influencing their purchasing decisions. Following the success over the past 20 years of city and state magazines and regional publications like *Southern Living* and *Sunset,* new regional magazines devoted to special-interest subjects have begun to appear.

Another development certain to grow in the 1990s is the computerized process known as "selective binding." Based on subscriber demographic information, computers are now able to instruct binding machines to include special sections based on the individual reader's demographic profile.

Whittle Communications pioneered the so-called captive audience market with its Special Reports, which are distributed for reading in the waiting rooms of 19,000 doctor's offices. Whittle and traditional publishers have created single-sponsor magazines like a special *TIME* magazine on photojournalism for Eastman Kodak, a Mickey Mouse birthday magazine for Walt Disney Company, and a *Money* magazine financial guide for Citibank's retail banking customers. Kraft General Foods will give away 5.5 million copies of its 92-page "Holiday Guide" magazine produced by *Family Circle* in supermarkets during the 1990–91 holiday season.

Publishers have also begun to offer magazines on videotape, hoping to reach heavy VCR users at home—and away, as portable VCRs catch on. Hearst Corporation is developing a video version of *Esquire* to play on video terminals in major airports.

Business and trade magazines also offer valuable opportunities for marketers to reach the trade. There were 2,775 business magazines published in 1988. As with consumer magazines, new titles have been added as new niches emerge and grow.

Marketers can effectively employ MPR to reach retail decision makers through articles about new products, new promotions, new sizes, new packaging, new store displays, new advertising, and new public relations programs in trade publications. Retail buyers, whether at the headquarters, regional, or store level, read the key trade books to keep up on what is new in their product category. A feature story on a successful promotion, or a byline by a vendor's marketing director, can also influence the buyer's decision to stock the item and the manufacturer's strategy to "push" the product through the distribution system.

Marketing public relations is of particular importance to business-to-business marketers. Product exposure in trade magazines reaches an end user who reads them thoroughly and specifically, to stay informed on new products, new methods, or new technologies.

3

Marketing and Public Relations: The New Partnership

Despite the increasing acceptance of public relations by marketing executives, considerable confusion surrounds the nature of the relationship. The confusion is attitudinal, organizational, and functional.

Marketing managers generally recognize that public relations is an available option in helping accomplish their task, but the public relations function is often associated with functions far removed from marketing. Here are just a few of them:

- Interacting with the financial community
- Maintaining contact with the financial media
- Writing speeches for corporate executives
- Handling corporate contributions
- Producing employee publications
- Administering corporate-identity programs
- Dealing with government agencies and regulators
- Conducting plant tours and open houses
- Dealing with social activists
- Managing corporate advocacy campaigns
- Standing in for top management at civic events
- And, in the worst-case scenario, defending the company from takeover.

Activities like these clearly relate to the corporate mission, but how these activities relate to the marketing mission may not always be apparent to the marketing manager. He or she must question whether the corporate public relations department (also known as "corporate communications," "corporate relations," or "public affairs") will have the time or the marketing expertise to make a significant contribution to the fulfillment of a plan, on the success of which the manager's career may be riding.

The confusion is further complicated by the corporation's organization chart. Marketing, a line function typically headed by a senior officer reporting to the president or CEO, stands with production, finance, and personnel as one of the principal functions of the corporation. Corporate public relations is a staff function that, in most cases, reports to the chairman, president, or chief financial officer. The relationship between the corporate public relations department and the marketing department is generally a dotted-line relationship.

The marketing manager rightfully wants his or her own team. If a manager wants to build a public relations component in a marketing plan, he or she will want to command the full attention of the public relations executive, to steep that person in the product and the plan, undiverted by other corporate considerations. The manager will want to be in a position to motivate and reward a successful effort with raises, promotions, bonuses, and the like. This objective may not be feasible with a person on loan for this assignment from another self-standing department with a different agenda and chain of command.

PUBLIC RELATIONS AND MARKETING MOVING TOGETHER

The growing interest in the relationship of public relations and marketing has resulted in more public forums devoted to the subject. The *Advertising Age* Creative Workshops have, for several years, included sessions on public relations led by public relations experts. The Association of National Advertisers invited me to speak at its annual Media Day alongside authorities on print and broadcast media, market and media research, and promotion. Many corporations include public relations speakers in marketing communications seminars for their top national and worldwide marketing executives.

In 1988, the Chicago Chapter of the American Marketing Association and the Public Relations Society of America held their first joint event, a seminar on "Marketing and Public Relations: Allies in Megamarketing." The seminar featured public relations and marketing experts from corporations, PR firms, and academia, led by Philip Kotler, whose article "Megamarketing" in the *Harvard Business Review* occasioned the seminar. The next year, a colloquium was held at San Diego State University called "A Challenge to the Calling: Public Relations versus Marketing."

At the colloquium, *PR Reporter* editor and counselor Patrick Jackson described the relationship between marketing and public relations:

> Whatever an organization offers to whichever publics, the hard fact is that success lies in its sales—getting someone to sign on the dotted line, actually or figuratively. No matter what type of organization we're talking about, without successfully selling something, it fails. Therefore, both public relations and marketing ultimately exist to serve sales—the purveying of goods, services, or ideas.[1]

Professor Glen Broom of San Diego State University described the relationship between marketing and PR as "an essential double helix." He explained that, "just as the two twisted chains of the DNA double helix are essential to life, so too are the two strands of marketing and public relations necessary to organizational life and success."[2]

MPR: A DISTINCT DISCIPLINE

The term *marketing public relations* is widely used today and was, therefore, selected as the operative term for this book; *MPR* is used throughout to distinguish this field from the broader one of PR, public relations.

This would seem to suggest fission sometime in the future, that is, the split-off of marketing-support public relations from those other public relations activities that define the corporation's relationships with its non-customer publics. The corporate public relations (CPR) function may well remain a corporate management function, and what is now known as marketing public relations will become a marketing management function. Under such a scheme, the mission of CPR would be to support corporate objectives. The mission of MPR would be to support marketing objectives.

Significant staff restructuring would, of course, be required. MPR practitioners would become marketing associates, and their career paths would be directed toward marketing management. CPR practitioners would continue to report to top management.

A close working relationship would be maintained between the two disciplines, not only because of the similarity of skills and experience, but also because of the need to integrate marketing objectives with corporate objectives. Relationships with government on all levels, for example, significantly affect the environment in which the company markets its products, as do the company's public positions on a variety of existing and emerging issues that affect the public as consumer.

Corporate response to crisis situations inevitably affects consumer perceptions and consumer behavior. The now-famous Tylenol case was for Johnson & Johnson both a corporate crisis and a marketing crisis that might well have destroyed a major product line had not responsive, responsible corporate action been taken and effectively communicated to all of the company's publics, especially the consumer and the trade.

The need for cooperation between CPR and MPR is essential now and will be increasingly so in the future. Some give and take will inevitably be required from both. Public relations will have to abandon its intellectual pretensions and its disdain of the marketing function, and marketers will have to become increasingly aware of how the social, political, and economic environment affects consumers and the opinion makers who influence attitudes toward companies and their products. This synergy cannot be achieved if marketing and public relations are seen as rivals rather than allies.

INTEGRATED MARKETING COMMUNICATIONS

The move to integrated marketing communications was underscored in 1990 when the largest U.S. car maker and its leading packaged goods company both took action to integrate their public relations and marketing activities. General Motors Corporation created a new communications and marketing staff to "integrate PR and marketing expertise to achieve communications goals." Procter & Gamble Company appointed Robert L. Wehling, formerly its Vice President-Marketing Services and longtime advocate of integrating PR, media, and promotion to head the company's public affairs and public relations department.

Other major companies cited by Philip Kotler as moving toward integrated marketing communications are McDonald's, the Limited, and IBM. All of them are taking steps to coordinate their communications planning so that it is consistent, impactful, and synergistic.

IBM believes that media relations plays an integral role in market-driven corporate communications programs and holds an important edge over every other tool of communications because of its high credibility. Media relations is one of the "balanced set of communications tools" used by the company to drive target audiences through the "purchase path" from (1) awareness to (2) interest to (3) desire to (4) action. Other tools include advertising, business shows, field network television, sales promotion, publications, and direct response advertising.

In its communications to marketing managers, IBM explains that the general public, despite some cynicism about advertising, continues to believe what is seen in the local and trade papers and broadcast on the evening news. Publicity has the impact of a respected third-party endorsement. When IBM activity is in the news, the report can generate far more word-of-mouth publicity than any advertisement. The company also believes that media relations heightens the impact of other communications efforts.

The implications of integrated marketing communication on the practice of public relations are far-reaching. Bob Dilenschneider expects to see more marketers pursue interdisciplinary careers, with stints in planning, product management, research, the advertising disciplines, and public relations. Dilenschneider says that "this lateral movement will be required to understand marketing problems in their total scope" and that "interdisciplinary backgrounds will be needed if people are to overcome the reflex action of selling their particular specialty as the optimum solution to any problem."[3]

On the consultant/agency side, the question ("Whose turf *is* this?") is accompanied by a question of practical fiscal concern ("Whose budget is this?").

At the San Diego colloquium (see page 33), Larry Jones, senior vice president of Foote, Cone & Belding, pointed out that:

> as clients grow they usually find an increasing need for more PR, more advertising or both. The result is often a competition between advertising and PR for the available budget dollars. Working separately can heighten the competition. However, integrated communications companies can bring both advertising and public relations to the planning stage and then develop the most targeted plan for investing the marketing funds—through advertising, PR or both.

In a keynote address called "The Future's Not What It Used to Be," president John O'Toole told the 1990 annual meeting of the American Association of Advertising Agencies that he recognized the need for integrated marketing communications and asserted the role of ad agencies in providing all of the pieces to clients:

> Advertising will—indeed must—be redefined to comprise all marketing communications directed to the consumer of the product or service.
>
> The lines between media, advertising, sales promotion, direct marketing, package design, public relations, directory advertising, and so forth will fade. Those distinctions are really more of our making than the consumer's anyway. What we're calling the New Advertising is, in the consumer's eyes, plain old advertising.
>
> The future belongs to those agencies that can truly integrate them into a seamless marketing communications force; that can credibly advise their clients as to the relative disposition of marketing dollars; that can demonstrate superiority in every aspect of the New Advertising.
>
> This could require significant restructuring; it will involve a good deal of retraining. It will necessitate a review of how and what they charge for their services. But in return for all this, the New Advertising holds out the promise of a renaissance of our industry.

The same theme was echoed by Keith Reinhard, chairman and CEO of DDB Needham Worldwide and new chairman of the 4As, in a speech to the Advertising Federation of Australia on April 5, 1990, in

Sydney. He admitted that advertising agencies have "in our arrogance, looked down our noses at anything that wasn't by definition 'pure,'" and said that:

> at one and the same time, we bought up sales promotion companies, public relations firms, direct marketing companies and others to capture some of the escaping dollars. . . . But most of these were supply-side maneuvers, pure and simple. They provided the client slight benefit. We spoke of one-stop shopping which, while it might be a good idea in convenience stores, in our business still leaves the shopping to the client. What we have as an industry body been up to has been diversification when what we need to be achieving is integration. We need to stop toying with the idea and, as an industry, commit to it. The New Advertising must encompass all the voices directed toward consumers in a brand's benefit.

Direct and Indirect Media

At a recent Advertising Research Foundation symposium at Northwestern University, Denman Maroney of the D'Arcy Masius Benton & Bowles advertising agency proposed that the impact of advertising or promotion results should not be looked at in isolation and that we must look at the impact of overall marketing communications. Maroney's proposed new model for marketing communications is of particular interest to MPR because he separates media into "direct" media (direct mail and point of purchase, which are free of any editorial environment) and "indirect" media (those which present messages in an editorial environment). He points out that the consumer does not come to the media for the marketing message; indirect media are passive, that is, the marketing message is always accidentally exposed.

But *not* always. Had Maroney examined marketing public relations, he could have concluded that the consumer does come to the media for the editorial message. Because of this, the MPR message is both direct and, it could be argued, more impactful than accidental exposure to advertising.

HOW CPR BENEFITS MPR

In the absence of increasing sales and market share, a company will wither and die. As Peter Drucker observes:

> Marketing is so basic that it cannot be considered a separate function. It is the whole business seen from the point of view of its final result, that is, from the customer's point of view. . . . The aim of business is to create a customer.[4]

An underlying assumption of this book is that unless an organization successfully markets its goods and services, it cannot survive and that, therefore, its relationships with its various publics are inevitably intertwined with marketing. Many of these publics influence, to a greater or lesser extent, the success of an organization's marketing efforts, but success in the marketplace depends on building healthy relationships with noncustomer as well as customer publics.

A company's community relations affect the marketplace because people want to do business with companies they know and trust. Clearly, questions of product safety and efficacy are a key concern of consumer and government and have an enormous impact on the marketplace. Marketers were once concerned only with delivering the right product to the right people at the right time and in the right place through the right communication and promotion. Now they must spend a great deal of time and energy anticipating or personally interacting with consumer advocates, environmentalists, political activists, legislators, and governmental agencies, whose influence on the marketing of their products is enormous.

All of these relationships with all of these publics inextricably bind public relations to marketing. These activities also closely link corporate public relations (CPR) with marketing public relations (MPR). Cutlip, Center, and Broom acknowledged that "in practice, public relations specialists are many times called upon to help in the marketing effort by writing publicity stories and arranging media coverage for new products," but they believe that "because some view publicity as the same as 'public relations,' product publicity is the source of much confusion between the marketing and public relations functions."[5]

This view fails to draw the needed distinction between MPR and CPR (see Table 3–1). It also assigns public relations a limited role of issuing new-product press releases. This approach does not square with recent developments, including dramatic increases in budgets for marketing public relations programs and the rapid growth of public relations firms that

TABLE 3–1   Marketing, MPR, and CPR Functional Responsibilities

Marketing	MPR	CPR
Market assessment	Product publicity	Corporate media relations
Customer segmentation	Sponsorships	Investor relations
Product development	Special events	Government relations
Pricing	Public service	Community relations
Distribution	Publications	Employee communications
Service	Media events	Public affairs
Consumer advertising	Media tours	Advocacy advertising
Sales promotion	Trade support	
Sales		

specialize in MPR. No recognition is given to the increasing role of MPR in maintaining markets for mature products and in winning consumer confidence for companies and products through sponsorship of and involvement in events and endeavors that consumers, market influencers, and sellers care about.

MPR AND THE FOUR Ps OF MARKETING

Today's marketers were brought up on the famous four Ps of marketing: product, price, place, and promotion. Under this scheme, promotion encompasses all the activities which the company uses to communicate the product's attributes to consumers in order to persuade them to purchase it. This is where MPR fits in, along with advertising, direct marketing, sales promotion, and personal selling.

Each of these disciplines employs a number of communications tools. Some of these tools are clearly the province of one or another of the disciplines. Others overlap, creating confusion and contributing to the turf battles among providers of each, as they seek new sources of revenue.

Table 3–2 lists some communications tools commonly used by advertising, sales promotion, and MPR. Person-to-person selling does not normally use these tools or overlap with these three nonpersonal forms of communication.

TABLE 3–2   Advertising, Sales Promotion, and MPR: Exclusive Functions

Advertising	Sales Promotion	MPR
Television commercials	Couponing	News conference
TV program sponsorship	Games, sweepstakes,	Media tours
Radio commercials	rebates	Newspaper publicity
ROP newspaper ads	Patronage awards	Radio publicity
Magazine ads	Price packs	Magazine publicity
Co-op advertising	Prizes	Television publicity
Business and trade	Premiums and	Seminars and symposiums
press advertising	incentives	Surveys
Direct mail		
Direct response ads		
and commercials		
Outdoor advertising		
Telephone direct		
advertising		
Motion picture advertising		
Car cards		

TURF WARS

As shown in Table 3-3, advertising, sales promotion, and MPR overlap in a number of areas. In some companies and advertising agencies, the lines are clearly drawn; in others, a particular project becomes the "property" of the party who created it and appropriates the right to implement it. Since there are no clear-cut boundaries, marketers have assigned grey-area projects to outside sources or to the inside support departments that are perceived to be best qualified to execute the projects because of experience, staff expertise, or assertiveness.

I once headed the public relations division of FCB Communications, an advertising giant that was beginning to diversify into allied communications areas. Both the public relations and sales promotions divisions were started at the same time, and both were anxious to stake their own turf. Media-related activity was recognized by both as clearly the function of public relations. Couponing, premiums, and games were accepted as the province of promotion. But endless discussion ensued about whose job it was to stage an event or create collateral material for a

TABLE 3-3 Advertising, Sales Promotion, and MPR: Overlapping Functions

Advertising	Sales Promotion	MPR
Advertorials		Advertorials
Promotional advertising	Promotional advertising	
Free-standing inserts	Free-standing inserts	
In-store media	In-store media	
Point-of-purchase	Point-of-purchase	
Tie-ins	Tie-ins	Tie-ins
Contests	Contests	Contests
Special events	Special events	Special events
Booklets and brochures	Booklets and brochures	Booklets and brochures
Public service tie-ins	Public service tie-ins	Public service tie-ins
	Trade shows and exhibits	Trade shows and exhibits
	Sampling	Sampling
	Demonstrations	Demonstrations
	Parades	Parades
	Festivals	Festivals
	Sports events	Sports events
	Entertainment sponsorships	Entertainment sponsorships
	AV presentations	AV presentations
	Meetings and conventions	Meetings and conventions

common client. The question was never resolved to anyone's satisfaction. The winner was whoever got an idea first and sold it to the client.

There is still no "whose-turf" definition about those in-between areas. Public relations firms find themselves competing for marketing-related assignments against sales promotion firms and often against advertising agencies as well.

Specialist suppliers have sprung up in such areas as sports marketing and special-event production. There are very successful sales promotion firms, for example, who do not do coupons and premiums, limiting their practice exclusively to games.

In the 1990s, turf battles are certain to accelerate as large communications firms (and even management consultants, accounting firms, law firms, and banks) seek to grow by selling new communications-centered services and as entrepreneurs seek specialized new niches in the marketplace. MPR firms will have to continue to aggressively market their expertise in the "life-style marketing" areas, capitalizing on the one exclusive area of expertise that they alone bring to the party—their ability to transform special events into media events, expanding the audience geometrically.

THE MARKETING/PR RELATIONSHIP: FIVE MODELS

The value of MPR as an element of promotional planning is gaining in prominence. In an influential article titled "Marketing and Public Relations," in the *Journal of Marketing* in 1978, Philip Kotler and William Mindak asked: "Where does marketing end and public relations begin, and where does public relations end and marketing begin?" (6). They pointed out the following similarities: "Marketing and public relations are the major external functions of the firm. Both functions start their analysis and planning from the point of view of satisfying outside groups."

But they noted that while each deals with the external environment as the starting point for planning, "one hopes to make the company more market-oriented, while the other hopes to make the company more public-oriented, objectives that are not necessarily compatible."

They suggested five different models for viewing the organizational relationship between marketing and public relations:

1. *Separate but equal functions: The traditional view that marketing and public relations are different in their perspectives and capacities.* Marketing exists to sense, serve, and satisfy customers' needs at a profit. Public relations exists to produce good will in the company's various publics so that these publics do not interfere in the firm's profit-making ability.

2. *Equal but overlapping functions: The view that marketing and public relations are important and separate functions but share some common terrain.* The most obvious overlap is in product publicity. The company can either locate product publicity in the marketing department or "borrow" it as needed from the public relations department.

3. *Marketing as the dominant function: The view that corporate public relations should be placed under the control of corporate marketing.* Public relations exists essentially to make it easier for the firm to market its goods; it does not exist in the corporate picture simply to do good deeds.

4. *Public relations as the dominant function: The view that public relations should control marketing.* The firm's future depends critically on how it is viewed by key publics, including stockholders, financial institutions, unions, employees, and community leaders, as well as customers. The task of the firm is to satisfy these publics as much as possible. Satisfying the customers is one part of the task, the part called marketing. Satisfying customers must be kept in balance with satisfying these other groups.

5. *Marketing and public relations as the same function: The view that the two functions are rapidly converging concepts and methodologies.* Marketing and public relations both talk in terms of publics and markets, both recognize the need for market segmentation, and both acknowledge the importance of market attitudes, perceptions, and images in formulating programs and the primacy of a management process consisting of analysis, planning, implementation, and control.

While I agree with Kotler that no one model will be appropriate for all enterprises, the advantages of the fifth model are, in my view, in the best interests of the corporation. The synthesis would lead to marketing decision making that recognizes the necessity of satisfying both consumer and nonconsumer publics who influence the company's ability to market its products effectively. The importance of maintaining the image of the corporation as an organization that understands the consumer and delivers products of quality and value would be recognized.

MEGAMARKETING

Kotler refined his view of public relations in another influential article, "Megamarketing," in the *Harvard Business Review.*[7]

The article dealt specifically with the need for companies that want to operate in certain markets to "master the art of supplying benefits to parties other than target consumers" who can singly or collectively block profitable entry into a market. These gatekeepers include legislators, government agencies, political parties, labor unions, public interest groups, and churches, among others.

Kotler believes that a new strategy, megamarketing, is called for, in order for companies to break into blocked markets. Kotler's article defined *megamarketing* as:

> the strategically coordinated application of economic, psychological, political, and public relations skills to gain the cooperation of a number of parties in order to enter and/or operate in a given market.

Kotler proposed that gaining access to blocked markets requires executives to address new multiparty marketing problems. In normal marketing situations, the skillful use of marketing's traditional four Ps— product, price, place, and promotion—can create a cost-effective marketing mix that appeals to customers and end users. In megamarketing situations, Kotler said, executives must add two more Ps—power and public relations. Power is a *push* strategy in winning multiparty support and public relations is a *pull* strategy.

Megamarketing clearly requires marketing executives to utilize the skills of corporate public relations and public affairs professionals and lawyers. It is my view that public relations relates to marketing in two different but complementary ways—one in straight-ahead promotional planning, the other in blocked-market situations:

1. Marketing public relations (MPR), used in normal marketing situations to influence consumers, is an important component of the Four Ps strategy, specifically supporting Promotion to facilitate a transaction.

2. Corporate public relations (CPR), used in megamarketing situations to influence nonconsumer publics in order to gain market entry. Together with the use of Power, CPR adds an important new component to a Six Ps strategy in blocked markets.

4

How MPR Adds Value: Push, Pull, Pass

Marketing public relations works because it adds value to products through its unique ability to lend credibility to the product message.

Professor Theodore Levitt of the Harvard Graduate School of Business, a former editor of the *Harvard Business Review*, has long recognized public relations as "the credible source." In his influential book *The Marketing Mode*, Levitt drew a distinction between the public relations message and the advertising message, pointing out that when the message is delivered by an objective third party, such as a journalist or broadcaster, the message is delivered more persuasively.[1] Levitt's recognition gave added clout to a claim long made by public relations practitioners.

In 1962, management consultant Chester Burger drew a finer line. In an article titled "Credibility: When Public Relations Works," Burger wrote:

> If the objective is to gain "free advertising," it will probably be unsuccessful in helping sell the product. If, on the other hand, the objective is to secure the independent editorial endorsement of product claims which the public may disbelieve, then editorial publicity may be desirable, and indeed necessary, for the successful launching of a new product.[2]

No less an advertising authority than David Ogilvy pointed out:

> Roughly six times as many people read the average article as read the average advertisement. Very few advertisements are read by more than one reader in twenty. I conclude that editors communicate better than admen.[3]

Ogilvy's advice to copywriters was: "If you make advertisements look like editorial pages, you will attract more readers."

It follows that a good article about a good product in a good publication will not only be read, it will be believed. A good interview about a good product on a good program will not only be viewed and heard, it will be believed because it is delivered by a trusted source with no commercial axe to grind. Consumers know instinctively that the program or publication exists to inform and/or entertain them and not to puff products. A publication or program that promotes undeserving products indiscriminately will soon lose its credibility, its user friendliness, and its audience.

James Arnold, now president of the Chester Burger Company, points out that in this age of attitudes, a company's success is in large part determined by perceptions of key audiences. Arnold believes

> the proliferation of media channels has made possible the amplification of attitudes many times over, increasing their influence and power. These trends have made public relations even more relevant to marketing than it might have been in the past. Not because PR is a cheaper form of advertising, but because PR can be more effective.[4]

COST-EFFECTIVENESS OF MPR

MPR gives companies a big bang for their marketing bucks. These days, marketers who are experienced in the use of MPR and recognize its value typically budget a quarter to a half million dollars or more for a brand program. Larger-scale multiproduct company-positioning programs often exceed $1 million. Multifaceted MPR programs for Coca-Cola, Anheuser-Busch, and McDonald's run into many millions.

Most public relations budgets are a fraction of advertising budgets. To a marketing decision maker, MPR is a bargain because the effectiveness of an entire public relations program can be evaluated vis-à-vis running a single, fleeting, 30-second spot on prime-time television.

MPR is such a bargain that some marketers may question how they can get so much for so little: "Where's the rub?" The marketing vice president of a major packaged-goods company once asked me whether I thought anything could really be accomplished for "only a million dollars."

While MPR adds value to brands, sales-promotion programs are usually designed to score a quick hit by giving something away—a deal to the trade, or a price-incentive premium, or a costly contest prize.

MPR's cost-effectiveness is usually measured in terms of total exposures generated and cost per impression. Kathy Rand, now executive vice president of Lesnik Public Relations, points out that frequently the cost per thousand MPR exposures is less than $1 and that marketers can buy a full year's MPR program for the cost of a single, 30-second, prime-time TV spot. Increasingly, these measures are being refined to consider cost-per-target market impression, which eliminates waste exposure to nonprospective consumers and applies especially to exposures in media that appeal to a mass audience. On the other hand, with narrowcasting or special-interest publications there is very little waste exposure. Whatever the media mix, the marketer is interested in how cost-effective MPR is in reaching a particular target audience.

Another widely utilized method of measuring MPR's cost-efficiency is by equating exposures to their "advertising equivalents." Many public relations people question whether an article can really be considered the equivalent of a print ad, or a TV interview the equivalent of a commercial. They believe that the implied editorial endorsement makes an article more valuable than an advertisement taking up the same amount of space in a publication or the same amount of time on a television program. They point out the difficulty of comparing a 30-minute interview with a 30-second spot on the same show. Yet, measuring MPR exposures by calculating what it would cost to buy the space or time persists, and likely will continue to, because marketing clients are familiar with advertising rates and the use of equivalencies gives them a convenient way to quantify exposures.

These kinds of measures will have to do until MPR budgets are sufficient to include more sophisticated measuring devices. Methods of tracking a cause-and-effect relationship between advertising and sales are still inadequate at best and the same holds true for MPR.

COHESIVE COMMUNICATION STRATEGIES

Public relations works best when it is integral to the marketing strategy and plays a specific role in the marketing plan. Whether it is used to stretch the marketing dollar, to make advertising campaigns or sales programs work harder, or to provide a silver bullet that generates real excitement in the marketplace, MPR brings a number of unique benefits to the marketing plan.

One benefit is the opportunity to gain positive product exposure in the ever widening selection of media. While it is becoming nearly impossible to cover the bases with the most generous advertising budget, there have never been more publications or television programs available as publicity outlets. An advertising plan typically concentrates on reaching the largest target audience at the lowest cost per thousand. MPR may be assigned the role of reaching primary and/or secondary markets through like and supplementary media. Women between the ages of 25 and 49 may buy 60 percent of products in a category, so ad dollars are allocated to reach this market at a high rate of frequency. Since MPR is not buying time and space, reaching this target market—plus the other 40 percent—through media they read, see, or hear is inexpensive. A cohesive marketing plan integrates media planning and assigns a specific role to MPR.

Horace Schwerin, founder of Schwerin Research Corporation and father of television commercial testing, sees publicity, promotion, and advertising as the troika of media available to marketers. He believes that, properly utilized, publicity is a valuable channel of marketing persuasion, that is, "the engineering of incremental sales gains through implementation of a deliberate strategy."

In *Persuasion in Marketing,*[5] Horace Schwerin and Henry Newell observe:

> Enlisting publicity in the service of a specific product, as opposed to broader long-term company goals, has historically had observable short-term marketing benefits. . . . The most dramatic example was the exploitation of fluoridation of Crest toothpaste, beginning with securing the seal of approval of the ADA and the wide dissemination of the favorable story, both in the press and in paid advertising.

Other instances abound. A 1974 article in *Reader's Digest* read in part as follows:

> Something may be missing from the American diet—sufficient fiber or roughage . . . mounting evidence suggests that the lack of this ingredient may be a contributing factor in a number of diseases, including appendicitis, intestinal polyps, diverticular disease, cancer of the colon and rectum and heart disease.
>
> Many vegetables and fruits have high fiber content. . . . However, cereal fiber appears to be the most effective. . . . In breakfast cereals the largest amounts of fiber are found in those with bran in their names. . . . Bran, itself, is the most concentrated form of fiber. . . . Research indicates that it may take restoration of only about two or three grams of cereal fiber in the daily diet to improve bowel functioning and health.

All cereal featuring bran benefited from this publicity, even those that had not advertised for some time. Retail-store audit data showed a sudden increase of 73 percent in sales after years of virtually static trends.

Successes like these, Schwerin and Newell conclude, "sometimes depend on being alert to newsworthy trends and exploiting them; in other times, on making the news yourself."

A TRIPARTITE APPROACH TO MARKETING
PUBLIC RELATIONS

The clout of MPR today on the sale of products from Trivial Pursuit to the Taurus, from Diet Coke to Disney World, is examined later in this book. This much is certain: product publicity is no longer a hit-and-miss proposition; it is now a strategic tool of MPR, which in turn is an integral element in the marketing communications plan.

I suggest a new approach to MPR that encompasses both traditional marketing strategy and the megamarketing dimension, that is, the need to communicate with parties who are not part of the traditional marketing chain.

Push-Pull

The first two dimensions of this approach are the "push" and "pull" strategies. Kotler states:

> A "push" strategy calls for using the sales force and trade promotion to push the product through the channels. The producer aggressively promotes the product to wholesalers; the wholesalers aggressively promote the product to retailers; and the retailers aggressively promote the product to consumers.
>
> A "pull" strategy calls for spending a lot of money on advertising and consumer promotion to build up consumer demand. If the strategy is effective, consumers will ask their retailers for the product, the retailers will ask their wholesalers for the product, and the wholesalers will ask the producers for the product.[6]

Larger MPR budgets are usually allocated to "pull" strategy programs, that is, those aimed directly at the end user, but both "push" and "pull" strategies can and are employed simultaneously.

For example, "pull" programs (such as those described throughout this book) may be designed to reach consumers through mass and/or specialized media, media tours, event sponsorships, special-audience programs, and the like. At the same time, aggressive MPR programs directed to the sales organization and the trade may be implemented to help "push" the product through channels.

"Pull" MPR results can be effectively "merchandised" to motivate the sales force. For example, particularly effective national-television news features about the product can be shown at a national sales meeting, or good local TV interviews can be presented at regional sales meetings. With the growing importance of regional marketing, it is important to demonstrate to salespeople how the MPR is specifically helping them in their territories.

"Push" tools used by MPR are:

- ○ Trade-show communications, including special publications and sponsored meetings, breakfasts, or receptions where the new product is introduced to the trade
- ○ Trade newsletters spotlighting new products and promotional support
- ○ Publicity reprints for use by salespeople on sales calls or mailed directly to buyers (the theory is that if the media consider this news, so will the consumer)
- ○ Trade-publication articles aimed at merchandise managers and buyers and covering product news items, stories about advertising and promotional support programs, including MPR, company-expert interviews and by-line stories, or retailer-success programs with the product line

Two of America's great marketing successes were accelerated through the use of "push" MPR techniques. Alvin Golin, chairman of Golin/Harris and longtime public relations counsel to McDonald's Corporation, recalled, "Our first job for McDonald's wasn't to sell hamburgers, it was to sell franchises." Publicity was used to draw attention to McDonald's as an attractive opportunity for investors who wanted to run their own businesses. For Sara Lee, an early feature story in *The Wall Street Journal*, "Sara Lee Builds Baking Bonanza on Heaping Slices of Quality," brought immediate demand for the company's cakes from supermarkets all over the country and led to national distribution.

Pass: The Third Dimension

In addition to "push" and "pull" strategies, I propose that a third dimension, the "pass" strategy, is required in today's increasingly complex marketing environment. It is occasioned by the factors Kotler describes in *Megamarketing*, especially the need to enter markets blocked or protected by parties other than end users. These parties include, but are by no means confined to, government policy makers, legislators, regulators, political parties, activists, and public-interest groups representing an ever growing agenda of causes, interests, and concerns.

Just as the media act as gatekeepers, determining which news will or will not enter, these parties act as gatekeepers to the marketplace. Marketers must make their way past them, to enter certain markets and to overcome or neutralize opposition, a task for which, Kotler points out, marketing executives are unprepared by training or experience.

Public relations' role is to devise strategies and conduct programs that permit the marketer to "pass" the gatekeepers and enter the market. In my view, both CPR and MPR must play a role in what I call "pass" strategic planning.

When customers make purchase decisions, they are in a very real sense deciding to buy two things: the product and the company. I strongly believe that people want to do business with companies they know and trust. Consumers' trust is earned by providing quality products at a good value. It is also earned by sponsoring activities and identifying with causes that demonstrate the company's appreciation of the consumers' patronage.

MARKETERS' SOCIAL RESPONSIBILITY

Another vital element in pursuing a successful "pass" strategy is related to the company's position on a variety of issues that are of concern to both gatekeepers and the consumers who share their views. The role of both corporate and marketing public relations advisors is to define these issues for management, to recommend action, and to communicate that action to the appropriate parties/publics.

The Council on Economic Priorities (CEP), a public interest research organization, has researched and produced publications that (1) inform communities about corporate activities and (2) convince companies that consumers care about corporate social responsibility. In 1987, CEP published a highly successful book, *Rating America's Corporate Conscience*. The following year, CEP's *Shopping for a Better World: A Quick and Easy Guide to Socially Responsible Supermarket Shopping* appeared. This pocket-size publication, designed for shoppers to take with them to the supermarket, lists more than 1,300 brand-name products and 138 companies.

Each company is rated in ten categories that represent issues of social concern: charitable giving, women's advancements, minority advancement, defense contracts, animal testing, social disclosure, community outreach, nuclear power, South Africa, and the environment. CEP pointed out that:

> Like it or not, the policies and programs of companies do influence your society—and you—for good or ill. Some makers of products you buy every day contribute to the dreaded "greenhouse effect," continue to sell strategic products to South Africa, or make parts for nuclear weapons. Some revitalize communities, fund higher education of disadvantaged students, and value the expertise of women among their top management. How can the average citizen possibly know which is which?

Here, for the first time in a pocket-size guide is information on corporate social responsibility that will help you cast your economic vote as conscientiously as your political vote. Of course, no one but you can decide which products to buy for yourself and your family. Quality, safety, nutrition and price may top your list of priorities. . . . But often in a sea of competing detergents or canned peas, differences are minimal. Product differentiations created by advertising can be trivial, artificial or just plain meaningless. That's where you can exercise your clout as a responsible shopper. Using the information gathered here, you'll have a greater chance to influence corporate policy than ever before.[7]

Parenthetically, CEP used the techniques of MPR as effectively as do the companies it scores. I learned about *Shopping for a Better World* when I saw Bryant Gumbel flipping through it with a CEP spokesperson on the "Today" show and I read about it the same week in a *Newsweek* article titled "Read the Fine Print First: A New Booklet Lets You Shop with a Clear Conscience." *Business Week* described the booklet, which was published in December, as "a stocking stuffer for that social activist on your list." The publicity and word-of-mouth it generated demonstrate not only the interest of consumers in corporate social responsibility but also the pulling power of publicity. CEP expected to sell 50,000 booklets but, in two years, it sold more than 700,000.

The booklet capsulized major social concerns of 1988, and CEP promises it will be revised and updated as new issues emerge and are identified.

The role of that corporate public relations function known as issues management must address all of the issues in *Shopping for a Better World*, and many more. The CPR professionals act as the corporate eyes and ears in identifying and assessing the present and potential impact of these issues on the company's ability to achieve its objectives. Since the profitable sale of its products is a primary objective, the ability and influence of senior public affairs officers and counselors have incalculable effect on the company's marketing efforts.

USING PUSH-PULL-PASS

"Push," "pull," "pass" strategies: In writing today's marketing plans, marketers must consider all three. "Pass"strategies involving company policy are primarily the function of CPR, while branded trust bonding programs, along with "pull" and "push" marketing strategies, are the responsibility of MPR, as outlined in Table 4–1.

Some products will succeed by pursuing an aggressive "pull"

TABLE 4–1   PUSH-PULL-PASS Strategies

Strategy	Target	PR Type	Tools
PUSH	Sales force Dealers Distributors Retailers	MPR	Trade shows Trade publicity Reprints Publications
PULL	Consumer/ End user	MPR	Media events Media tours Story placement Product placement Teleconferences Exhibits Demonstrations Sampling Surveys Newsletters PSA's Symposia Publications

PASS	Gatekeepers
	  Public interest groups
	  Government
	  Community leaders
	  Other influencers
		CPR	Assessing issues
			Advising action
			Communication

	Consumers as publics	MPR	Charity tie-ins National sponsorships Local sponsorships

strategy alone. But, as retailers exert ever increasing influence over the marketplace, equal attention must be paid to "push" strategies.

The "pass" strategy I am suggesting comes into play with society and media attention intensifying not only on product safety and efficacy but, as has been demonstrated, on the corporation's response to critical issues facing the society at large. Marketing public relations can and should play a part in all three and in concert with corporate public relations when corporate policy issues are at stake.

5

Circumstances
for Success:
The Harris Grid

Public relations counselor Daniel J. Edelman has, over the past 40 years, been responsible for some of the most successful and innovative marketing public relations programs.

In an address in Sydney, Australia, Edelman contrasted the roles of advertising and public relations:

> The role of advertising is to reach the consumer in a quick, exciting, and emotional way to motivate a sale. But public relations has the unique advantage of presenting the message in the context of the day's news. The story is told in greater depth. Its impact can be enormous.

Edelman went on to state:

> It's not going to happen for every product or service. There's a time and a place for public relations.
> My experience over these many years has demonstrated to me that in proper circumstances, and when handled expertly, public relations can often be the best and most cost-effective marketing technique.
> Here are some, but certainly not all, of these circumstances:
> 1. There's a revolutionary, break-through type of product—one that can make news.
> 2. The company is new or small—there's little, if any, money available for advertising.
> 3. Television isn't available for regulatory reasons—for example, distilled spirits cannot advertise on U.S. television.
> 4. The environment is negative and has to be turned around quickly.[1]

In a 1989 speech in Dallas, at the annual conference of the Public Relations Society of America, Edelman expanded the list to include six more ways in which public relations can be more effective than advertising.

   5. When generating new excitement about an existing product
   6. When a company is having difficulty distributing its product
   7. When advertising is well-liked, but fails to build brand recognition
   8. When a product takes time to explain
   9. When you cannot advertise your product to consumers
  10. When established companies or brands are aligned with a cause.

WHERE MPR WORKS

MPR certainly works well in the circumstances Edelman listed. But public relations can also build demand for a mature product by creating new news about that product, expanding the market for a product category, enabling competing brands to fight for a share of a larger pie, and building business by generating consumer trust.

Some product categories particularly lend themselves to public relations. Here are a few of them.

Books

Publishers agree that one of the best ways to make a best-seller is to get the author on TV shows like "Today," "Good Morning America," "Donahue," or "Geraldo." *The New York Times* reports than an appearance on "Oprah Winfrey" can create an instant best-seller. Barry Lippman, president of Macmillan's general book publishing division, told the *Times* that the company had studied the factors shared by the company's last 10 best-sellers and found that all had been featured on national television shows. While traditional advertising is still used, publishers say that what they call "free advertising" resulting from marketing public relations efforts is the most effective advertising. It is also the most cost-effective. At $1,000 a city, an author can visit dozens of cities for media interviews for the cost of a single ad.[2]

Cars

Americans have long held a love affair with the automobile. The media have been willing matchmakers. News of new models is always reported in newspapers and magazines and on television.

Fashion

The mass media have traditionally reported on the latest fashions. Paris creations, once the stuff of movie newsreels, are now seen on the network morning shows and sometimes on the evening news. Those who really want to be in the know read *Vogue* and a host of new women's magazines like *Elle* and *Mirabella,* which regularly feature fashion.

Food and Ingredients

Food publicity has long been a staple of MPR. All the major food companies provide a flow of recipes, serving suggestions, and new-product news to magazines and newspaper food editors. Some of the most successful food publicity programs are those that offer consumers ideas for using products as cooking ingredients. Two perennials for recipes are Tabasco Sauce and Campbell's soup.

Healthy Foods

Americans are health-happy and read all they can about what to eat and what not to eat. Nearly half those surveyed in a 1989 poll conducted for *Advertising Age* by the Gallup Organization said they had bought a food product marketed as promoting good health in the previous 30 days. Entenmann's made big news and built a $200 million business in 1990 when reporters tried, liked, and wrote about a new line of fat-free, cholesterol-free baked goods with fewer than 100 calories per serving. On the other hand, bad publicity has damaged egg consumption and destroyed MSG as a consumer product. (Remember Accent?)

Sports and Fitness

The fitness boom of the 1980s gave rise to the athletic-shoe explosion. The latest shoes from Reebok, Nike, and L.A. Gear combine fashion and fitness and are seen everywhere, especially on TV sportscasts. The newest exercise equipment and sports apparel are also widely publicized because of their high interest to the fitness crowd.

Pills

In recent years, pharmaceutical companies have been among the heaviest users of marketing public relations. They once confined their communications activities to reaching doctors and healthcare professionals; they now spend big bucks to reach consumers directly with messages about new and existing products, especially those moving from Rx to over-the-counter. Because of burgeoning consumer interest in health-related news and especially in drugs that treat personal medical problems, the major media have greatly expanded their coverage of medical subjects. The networks and TV stations in major markets all have medical reporters, many of them doctors. Doctors Art Ulene on NBC, Tim Johnson on ABC, and Bob Arnot on CBS are familiar to and trusted by viewers of the network morning shows. Consumer print media have followed suit with health columns and more health features, and a new category of magazines like *Prevention* and *American Health* has prospered.

Buff Products and Activities

Golf, tennis, and skiing fanatics, video and stereo buffs, shutter bugs, computer jocks, gun nuts, and other devotees not only read their buff books from cover to cover, but they also absorb what they read and discuss it with fellow buffs and nonbuffs who look to them for product information and advice.

Multiuse Products

Arm & Hammer baking soda became a marketing classic by devising new ways to use a very old product. The public relations program for Saran Wrap and Ziploc bags promotes multiuses of these products. These uses are of interest to consumers and to media that feature service copy.

Arts and Entertainment

Movies, records, and newly released videos are regularly reviewed in newspapers and magazines and on radio and television. The media and the entertainment industry feed off one another. Major films make the covers of the newsweeklies and other big consumer magazines and are featured on local news programs and special TV shows like "Sneak Previews" and "At the Movies." *TIME* Warner's *Entertainment Weekly,* introduced in 1990, reviews and grades the latest TV shows, films, music, video, and print. It points out that "morning television tied itself to the celebrity-culture boom of the '70s when Americans couldn't seem to read enough about their favorite TV, movie, and rock stars." "Good Morning America," "Today," and "CBS This Morning" try to "woo the biggest names onto their broadcasts, often promising lots of air time, even a week-long series of interviews, in exchange for exclusive appearances to tout a new TV show or film." Publicity-generated word of mouth sells out the really big rock shows precluding the need to advertise at all.

Travel and Leisure

Americans are traveling more than ever before. Sunday travel sections of major metropolitan newspapers have expanded their editorial pages to support the growing number of ads for airlines, cruise lines, travel destinations, and travel packages. Travel magazines are growing. There are opportunities to gain exposure on TV newscasts and even in sports postgame pronouncements from winning athletes. ("I'm going to Disney World"). Exposure of exotic locations on TV shows or movies has incited travel booms. Puerto Vallarta was a sleepy Mexican fishing village until Elizabeth Taylor and Richard Burton filmed *The Night of the Iguana* there. Travel and leisure is such a hot area for MPR that *Relate* magazine singles it out for inclusion on the PR All-Star Team.

Trendy Products

What is "in" is what is news. One year it was wine coolers and CD players. Another year it was frozen yogurt, cellular phones, and Nintendo. Next year voice activated phones will be introduced and the consumer-electronics industry will try to follow the success of Walkman and Watchman with portable VCRs.

Fads

Fads have always been fed by the media. In 1958, publicity, including a musical-production number on the popular Sunday-night *Dinah Shore Show,* convinced 30 million Americans to buy a three-foot-diameter plastic ring called a Hula Hoop. While the hoops were at least good for hip exercise, there was no accounting for the 1975 fad that caused a million people to part with $4 for an ordinary stone named Pet Rock. That was news. In 1989 Batmania hit the world again, and persons wearing Batgear were seen everywhere, including on TV, acting as walking advertisements for the summer's big film, *Batman.* The next year Turtlemania of the Teenage Mutant Ninja Turtle kind arose from the sewers to eclipse the caped crusader.

THE HARRIS GRID

Professor Kerri Acheson suggested that a grid could be created to plot out circumstances where public relations works best. As has been shown, certain product categories are more newsworthy than others and lend themselves to a news approach. Other product categories are generally not newsworthy enough to justify coverage from the media and are required to "borrow interest" by identification with something that is of greater interest to the target market.

The grid introduced in Figure 5–1 defines products in terms of (1) their interest to target consumers and (2) their potential interest to the media, that is, their newsworthiness.

The upper left quadrant, A, consists of those products that are of high interest to both the consumer and the media.

The lower left quadrant, B, is of lesser interest to the media and the consumer.

The upper right quadrant, C, is of interest to the consumer but not the media.

The lower right quadrant, D, is of low interest to both the consumer and the media.

Of course, within the listing of product categories in each quadrant, some are of higher or lower interest to consumers and media than are others.

Some major consumer product categories have been selected for purposes of illustration. By looking at products (and sometimes the companies that make them) in this way, marketers can select the most appropriate MPR strategic option. Clearly, products in the A quadrant should conduct high-visibility product campaigns; those in the B quadrant should also conduct product programs but recognize that the product may not be enough to carry the story alone. Therefore, new news about the product is needed to generate media exposure.

When there is no product news but the product is of high interest to consumers, as in quadrant C, an MPR sponsorship strategy enhances the brand image.

		Media	
		High News	Low News
C O N S U M E R	High Interest	Ⓐ Computers Cars Entertainment	Ⓒ Beer Soft drinks Athletic shoes
	Low Interest	Ⓑ Soup Cereal Aspirin	Ⓓ Cigarettes Car mufflers Cookies

FIGURE 5–1   The Harris Grid

	Product Category	Product-Publicity Opportunity
(A)	Computers Cars Entertainment	Announcement of Next Introduction of Taurus Release of *Batman*
(B)	Soup Cereal Aspirin	"Soup is good food." Quaker Oat Bran health benefits Heart-attack prevention

FIGURE 5–2   MPR News Strategy

When the product reaches the maturity or decline stages of the product life cycle, as in quadrant D, there may be no new news about it. This recommends that a borrowed-interest MPR strategy be employed, to link the brand with a program or event that will attract target consumers.

STRATEGIC APPLICATION OF THE GRID

How does the Harris Grid apply to familiar MPR efforts in these product categories? Quadrants A and B are illustrated in Figure 5–2, and quadrants C and D in Figure 5–3.

In the high-news, high-interest (A) quadrant, are the announcement of the Macintosh or PC2 or NeXT computer, the introduction of the Taurus or other breakthrough car, and the release of *Batman, Teenage Mutant Ninja Turtles, Dick Tracy,* or other major motion picture.

In the high-news, lower-product-interest quadrant (B), examples abound as companies look for new "reasons why" the consumer should buy. Campbell Soup publicized research on the nutritional "goodness" of soup. Quaker Oats led other cereal companies in publicizing the health

	Product Category	Product-Linkage Opportunity
(C)	Beer Soft drinks Athletic shoes	Budweiser Rolling Stones tour Celebrity advertising Celebrity brands
(D)	Car mufflers Cigarettes Cookies	Midas "Toys for Tots" Virginia Slims Tennis Nabisco Dinah Shore Golf Classic

FIGURE 5–3   MPR Borrowed-Interest Strategy

benefits of oat-bran cereal. Bufferin, Bayer, and other aspirin marketers boosted sales by making major news of research that showed the product's benefits in reducing the chance of heart attack.

In the low-news, high-interest quadrant (C), companies have followed the borrowed-interest MPR strategy. Budweiser is a major sponsor of national and local sports events and sponsored the thirtieth anniversary tour of the Rolling Stones. Like Bud, Pepsi gained major media coverage for the brand when it sponsored a hugely successful Michael Jackson tour tied to a commercial tied to a music video tied to a record. Nike has long gained exposure when big-name athletes wear the shoes with the easy-to-recognize Nike design, but Michael Jordan and the Air Jordan shoe was a publicity slam dunk in every way.

Then there are those products of low interest to the consumer and even lower interest to the media (quadrant D). No one thinks about a car muffler until they need one, but Midas wins friends and creates store traffic through its sponsorship of "Toys for Tots" with the U.S. Marine Corps. Cigarette companies, banned from television advertising, are big in sports sponsorships like Winston Cup NASCAR racing and Virginia Slims tennis. Packaged cookies and crackers are likewise low-interest products, but Nabisco gets mileage from its sponsorship of the Nabisco Dinah Shore Golf Classic.

While a new product or new-and-improved model may be the biggest news in a marketer's life, it may not have inherent news value to the media or be of high interest to the consumer. Early in my career, an exuberant marketing manager expected for his product publicity equal to that received by the then-hot car, the Toronado. His product was a new model electric organ.

Using the grid, marketers can plot where their product is located as the first step in MPR planning. In a low-interest category and in the absence of news or credible product benefits, even advertising may have to substitute emotional appeals for product appeals by producing commercials portraying the product in life-style situations that targeted consumers can identify with or aspire to. In other words, advertising, like marketing public relations, can be of the "borrowed-interest" variety. The MPR program should focus on increasing brand-name awareness by identifying the product with something consumers value.

6

The MPR Plan

As with all corporate strategic planning, effective MPR planning must begin with a clear understanding of the company's mission. The mission statement defines the company's business in terms of the industries the company operates in, the customers it serves, and its geographical scope. The statement focuses on the company's distinctive values and competitive domain.

The mission statement provides direction for the company's business units, each of which must in turn define its specific mission, goals, and values. Most business units pursue a mix of objectives, including profitability, sales growth, market-share improvement, risk containment, innovativeness, reputation, and so on. The business unit sets these objectives and manages by objectives.

Setting return-on-investment goals leads to the development of marketing strategies and plans. Often overlooked is the fact that the mission statement defines the company's relationships with its various publics—employees, stockholders, community, suppliers, dealers, and consumers—and reveals much about the company's corporate culture and marketing orientation.

Johnson & Johnson states:

We believe our first responsibility is to the doctors, nurses and patients, to mothers and all others who use our products and services.

Ford declares:

Our mission is to improve continually our products and services to meet our customers needs, allowing us to prosper as a business and to provide a reasonable return for our stockholders, the owners of our business . . . To achieve customer satisfaction, the quality of our products and services must be our number one priority. Customers are the focus of everything we do.

Celestial Seasonings, the archetypal 1960s company, transforms its mission into a statement of beliefs.

> We believe in marketing and selling healthful and naturally oriented products that nurture people's bodies and uplift their souls. Our products must be superior in quality, of good value, beautifully artistic, and philosophically inspiring. . . . We believe that our past, current and future successes come from a total dedication to excellent service to those who buy our products. Satisfying our customer and consumer needs in a superior way is the only reason we are in business, and we shall proceed with an obsession to give wholeheartedly to those who buy our products. Our customers and consumers are king, and we are here to serve them.

Schultz, Martin, and Brown define the marketing plan as "the document that defines and describes the overall marketing program developed for a particular organization and includes decisions and plans for various products, the pricing, the distribution systems, and the promotional activities."[1]

The plan defines brand objectives in units, sales, and expenditures needed to achieve those objectives. It provides relevant background information about the product and the market, defines opportunities and problems, and recommends strategies for achieving the desired objectives.

Marketers who understand the value of marketing public relations incorporate a description of and budget for MPR programs in their marketing plans. Unfortunately, far too many inexperienced product managers have neglected to adequately budget for MPR at the beginning. If a decision is made to mount an MPR campaign after the adoption of the marketing plan, monies must be borrowed from advertising or sales-promotion budgets, which can result in conflict with the managers and outside sources—or worse, with public relations budgets inadequate to the job.

Public relations people have long complained, with some justification, that they are called in too late, after marketing plans and budgets are finalized. They rightfully contend that they can significantly contribute to the development of a truly integrated marketing plan in which advertising, promotion, and public relations are assigned complementary roles that work together to achieve marketing goals.

THE MPR PROCESS

Clearly public relations is operating from a new depth of understanding of the marketing process and MPR planning is becoming ever more sophisticated. Product publicity may have once been a seat-of-the-pants business. Ideas were pulled from the sky. Stunts were staged to "get ink."

But in the past, public relations was far too often an afterthought, under-budgeted and misunderstood.

While media exposure is still at the heart of most MPR, programs are more closely focused on meeting preestablished marketing goals, and increasingly there are opportunities for MPR to provide input in the creation of those goals. Today MPR strategies are good only insofar as they meet marketing objectives. Ideas are good because they are on strategy.

Marketers have begun to recognize that the marketing public relations plan, like the advertising plan, should be an integral part of the marketing plan and should describe how MPR supports marketing objectives and strategies. The MPR plan should be the result of the application of the public relations process to the solution of marketing problems.

The following is the classic four-step public relations process designed by Cutlip and Center:

1. *Defining the Problem.* This step involves research and fact-finding, as well as probing and monitoring knowledge, opinions, attitudes, and behaviors of those concerned with and affected by the acts and policies of an organization. In essence, this is an organization's intelligence function; it requires determining "What's happening now?"

2. *Planning and Programming.* This step involves bringing the intelligence to bear on the policies and programs of the organization. It results in decisions affecting the program publics, objectives, procedures, and strategies in the interests of all concerned. It answers the question "What should we do and why?".

3. *Taking Action and Communicating.* This step involves implementing the plans and program through both action and communication designed to achieve specific objectives related to the goal. With respect to each of the publics, the question is "How do we do it and say it?"

4. *Evaluating the Program.* This step involves determining results of the program, as well as assessing the effectiveness of program preparation and implementation. Adjustments can be made in the continuing program or the program can be stopped after learning "How did we do?"[2]

The process as applied specifically to marketing public relations would address each of these four questions with a series of specific questions related to the marketing problem at hand.

1. *Defining the Problem.*

Principal PR Question: What's happening now?

Specific MPR Questions:
o What is the product?
o What are its benefits to the consumer?

- What is its price?
- What is the primary market for the product?
- What are the secondary markets?
- What are the channels of distribution?

- If an existing product:
  - —What is its recent sales history?
  - —What is its share?
  - —What are sales projections?
  - —Where will new sales come from?

- If a new product:
  - —Where will the product be introduced?
  - —What are plans to expand distribution?
  - —Where will it be sold? (geography)
  - —When will it be sold? (seasonality)
  - —What are the competitive products?
  - —What is the market share of each entry?
  - —What are benefits of each?
  - —What are positioning strategies for each?
  - —What are advertising and promotions for each?
  - —What environmental factors impact marketing?
  - —What influencers should be reached?

2. *Planning and Programming.*

   Principal PR Question: What should we do and why?

   Specific MPR Questions:
   - What are we trying to achieve?
   - How do MPR program objectives support marketing objectives?
   - Who are our publics?
   - What do we know about them?
   - What do we want them to know?
   - How are we going to communicate with them?
   - What do we want them to do?
   - How are we going to persuade them?
   - What is the major MPR message?

3. *Taking Action and Communicating.*

   Principal PR Question: How do we do it and say it?

   Specific MPR Questions:
   - What program elements will be used to reach each target market group?
   - How will each of these programs be implemented?
   - What materials will be required?
   - What is the media plan?
   - What is the timetable?
   - How much will it cost?
   - Who will be responsible for implementing it?
   - Will a PR firm be used?
   - How will it be selected?

4. *Evaluating the Program.*

   Principal PR Question: How did we do?

   Specific MPR Questions:
   - How well did we meet MPR objectives?
   - Did we reach the right people?
   - How many people?
   - What was the cost per impression?
   - Did we increase awareness?
   - Did we interest consumers in the product?
   - Did they buy it?
   - How do we know?
   - How will we measure results?
   - How much money is there to evaluate results?
   - What did we learn that will make the program better?
   - How can the program be changed?
   - Should we change it?

RESEARCH IN MPR PLANNING

Both the marketing process and the public relations process begin and end with research. Perhaps the greatest difference between marketing public relations as practiced today and the product publicity of earlier times is the use of research in the planning stage.

Today MPR programs are grounded in research about the marketplace, the category, and the consumer. Since advertising and public relations support the same marketing objectives, they usually have access to the same market research conducted by the company. However, the same research may be interpreted in different ways. Advertising may take its creative cue from one research finding, and MPR may take its direction from another finding from the same study. The media plan may also lead to different, although complementary, directions. The old half-empty, half-full analogy may apply; that is, the advertising plan may concentrate on reaching heavy users to maintain market share, while the MPR plan may try to build demand by influencing light or new users.

In addition to client-developed shared research, both advertising and public relations may recommend conducting supplementary research, either original research directly related to consumer attitudes about the product, or the use and interpretation of secondary data from existing sources.

Using Secondary Research

Information about the target audiences is obtained from the client and its advertising agency. However, many public relations firms today conduct their own runs of demographic, psychographic, and media research since both their message and their media recommendations may be complementary rather than supplementary to those of advertising. In addition to using secondary research to define primary and secondary consumer audiences, MPR places particular emphasis on examining those individuals, groups, or organizations that influence the target audience. These influencers, often overlooked in marketing plans, are often addressed specifically in the MPR plan.

Finally, secondary research is used to draw a picture of the environment in which the client is or will be competing. The components of this environment that may have significant impact on marketing the product include the natural environment, the social–cultural environment, the political environment, the technical environment, and the economic (marketplace) environment. This phase includes examination of events, trends, and constituent demands that affect marketing.

Use of Data Bases

Public relations people make particular use of data banks that retrieve articles that have appeared about the company, the product, the category, and the competition in the print media. The same sources are used to gain information that supports proposed programs. For example, the MPR plan may call for the selection of an expert spokesperson. A data-bank search will identify experts who have written books and articles or have been quoted in the media on the desired area of expertise.

The most popular of these data banks is Nexis, a division of Mead Data Central. Nexis, the world's largest full-text database, can access the user to more than 32 million articles from newspapers, wire services, magazines, and newsletters. Another frequently used data base is Dow Jones News/Retrieval Service.

CompuServe is particularly popular among PR people for tracking the competition and the results of their own efforts. It provides Associated Press (AP) stories run in the preceding 24 hours and has access to AP, United Press International (UPI), and 700 other publications and media dating back as much as 25 years. Since most major public relations stories run on the PR Newswire, this service is particularly useful in keeping track of what the competition is doing and saying before it runs in the media.

Life-Style Research

Data bases are valuable to MPR in accessing the media environment, but MPR people are also becoming more focused on understanding the consumer. They are moving from a message orientation to learning more about the consumer to whom the message is directed.

The two major life-style classification systems are VALS and Yankelovich Clancy Schulman's Monitor. VALS, the acronym for values and life-styles, has been used by a number of public relations counseling firms to define audiences, develop strategies, and select media targets. The original VALS, introduced in 1978, utilized a typology divided into four major categories with a total of nine life-styles. These now familiar categories became widely used by marketers.

VALS has been utilized in recent years to shape the strategy of many MPR programs. Burson-Marsteller, for example, used VALS to design a program for the National Turkey Federation to encourage turkey consumption throughout the year instead of just at Thanksgiving and Christmas. Specific messages were targeted to three VALS groups through media they read. For the Survivor and Sustainer group, the message stressed bargain cuts of turkey that could be stretched into a full meal. For the highly traditional Belonger group, the message focused on serving turkey the year round. New, innovative recipes and gourmet cuts were featured in communications to the better-educated, higher-income Achiever group.

After a decade in use, VALS, which revolutionized market research, was completely updated in 1989. VALS 2 places less emphasis on values and more emphasis on the psychological underpinnings of behavior. It is described as a system that explains not just what consumers buy, but why and how they make purchase decisions. The VALS 2 typology has eight segments of adults, each exhibiting distinct attitudinal, behavioral, and decision-making patterns.

Simmons Market Research Bureau, in its 1988 survey, classified 19,000 consumers by VALS 2 types to determine how many people belonged in each segment and to show their product-purchasing and media-usage habits and demographic characteristics.

The Yankelovich Monitor defines life-style segments in terms of neotraditional values resulting from a synthesis of the traditional values of the 1950s with the newer values of the 1970s.

How MPR Uses Psychographics

The importance of Monitor, VALS, and other psychographic research systems is not in the labels but in understanding why the members of each group act as they do. The systems provide another link between marketing and MPR and will increasingly be used by PR counselors in several important ways.

1. *Strategic Planning.* Monitoring life-style changes enables MPR to identify emerging and declining social forces and trends and to devise strategies that reflect those changes.
2. *Creative Development.* Getting a greater feel for the prospective audience helps MPR to position products and services and to design campaigns and direct messages that match the market.
3. *Media Planning.* MPR campaigns can be directed to media whose targets have a profile similar to the audience in terms of their defined life-styles.

FROM PROCESS TO PLAN

Contemporary public relations plans must be written in clear, concise language that fits the format of the marketing plan. This was not always so. Not long ago, public relations proposals were ponderous selling documents that covered every idea of everybody connected with its writing. They were regarded as exercises in persuasive writing: the more excess verbiage, the better. It was widely assumed that the decision makers would read every word of the proposal, no matter how long and detailed, and give gold stars on how well it was written. It was felt that the readers would be impressed by the heft of the document and by the sheer energy that went into its making. The bulk of the document was a recitation of ideas to gain media coverage with little attention paid to how well these ideas supported marketing objectives and strategies. The "laundry list of ideas" approach generated by public relations firms was based on the assumption that among them there should be something the client would buy.

Today's marketing public relations plans are more precisely tuned to marketing strategies and presented in the language of marketing. Public relations jargon and detailed descriptions of public relations mechanics are disappearing. The purple prose has been reduced, if not eliminated. There has been a realization that the "client" wants only the facts and will not wade through a tome to find them. The "leave behind" is nearly identical with the oral presentation, but contains additional information and detail necessary to support the recommendation. Since most oral presentations are of 60 to 90 minutes' duration, including questions and answers, time constraints require that the plan be focused, concise, and easy to understand. Most "go" or "no go" decisions are made on the effectiveness of the oral presentation and the ability of the presenters to defend their MPR recommendations.

ELEMENTS OF THE MPR PLAN

MPR plans, in fact, borrow heavily from the format of advertising plans. While the tactics are different, both exist to achieve the same marketing goals.

MPR objectives must be sharply defined as they relate to marketing objectives. The decision to utilize MPR and the explanation of its purpose is itself a marketing strategy. A comprehensive marketing plan should also explain how the principal promotional functions—advertising, sales promotion, personal selling, and MPR—complement and supplement each other. A publicity effort might be used, for example, to bring attention to the advertising campaign, or advertising might be used to promote attendance at a sponsored special event.

The MPR plan, like the advertising plan, must show how MPR strategies support marketing strategies and must explain why the tactics proposed are on-strategy. How the tactics (MPR programs) will be implemented must be spelled out in detail and accurately budgeted. Finally, the public relations plan should always include an evaluation component to measure how well the program succeeds in meeting its objectives.

Marketing management might place greater or lesser emphasis on measurement depending on which is greater, the need to justify MPR spending or limitations of the research budget. Some marketers build in a research component to specifically measure MPR effectiveness. Others include measurement in a plan to evaluate how well the overall marketing plan works. Still others prefer to concentrate MPR dollars on program planning and execution and evaluate its effectiveness by clip count, "big hits," or "gut feel."

MPR should be considered a distinct subset of the marketing plan, designed to support the other promotion disciplines but employing different tactics to get there. The elements of a comprehensive MPR plan are shown in Figure 6–1.

USES OF RESEARCH

MPR uses research in planning communications campaigns to define objectives, identify audiences, design messages, and devise media strategies. Research is also being used increasingly to test MPR campaigns. Message testing has long been used in advertising. Some sophisticated marketers investing in larger PR budgets are now looking for ways to test the PR message or campaign idea. Research is also beginning to be employed to test tactics such as the credibility of spokespersons and the effectiveness of PR materials.

This testing can be done under simulated market conditions prior to launch or can be conducted in the field under real market conditions so that the campaign can be fine-tuned and improved along the way. In this way, research is used to help manage the communications process.

Finally research is being used increasingly to evaluate the results of completed public relations campaigns and determine how well they met their objectives.

EVALUATING THE RESULTS OF MPR

Traditionally, public relations results have been measured in terms of numbers of clips obtained, total circulation of print media coverage, and TV- and radio-audience data as compiled by such sources as Standard Rates & Data Service. Circulation of print media has largely been replaced by "reader impressions," an estimate of total readership of the publication, including pass-along readers. These figures are either provided by the publications themselves or calculated by an arbitrary formula.

In recent years, clip counting has become more sophisticated and exacting. Organizations such as PR Data Systems and News Analysis Institute (NAI) have developed techniques and technology to measure media coverage quantitatively and qualitatively. NAI tailors its analysis criteria to assess results in terms of specific public relations objectives met for each program it measures. Clippings are carefully reviewed to identify articles on the basis of positive, negative, or neutral coverage to determine the extent to which media coverage supports or detracts from the campaign's objectives. Content analysis can determine the use and treatment of specific messages, placement location within the publication, use of photos or charts, and geographic coverage.

Porter/Novelli has developed a system called PRESS (Public Relations Evaluation and Support System), which initially uses psychographic

I.   Executive Summary

This is a one- or two-page summary of the entire plan, outlining what is proposed and why, what it is intended to accomplish, and what it will cost. The summary gives management a roadmap of the elements of the program, stripped of their details.

II.   Situation Analysis

This section summarizes relevant background facts and important information necessary to understand the marketing problem and opportunity. The essential parts of the analysis are:

A.   The Product

This section discusses the background on the product—description, benefits, sizes, shape, price, channels of distribution. If it is not a new product, the product's sales and promotion history should also be included.

B.   Target Markets

This section defines target markets in terms of demographic and psychographic profiles. It differs from the advertising plan, which is usually focused on the single best target audience, for example, that traditional packaged-goods target, the married woman between the ages of 25 and 49 who has a high school education and family income of $30,000, and who keeps house, raises kids, and watches television. (Are there any left?) The prevailing thinking is that all advertising dollars should be concentrated on reaching the market that represents the best return on investment. Since MPR can reach additional targets at lower levels of spending than advertising, the MPR plan suggests reaching not only the principal target market, but also secondary consumer audiences, opinion leaders, and trade audiences to be targeted in the PR program. The plan should provide information on each of these secondary markets and possibly add new information and insights about the primary market, such as psychographic data indicating a concurrent or alternative public relations approach to reach the same market.

(continued)

FIGURE 6–1   A Comprehensive MPR Plan

C. Environment

This section should include information on market share and explanation of share changes. Direct and indirect competition, strengths and weaknesses of competing brands, geographic differences, and a description of promotional programs are part of the marketing environment. So are threats to the product or category that, because of safety or efficacy, may put it at risk. "Megamarketing" factors that block entry into markets should also be discussed here.

III. Market Goals

This section reviews objectives and strategies set by marketing management. They must be included to show how the proposed public relations program will support those goals and help the company meet them.

IV. MPR Recommendations

A. MPR Objectives

Clear MPR objectives must state what the program is designed to do. The program will be evaluated on how well these objectives are met. Objectives are usually cast in terms of communicating information, increasing awareness, and influencing behavior, that is, predisposing consumers to buy the product.

B. MPR Strategies

MPR strategies are stated in terms of ways that the program will cause the objectives to be achieved. For example, to communicate news about the product to target markets through publicity placement in relevant media.

C. MPR Recommendations

This is the guts of the program, the tactics that will be used to support the strategies stated above. Here is the place to describe those good ideas and show how they will contribute to the overall marketing effort. The section consists of:

1. The Message

There will usually be a single message, which gives the consumer a reason to buy the product. While the

FIGURE 6-1 *(continued)*

message may include common copy points with the advertising, it is not likely that the media will transmit the message in the same words. Nor is it possible for the MPR program to be built around a selling slogan. While the MPR message often supports the advertising, it cannot emulate an ad campaign that depends on sloganeering, imagery, or emotional appeals like "Coke is it" or "The heartbeat of America: that's today's Chevrolet." MPR cannot use a slogan like "The Right Choice is AT&T," but it can generate stories that give target consumers reasons for choosing AT&T as their long-distance carrier.

While advertising puts all of its firepower behind a slogan or single selling point, the MPR program may redirect different strategically correct messages to audiences differentiated demographically, psychologically, or functionally (in the case of opinion leaders and trade audiences).

2. **The Media**

Since most MPR programs are media-centered, most MPR plans include a media plan. The MPR media plan should describe the means for disseminating useful information in selected target media. The cost is professional staff time, which does not rise incrementally with each media contact. It should not be confused with media buying, which paradoxically is also sometimes called placement. MPR placement is the result of selling, not buying.

The MPR media plan might include mass media like network television and national magazines. But it will also be likely to also include a wide variety of specialized media vehicles to reach primary and secondary target audiences and media to carry the story to the local level, for instance, media directed specifically to opinion leaders and trade audiences and "created media" like newsletters, service booklets, teaching or program materials, and audio-visual aids.

The MPR media plan should not be confused with the advertising media plan, which details how advertising dollars will be spent to achieve optimum reach and frequency against the target audience.

(continued)

FIGURE 6–1 *(continued)*

3. The Program

This section spells out the specific tactics that will be used to deliver the product message to the target audience. Some tactics will be designed to generate publicity in media selected for their ability to reach defined audiences. The program section details the methods that will be employed to achieve media coverage—for example, one-on-one media interviews, media tours and news conferences—and the tools such as press kits and video news releases necessary to support this effort. This section also recommends events, sponsorships, and other tactics designed to reach target audiences directly rather than through the media. Media created to support the program, such as printed materials and audio-visual aids are also described here. The variety of MPR tactics, as we will see in Chapter 7, is as broad as the imagination of the people charged with creating and implementing the program.

4. The Timetable

The plan should provide a detailed calendar that shows the amount of time that will be required to prepare, produce, and implement each element of the program. Key dates should be coordinated with cost commitment requirements.

5. The Budget

This section will be of key importance to the marketing decision makers. They must weigh the MPR recommendations against other promotion options in terms of relative cost effectiveness in reaching and influencing target audiences. It is therefore imperative that each element of the MPR program be budgeted accurately. This involves obtaining cost estimates from suppliers, event locations, spokespersons, and others. Estimated costs of expanding or reducing the program should be available and the presenter should be prepared to prioritize recommendations in terms of relative importance of tactics in meeting strategies and marketing objectives.

FIGURE 6-1 *(continued)*

V. Evaluation

This section outlines a plan to measure results. Results have usually been stated in terms of print circulation and broadcast audience or estimated numbers of consumers exposed to the newspaper or magazine and to the particular article about Porter/Novelli has developed a system called PRESS (Public Relations Evaluation and Support System), which initially uses psychographic advertising-oriented consumer-product companies. Whether these exposures are truly equivalent is a matter of considerable conjecture, but it gives the client a somewhat better idea of what he got for his MPR dollar.

Some MPR programs are evaluated on their ability to achieve a predetermined number of gross or target-consumer impressions, but MPR is moving from exposure measurements to behavior measurements. These measures might include primary pre- and post-research determining the effect of MPR exposures on decisions to purchase. (They should be included in this section if budget allows.) Other measures that can be used to assess consumer interest in the MPR message are number of booklet requests from offers made in publicity, number of entries in MPR-generated contests, and number of consumers calling in to ask questions to company spokespersons appearing on television and radio interview shows.

VI. Conclusion

This section may or may not be included in the plan. If the plan is being sold to management, it offers an opportunity not only to restate why the program will work, but, in the case of competitive presentations by PR firms, why the firm should be chosen for the job. In asking for the order, the firm will likely try to demonstrate why it is best qualified for the assignment on the basis of experience, expertise, proven record of results, dedication, and fit with the client-company culture.

FIGURE 6–1 (continued)

and demographic research to target audiences and select media that reach these audiences. Then, after the campaign, the media coverage is compared with preagreed strategies to determine the extent to which media coverage was on or off strategy. The firm quantifies clips, circulation, and message and media vehicles, measures gross impressions for the specific target audience, and then weighs the quality of each placement in an effort to identify cause-and-effect relationships.

Ketchum Public Relations, a pioneer in the field, introduced its Publicity Planning and Tracking System in 1982. The system evaluates individual media vehicles to determine how many people in the target demographic group are found in that vehicle's audience. VALS is used similarly to determine media best suited to reach the psychographic profile or target audiences. Media are also analyzed on their ability to deliver users of the product category. The system measures the exposure value of placements based on size (print) or length (broadcast) and evaluates the message elements that can be identified and tracked. These elements are then checked for number of mentions and prominence within a given placement. Impact is measured by applying a multiplier that takes into account how effectively the message was presented.

In Dallas in October 1989, Ketchum introduced an updated version of the system with three new features: a publicity-planning component that gives audience data for major media nationally as well as for the 50 largest markets; a component that tracks competitors' media placements; and an issues-tracking component.

In April 1988, Ketchum conducted its Nationwide Survey of Public Relations Research, Measurement, and Evaluation among public relations executives at major corporations, trade associations, nonprofit organizations, and public relations firms, and among university academicians. Two out of every three public relations counselors and academicians felt that the volume of public relations research had increased moderately or greatly in the United States in the period 1985–1987. Almost half of those surveyed said that they had been involved in measurement and evaluation research related to media relations and publicity activities in 1986 and 1987. Eighty-one percent of the PR practitioners said they occasionally or frequently conduct publicity-tracking or media-monitoring studies.

Dr. Walter K. Lindenmann, vice president and director of research at Ketchum, believes that "what is most encouraging about the findings is that a solid 57 percent of all PR executives who were interviewed have come to recognize that it is possible to try to measure PR outcomes, impact, and effectiveness in precise terms." He concludes that "research in PR is beginning to come out of the Dark Ages and is starting to become accepted as a 'given' part of the field."

OUTCOMES VS. OUTPUTS

In a 1988 *Public Relations Journal* article titled "Beyond the Clipbook," Lindenmann pointed out:

> No matter how sophisticated, clip-counting systems measure only public relations outputs (how publicity is presented in the media), not the more desirable public relations outcomes (the overall impact or effect of that

presentation). Output systems do not measure the most important areas of evaluation: Did people actually pay attention to the publicity? Did they comprehend the message and retain it over time? Did they change their opinions or beliefs based on the content? And, perhaps most important, did they take any actions as a result of that publicity?[3]

Among the techniques being used today to measure outcomes, the most used is a pre- and post-test where a sample of the target audience is surveyed before and after a campaign to determine changes in awareness, interest, and purchase intention. A variation is tracking polls that measure opinion before, after, and during the campaign.

Focus groups are being used not only in the planning stage, to test message appeals, but also to evaluate the effectiveness of program components. Other techniques borrowed from advertising and market research are now being used by MPR, including day-after recall. Participants are asked to watch a specific TV program on which a company spokesperson is to appear. The next day they are called to determine whether they remembered seeing the spokesperson, recalled the message, and were more inclined to try the product discussed. A variation is the mall-intercept in which a group of qualified target consumers is asked to view a videotape of a talk show on which the spokesperson appeared. Participants are asked to play back the messages they heard and tell whether what they learned would interest them in buying the product. These results are measured against a control group that did not watch the program.

Another research method borrowed from advertising is setting up matched markets with and without public relations and measuring the effect not only on awareness but on sales. While it is difficult to isolate consumers in test communities from all non-PR stimuli, and while matched market tests are expensive to conduct, the tests can prove valuable not only in assessing the value of public relations but in determining the right marketing mix before the product is rolled out or taken national.

The Campbell "Soup is Good Food" campaign worked best in a California test market where PR and advertising were used in tandem; neither moved the needle in matched markets where they stood alone. Lloyd Kirban, executive vice president and director of research at Burson-Marsteller, cites a similar test involving a new product launch in Canada. Like the Campbell test, the product was supported by advertising in one province, PR in another, and a combination of both in a third province. Sales were highest where both advertising and PR were used. However, sales were better in the PR-only market than in the advertising-only market.

Kirban points out that "all placements are not necessarily equal. One placement may have more news value, may be more believable, or just may have had better message delivery by the spokesperson."

7

MPR Tactics from A to Z

The tactics that can be employed by MPR are limited only by the practitioner's imagination and ability to execute. It is not demeaning to refer to this variety of tactics as PR's "bigger bag of tricks," especially when contrasted to advertising, whose tools are basically limited to print ads and broadcast commercials.

The bigger bag could cover several alphabets. But the tactics listed here alphabetically are frequently used to gain media and consumer attention for new and established products.

AWARDS have been used by sponsors to honor the worthwhile and the simply interesting, for example, best dressed, best coiffed.

Blistex's Most Beautiful Lips

Blistex, Inc., of Oak Park, Illinois, manufacturer of lip-care products, conducts a public relations program designed to create a preference for its products by positioning Blistex as "the" authority on lip care. A publicity feature that has been popular with both the print and broadcast media since it was created by Golin/Harris in 1980 is Blistex's Beautiful Lips Contest. Every year, "the lip-care experts at Blistex" select a dozen people with the "World's Most Beautiful Lips." Photos of the winners and their citations are distributed by the Associated Press to newspapers across the country and the contest is covered extensively by radio and television.

The popularity of the Beautiful Lips Contest results from combining names that made news with humorous citations, for example:

1980	Loretta Swit (star of TV's "M*A*S*H")—"hottest lips"
1981	John McEnroe (tennis player)—"most self-serving lips"
1982	Richard Simmons (TV star)—"most exercised lips"
1983	Paul Volker Jr. (Chairman, Federal Reserve Board)—"most reserved lips"

1983	Eddie Murphy (comedian)—"least reserved lips"
1984	Margaret Thatcher (British Prime Minister)—"stiffest upper lip"
1984	Wayne Gretsky (hockey player)—"most puckered lips"
1985	Sylvester Stallone (movie star)—"most rambunctious lips"
1985	Joan Collins (TV star)—"Dy-nastiest lips"
1986	Jim McMahon (football player)—"most over-Bearing lips"
1987	Spuds McKenzie (party animal)—"best doggone lips"
1987	Lt. Col. Oliver North (USMC)—"most Contra-versial lips"
1988	Leona Helmsley (hotelier)—"most harried lips"
1988	Ronald Reagan (retiring President)—"most outgoing lips"
1989	George Bush (President)—"read my lips"

The Chicago Bureau Chief of AP told a meeting of the Publicity Club of Chicago that "Beautiful Lips is the kind of feature we are looking for" and reminded his audience that AP must judge 600 to 800 stories a day. Because of the selection of foreign winners, the Beautiful Lips awards have been featured in media all over the world. Company executives have been interviewed by media in England, Canada, and Australia. The company's president received from Blistex's Japanese distributor an article from one of the most widely circulated magazines in Japan with a note stating, "These kind of PR activities are a great help for the brand."

Blistex has received thank-you notes from recipients ranging from Joan Collins to Queen Elizabeth to Barbara Bush. TV news commentator Diane Sawyer personally discussed her award with a *Ladies' Home Journal* interviewer. Joan Rivers wrote to Blistex, "I am extremely honored to have been among the twelve chosen for your Beautiful Lips award. The plaque hangs proudly in my den and every time I pass it I can't resist the urge to pucker up. Thank you, thank you, thank you so very much for this wonderful recognition." Paul Volker's letter stated simply, "I will hang the certificate proudly, but without comment."

The secret of the Beautiful Lips success was capitalizing on names that made news in the 1980s' style of mixing world leaders with nouveau celebrities who were enjoying Andy Warhol's often-quoted fifteen minutes of fame. All were juxtaposed in *People* Magazine style because of their attention-getting celebrity status. Each year, the winners are famous for being famous and are highly attractive to the media that made them famous in the first place.

BOOKS, ranging from General Mills' *Betty Crocker Cookbook* to Maytag's *Encyclopedia of Laundry*, in addition to literally thousands of service and "how to" booklets published by manufacturers, are used to promote products.

CONTESTS, COMPETITIONS, AND CREATED EVENTS range from the Pillsbury Bake-Off to Gainesburgers Dog Frisbee Catch to the Combat Quest for the World's Largest Roach.

Soap, Sticks, and Specs

A media-attracting MPR contest was the "Coast to Coast Shower Sing-Off" sponsored by Procter & Gamble's Coast Deodorant Soap and created by Hill & Knowlton. Regional competitions to pick the area's best shower singers were held in nine shopping malls. In each, shower-costumed contestants were given two minutes to sing *a cappella* or accompanied by a prerecorded tape in a custom-designed shower stage set. The winners were selected on the basis of originality, overall performance, and entertainment value.

Stimulated by pre-event local publicity and radio-station promotions, the events each attracted an average audience of 1,000 spectators and widespread coverage in the local newspapers and on local television. The national finals at New York's Radio City Music Hall, featuring Bert Parks as emcee, were covered on all network news programs. The program generated more than 165 million consumer impressions, revitalizing interest in an established brand. A research study showed that 85 percent of all event attendees knew that the shows were sponsored by Coast soap, and 76 percent said that the events made them want to buy the product.

In recent years, MPR people have worked closely with major magazines to create contests that involve readers with both the sponsor and the magazine. In these contests, readers are offered the opportunity to both win prizes and be featured in the magazine.

Popsicle's Stick Art Contest invited moms and their 6-to-12-year-olds to create art objects using Popsicle sticks. *Woman's Day* craft editors selected the winners. The magazine hosted an awards ceremony for winners and parents and ran photos of the winning entries.

Pearle Vision Center's Spectacular Specs Makeover Contest invited *Woman's Day* readers to send the magazine a color photo of themselves wearing their favorite pair of glasses and a 100-word answer to the question, "Why I Want a Spectacular Specs Makeover." The grand prize was a trip for two to New York City for a *Woman's Day* makeover. Second and third prizes were cash and new Pearle prescription eyeglasses. Even more important to Pearle (and attractive to readers) was the fact that all entrants received a discount certificate worth $30 off on any pair of eyeglasses at any Pearle Vision Center. The contest was a huge success. More than 5,000 women took the time to enter, win discount certificates, and redeem them at a Pearle store. Results showed the power of MPR to attract and involve consumers, build store traffic, and move merchandise.

CHOTCHKES are widely used in public relations to entice press and public alike. Billions of T-shirts, sweat shirts, sweaters, caps, aprons, umbrellas, tote bags, and more are walking promotions for brands and branded sponsorships. So popular are these chotchkes that the sale of branded merchandise has become a mini profit center for beer companies and others. The Hard Rock Cafe is world famous because of its T-shirt.

DEMONSTRATIONS are conducted in stores, shopping malls, and elsewhere by company spokespersons; products range from food processors to cosmetics to adult toys.

EXHIBITS consist of both the permanent variety, in high-traffic locations like Walt Disney World's Epcot Center and Chicago's Museum of Science and Industry, and traveling exhibits, which range from Campbell Soup's soup tureen collection and Bally Corporation's exhibit of lottery memorabilia to interactive exhibits in shopping malls.

NutraSweet sponsors a traveling exhibit that appears annually at high-traffic state fairs during the summer months and is visited by more than 2 million consumers. These family outings provide an opportunity to talk with NutraSweet dieticians, sample recipes made with products sweetened with NutraSweet, and walk away with a Nutra-Sweet tote bag filled with recipe booklets, coupons, and dry product samples.

Allied Van Lines' Move to Freedom

In an effort to strengthen its ties to local communities and its number-one position in the moving industry, Allied Van Lines developed the "Move to Freedom" exhibits. Two identical traveling displays were housed in 48-foot Allied vans, as shown in Figure 7–1. The exterior was specially painted with "Move to Freedom" graphics and the exhibit featured historical artwork, rare photographs, and sculpture depicting the history of the Statue of Liberty and Ellis Island. Visitors to the exhibit viewed an elaborate multimedia production recreating the sights and sounds of the immigrant experience.

Over a two-year period leading up to the Statue's Centennial Celebration on July 4, 1986, the exhibits traveled to more than 300 cities and towns, collecting donations for the restoration of the Statue of Liberty. In 75 percent of the cities visited, mayors honored the exhibit's arrival by proclaiming local Liberty Days. Dozens of local schools visited the exhibit and hosted special fundraising events, ranging from concerts to walkathons. Some cities staged swearing-in ceremonies for new U.S. citizens at the exhibit site. More than 800 newspapers and radio and TV stations covered the exhibit, including an NBC "Today" feature that highlighted the tour.

FAN CLUBS, once the province of entertainers, now encompass the fans of products ranging from Barbie Dolls and Mustangs to peanut butter, catfish, and even NutraSweet. Fan paraphernalia typically includes membership cards and certificates, brand-merchandise offers, newsletters, and booklets. Periodic fan-club meetings keep interest high and generate publicity and word of mouth.

FIGURE 7–1 The Allied Van Lines "Move to Freedom" exhibits visited more than 300 U.S. cities to celebrate the Statue of Liberty centennial in 1986. Two identical traveling displays recreating the images and impressions that immigrants shared of Ellis Island and the Statue were housed in Allied vans.

FESTIVALS are so plentiful that a directory of them is published to attract potential corporate sponsors. Some sponsor their own, like Hershey's Great American Chocolate Festival.

GRAND OPENINGS can range from ribbon cuttings and tours of automated manufacturing plants to black-tie galas run by department stores to benefit charities to the opening of local franchised restaurants and stores.

HOTLINES have proliferated with the advent of 800 and 900 telephone lines. One of the best known is Butterball's Turkey Hotline, which answers 150,000 calls a year from consumers looking for new and better ways to prepare turkey dinners, and has become Butterball's principal marketing tool.

INTERVIEWS of high visibility CEOs bring attention to their company's products. Lee Iacocca says he will not give an interview unless it will sell cars.

JUNKETS are used to bring the media to the story. They often include plant tours or visits to research or training facilities.

KEY ISSUES can help build loyalty when the company takes a stand on issues that show that it is on the consumer's side.

LUNCHEONS and press parties are the tried-and-true way for companies to foster personal relationships with the media and generate news.

MEETINGS such as seminars, symposia, and teleconferences are sponsored by companies to discuss trends, reveal research, and stimulate discussion related to the company's products and consumers.

MUSEUMS assembled by companies like Hershey Foods and Anheuser-Busch have been popular with tourists for years. In 1990, the Coca-Cola Company opened a freestanding three-story museum in Atlanta called "The World of Coca-Cola." The museum, which Coke estimates will be visited by as many as a half million people a year, houses more than 1,000 items of memorabilia, exhibits, movies, a high-tech fountain that shoots a stream of Coca-Cola 20 feet in the air, and what the company calls "the most remarkable Coke sign ever created."

The New York Times pointed out that "The Coca-Cola museum is the latest—and perhaps most ambitious—example of the growing use of corporate historical exhibits as promotional tools." The *Times* said that, "seeking fresh ways to reach an advertising bombarded public, companies are converting themselves into nothing less than tourist attractions through a confluence of marketing, education and entertainment."[1]

NEWSLETTERS are used by MPR to communicate news and keep products, places, and personalities top-of-mind among consumer and trade audiences. Companies build mailing lists from in-pack buyer questionnaires, visitors to company exhibits and events, people who write for booklets offered in publicity, and 800-number callers.

OFFICIAL ENDORSEMENTS from government officials and respected organizations provide third-party endorsement and support market positioning. The endorsement of Crest toothpaste by the American Dental Association propelled the brand to category leadership. Mayoral, gubernatorial, and even presidential proclamations focus attention on company sponsorships and enhance the corporation's image.

PRODUCT PLACEMENT in movies and on television shows has become a mini-industry since Reese's Pieces achieved a remarkable sales boost when the candy was featured in *E.T.*

The Trail of *E.T.*

The marriage of brand names and Hollywood films has a long history. But marketers really took notice when an extraterrestial visitor called E.T. took a fancy to Reese's Pieces in one of the top-grossing films (and subsequently, videos) of all time. The story of how Reese's Pieces were substituted for Mars Company's M&Ms when Mars declined to provide product samples for the filming is by now well known. Hershey paid nothing for the exposure, yet by a month after the film's release, sales of Reese's Pieces had increased 65 percent. Hershey got behind the film, spending $1 million for promotion and public relations, the largest such budget in the company's history. Reese's Pieces were billed as "E.T.'s Favorite Candy" and the brand offered E.T. T-shirts and posters free with proofs of purchase. The sales increase for Hershey Foods' relatively new brand was so significant that E.T. was honored on the cover of Hershey's annual report to shareholders.

While some companies may provide products free and take their chances that their brands might end up on the cutting-room floor, the trend has been toward so-called "back-end" promotions incorporating promotion, PR, and advertising. Companies may pay promotional-consideration fees for critical product placements in films with big box-office potential. Others provide promotion of the film in prerelease product promotions and advertising, in exchange for product exposure in the film. This exposure is critical to the success of the film since the box-office fate of most films is decided on the first weekend of release. In the movie business, however, there are no guarantees of success and a product promotion may die with the film. Then there is that rare situation where the film dies but the product promotion is a success. This happened to a Glad Bags promotion tied to a box-office flop named *The Million Dollar Movie.*

The business of getting feature-film or TV exposure for an auto maker's cars and trucks has become "a big and competitive business" according to *The Los Angeles Times* report that auto makers annually turn over some $10 million of free cars to Hollywood. The studios save the hundreds of thousands of dollars it would cost them to buy or rent needed cars and in turn provide free exposure in an entertainment context. The M&M debacle with *E.T.* was replayed in the auto-placement business when Porsche refused to provide a car with a special sunroof to the producers of *Magnum, P.I.* Tom Selleck ended up driving a now famous Ferrari in the long-running TV hit show.

The latest wrinkle in product placement was the showing of a made-for-the-movie full-length TV commercial for a real product in the context of a film. The movie was the big summer-of-1989 hit, *Lethal Weapon 2.* What made this particular product placement especially intriguing was that the commercial was for Ramses condoms, a product that cannot be advertised on television. *Newsweek* reported that the tie-in did not stop there: "Risking more predictable jokes, the studio has handed out as many as 15,000 condoms in packages bearing the *Lethal Weapon 2* logo at dance clubs from the Palladium in San Francisco to Atlanta's Club Rio."[2]

This equating of product placement to advertising has raised questions of whether it should be regulated under the laws and rules that apply to advertising. The Center for Science in the Public Interest has asked the Federal Communications Commission and state attorneys general to require that the use of paid product placements in movies be disclosed in the movie's opening credits and even that the word "advertisement" be superimposed on the screen when the movies are shown on television. An Ohio Congressman has introduced a bill that would ban cigarette companies from paying to have their brands shown in movies because they do not include the warning label required in cigarette advertising. He cites a scene in *Superman II* in which Superman demolishes a Marlboro truck. The movie is shown on television where cigarette advertising is banned.

Despite such criticism, product placement is likely to be here to stay, not only because it saves studios money and helps them promote pictures, but because realism in movies requires it. In portraying real-life situations, actors drive brand-name cars, shop in real stores, eat and drink brand-name products, and wear brand-name clothing. Their kitchen and bathroom shelves are not filled with Brand X products. Generics did not sell in the supermarket and will not work in the movies.

PUBLIC SERVICE ANNOUNCEMENTS (PSAs) are used by companies and trade groups to identify themselves with subjects and issues of interest to the public. Widely used on both radio and television, they link commercial sponsors with good causes ranging from literacy to fire safety to pet adoption.

QUESTIONNAIRES not only provide marketers with valuable consumer information, but they also give MPR programs quotable survey material favored by the news media. Surveys on fashions, favorite foods, and lifestyles are widely publicized. Orkin even releases an annual survey on cities where termites eat the most wood.

RADIO TRADE-FOR-MENTION CONTESTS generate frequent on-air product mentions which are traded for prizes provided by the manufacturer.

ROAD SHOWS can achieve headlines, trade interest, and marketplace excitement.

Roger and Lee

In 1988, General Motors Chairman Roger Smith personally led a marketing public relations campaign to regain consumers' trust by repositioning GM as a leader in technology "for today and tomorrow." The show, instantly dubbed "Rogerama" by the media covering its opening in New York, included one-of-a-kind vehicles and 1988 production cars and trucks, plus a number of exhibits designed to demonstrate the company's commitment to teamwork and technology. Large-screen video projection was used to dramatize new-product features and high-tech activities.

The road show moved on to Chicago, Los Angeles, Dallas, Atlanta, and finally Detroit where, according to a company press release, "thousands of invited guests representing a cross-section of GM's many publics—GM dealers, stockholders, employees, union representatives, suppliers, and news media, plus leaders from business, government, education, and the arts—are learning about the corporation's accomplishments and its confidence in the future." The "Teamwork and Technology" show was designed to achieve optimum public relations impact. Chairman Smith described it as "a progress report to our many stockholders and publics" and a way of "telling the world that our vision is paying off."

Two years later, it was Lee Iacocca's turn. Chrysler Corporation's Chairman and CEO brought his special brand of personal salesmanship to a six-city tour called "Chrysler in the 90s."

The tour featured 1990 production vehicles from Dodge, Chrysler-Plymouth, and Jeep-Eagle; 1991 cars and minivans; and concept cars, that could become production vehicles in the 1990s. In addition to cars and trucks, there were exhibits on air bags and engines and a look at Chrysler Technology Center, the company's new billion-dollar design and engineering center.

But the real star of the show was America's best-known businessman, Lee Iacocca.

He did not disappoint. "Iacocca declares war on foreign cars," declared *USA TODAY* in its lead story. The paper's report from the tour kickoff in Washington, DC, quoted the colorful Iacocca prose: "We have this obsession that anything built overseas is better; we're not going to let that kind of crap go unchallenged." Another Iacocca-ism was widely picked up in the nation's news media: "Japan today is wrapped in a teflon kimono, especially when it comes to cars, and maybe it's time to start peeling back the kimono a little bit."

Iacocca used the Washington event as the occasion to unveil a new Chrysler advertising campaign called "Advantage Chrysler"—starring Lee Iacocca. He explained the reason for the roadshow this way at a Washington press conference:

> We're in a business where our sales get measured and talked about every ten days. At "Chrysler in the 90s," we'll talk about how to measure Chrysler over the next ten years. The bottom line is that Chrysler is going to be competitive with the Japanese and anybody else.
>
> I don't happen to subscribe to the current theory that everything Japanese is better than anything American. I don't think that's true for Chrysler or for American industry or products in general. Chrysler has $15 billion committed over the next five years to assure that we remain competitive in the future. "Chrysler in the 90s" will give us an opportunity to tell that story.[3]

The morning press conference was followed by a day-long series of events that included one-on-one interviews with key news media, a luncheon for fleet car buyers, government officials, and automotive analysts (whose views were sought by the media), and a reception for 2,000 VIPs in the evening.

The routine was repeated in each of the other tour cities—Dallas, Atlanta, New York, Chicago, and Los Angeles. During the three-month tour, Iacocca took the message "Chrysler is alive and kicking and in business" directly to 12,000 invited guests, including politicians, bankers, and opinion leaders. Displaying his legendary media savvy, Iacocca made national news at each stop, concluding the tour in Los Angeles with the announcement that the Dodge Viper sportscar introduced at the show would be put on sale in 1992. He said that more than 3,000 people had written or called about the car, proof positive of the power of product publicity, Iacocca-style.

———————

SAMPLING of products is a longstanding weapon in the marketing arsenal. New products are mailed to residences in selected zip codes, given away in stores and on street corners, and packed with established products. MPR sampling is designed for a different purpose. Sampling (or in the case of high-ticket items, loaning) products to reporters has long been standard public relations practice. Increasingly, public relations has provided samples to other opinion leaders and taste makers from executives to extension home economists. Another function of MPR sampling is to gain visibility. Having the right product in the right place at the right time will result in trial and start word-of-mouth endorsement. It can also offer an opportunity to reach a larger audience if a strong publicity angle can be created around the sampling occasion.

In 1981, millions of people got their first taste of the new sweetener NutraSweet in, of all things, a gumball. In the first year, nearly 3 million people wrote the company for a free sample sleeve of four brightly colored NutraSweet sweetened gumballs. Since that time, gumballs have become the brand's signature and the one thing that everyone identifies with NutraSweet. Gumballs are still given away at trade shows and company exhibits.

———————

Halls' Silent Nights at the Symphony

Halls Cough Suppressant Tablets, a 60-year-old brand, is the number-one-selling brand in the United States and the world. With the exception of new flavor additions, there is very little news about Halls. In 1988, Warner-Lambert set out to create news about Halls cough-suppressant benefits.

The company distributed a survey to 2,500 patrons at three leading symphony orchestras—the Atlanta Symphony, the St. Louis Symphony, and the Los Angeles Philharmonic—to determine the most distracting audience noises encountered during symphony performances. Whispering, coughing, and sniffling ranked first, second, and third, respectively, followed by rattling of candy wrappers, humming along, and constant moving about in one's seat.

Publicity about the survey was released in conjunction with an innovative antinoise campaign launched at the onset of the 1988–1989 concert season. In an effort to create "Silent Nights at the Symphony" during winter's cough-and-cold season, Warner-Lambert began providing complimentary wax-wrapped Halls Cough Suppressant Tablets to patrons at the New York Philharmonic and the Dallas and Chicago Symphony Orchestras, as well as audiences in Atlanta, St. Louis, and Los Angeles.

Chicago Tribune music critic John von Rhein picked up the theme. In an article introducing the 1988 CSO season, he wrote:

Perhaps the most intriguing item on the press release heralding the 98th Chicago Symphony Orchestra season is the news that Warner-Lambert now will provide free cough lozenges to those attending Orchestra Hall performances. The lozenges, available in five flavors, will be wrapped in noiseless wax paper and dispensed in all lobby areas. Warner-Lambert has performed a similar service with other orchestras across the nation and reports—I am quoting here—"considerable reduction in coughing noises during concerts. Any way you unwrap it, this is a historic boon to musical mankind. Cough-free Copland! Low-noise Lizst! Silent Schubert! The prospects are endless and tantalizing. If the idea clicks, Warner-Lambert will have earned the deathless gratitude of the silent majority of subscribers, not to mention the long-suffering performers on stage."[4]

SYMBOLS like Ronald McDonald, the second most recognized figure to the children of the world (outranked only by Santa Claus), the Campbell Kids, Ernie the Keebler Elf, and the Pillsbury Doughboy are highly visible and personalize a company to consumers.

Show Horses and Showplaces

Of all the vast array of promotional vehicles and programs used by Anheuser-Busch to carry the Budweiser name and colors to the public, the most famous and potent promotional vehicle of them all is the Clydesdales. To celebrate the end of Prohibition, the promotional-minded August Busch, Jr., put together a hitch of Clydesdale horses and delivered a case of Budweiser to President Franklin D. Roosevelt. Since then, reports *The New York Times*, "the Clydesdales have been transformed into a highly visible marketing force for Budweiser . . . the big horses have become one of the best-known corporate symbols in the world."

Today the company maintains three hitches, in St. Louis, in California, and in New Hampshire. Each appears in more than 100 parades and county fairs a year in response to requests by Anheuser-Busch's 950 wholesalers. The company says it cannot come close to accepting the thousands of appearance invitations received each year for the Clydesdales. Wherever they do appear, however, they are backed with advance publicity, feature stories, and local event coverage.

Another vehicle for attaining high visibility for Anheuser-Busch products is the company's theme parks. In addition to its two Busch Gardens parks, the company owns Sesame Place and Adventure Island, and recently acquired four Sea World parks and two other amusement parks. In all, these parks entertain 20 million visitors annually. Busch Gardens in Tampa, Florida, celebrated its 30th anniversary in 1989. The enormous number of stories generated by Anheuser-Busch's longtime PR firm Fleishman-Hillard, about such attractions as giant pandas from Beijing and Koala bears from San Diego in both national and local media is credited with helping attract 3 million visitors to the park. While its family-entertainment business is dwarfed by the beer business, the company takes full advantage of the opportunity to gain positive visibility for its beer brands at the parks.

August Busch III told *The New York Times*, "When one of those 20 million people come through one of these theme parks, we think he will leave with his image of this company enhanced. Our beer products and snack products will be enhanced." He might have added that hardly a person leaves the park without having become a walking advertisement of his favorite A-B brand by buying a Budweiser, Michelob, or Busch cap, jacket, sweat shirt, or T-shirt.

TOURS of the media in person or especially on TV via satellite, are a proven way to obtain exposure for established products, in key markets.

THONS including telethons, marathons, bikeathons, and walkathons link brands with good causes like the Muscular Dystrophy Association, Easter Seals, the United Negro College Fund, and the March of Dimes, and generate positive media exposure and brand loyalty.

UNDERWRITING events of all sorts from professional and participant sports to sponsorships of the fine and performing arts offers marketers opportunities to identify with the interests of their target consumers.

VEHICLES, including hot-air balloons, sailing ships, planes, trains, and racing automobiles, are rigged up by companies to gain visibility for their brands. The grandaddy of them all, the Goodyear Blimp, always seems to appear where the action is.

The Wiener on Wheels

Kids who grew up in the 1950s recall the time they saw a 23-foot four-wheeled hot dog come down the street in their hometown. The first of Oscar Mayer's famous Wienermobiles hit the streets of America in 1936 and subsequent models visited hundreds of U.S. cities until the late 1970s, leaving behind memories and a bit of marketing Americana.

In the 1980s, the company used the last driveable vehicles for two anniversary tours. They were so successful in attracting attention and headlines that the company brought back the Oscar Mayer Wienermobile "by popular demand" in 1988. A fleet of 6 new Wienermobiles converted from Chevy Vans took off on a tour or more than 500 cities across America.

The revival of the Wienermobile was tagged by the company as "a return to family values and traditions and a familiar link between parents who remember the Wienermobile and their children who are seeing it for the first time."

FIGURE 7–2 Hundreds of college students competed to become the baker's dozen "Hotdoggers" who escorted the new fleet of Oscar Mayer Weinermobiles that toured 500 cities across the country in 1988. The 23-foot, four-wheeled hot dogs continue a tradition dating to 1936.

The tour was updated in a number of ways. Little Oscar, the company's goodwill ambassador who escorted earlier Wienermobiles to such activities as parades and grocery-store openings, retired and was replaced by a "baker's dozen" of Oscar Mayer "Hotdoggers," shown in Figure 7–2. They were selected from hundreds of graduating college seniors who competed for the jobs. Their job is to drive the sleek, futuristic-looking, new Wienermobiles "painted wiener-red with a splash of mustard yellow on a lightly toasted bun" around the country; hand out balloons, stickers, and buttons; and make special appearances at festivals, parades, picnics, ball games, orphanages, and nursing homes.

The Wienermobile Hometown Tour was launched as a year-long Salute to Kids; with the help of the National PTA and *Weekly Reader Magazine,* the company conducted a search for young entrepreneurs, artists, and inventors and named five kids as the Oscar Mayer Rising Stars of 1988. Each finalist received a certificate from Oscar Mayer honoring them for exhibiting "creativity and ingenuity and promise to be one of America's best and brightest entrepreneurs." In addition to the high visibility of the Wienermobiles themselves, the search resulted in hometown publicity for the finalists. National publicity was assured when the tour was launched and the fleet of Wienermobiles paraded down Broadway in New York City.

———————

VIDEO NEWS RELEASES (VNRs) are almost universally used to transmit newsworthy product news and event sponsorships to television networks and stations both in edited and extended (B-roll) form, allowing users to localize their reports. Nielsen Research reports that 75 percent of all local TV stations now use VNRs regularly.

WEEKS, months, and days are used by companies and trade associations to focus consumer attention and provide media with a reason to feature their products. My first public relations assignment in 1957 was to promote National Hot Dog Month for a weiner casing manufacturer. More recently, I have been involved in such events as Ziploc National Sandwich Day and National Soup Month for Campbell Soup Company.

EXPERT COLUMNS (OK, I cheated) written by real, or, in some cases, invented company spokespersons run in hundreds of newspapers. Some examples are "Deere John" columns, where John Deere Company experts answer readers' questions about lawn and garden care, and "Ask Dr. Pearle," a Pearle Vision written-column series about eye care and eyewear fashion.

YOUTH PROGRAMS range from popcorn art contests to science awards and athletic competitions. Panasonic and Steven Spielberg cosponsor a Boy Scouts of America merit badge in cinematography. McDonald's reaches the difficult to reach youth market through nationally televised public service programs.

———————

McDonald's TV Events

More than 7 million schoolchildren, teachers, and citizens from around the world sang and played the same concert program simultaneously in the McDonald's World's Largest Concert. The 1989 concert was broadcast on PBS and the Armed Forces Radio and Television Service, which reaches 1,000 U.S. military bases.

Produced by the Music Educators National Conference (MENC), the concert was the highlight of "Music in Our Schools Month," focusing national attention on the importance of music in schools.

The McDonald's World's Largest Concert was taped before 2,500 schoolchildren at the Brooklyn Center for the Performing Arts. It featured the 102-piece McDonald's All-American High School Band performing a concert of music beginning with "The Star Spangled Banner," concluding with "God

Bless America" and including the Music in Our Schools Month theme song. At the appointed time, students sang along with the concert via their school televisions.

Cartoon All-Stars to the Rescue was a television first. Aimed at children ages 5 to 11, the animated half-hour anti-drug-abuse special was the first entertainment program ever simulcast by all three major U.S. networks and the first appearance together in a television program of characters from the major animation studios. The program, underwritten by McDonald's and Ronald McDonald Children's Charities, featured a "dream cast" including Bugs Bunny, Daffy Duck, Huey, Dewey, and Louie, Garfield, the Muppet Babies, Alf, Winnie the Pooh, and the Smurfs. The show was repeated on hundreds of independent stations and cable networks. To extend its life and the impact of its message, McDonald's loaned 250,000 video cassettes free to video stores, libraries, and the nation's 72,000 elementary schools. McDonald's also created teachers' guides on the drug-abuse subject and student handouts featuring the cartoon characters from the show.

ZONE PROGRAMS are gaining in importance with the rise of micromarketing. MPR programs tailored to key regions, local markets, or company marketing zones are a way for manufacturers to identify their brands with local interests.

8

Using MPR to Reinforce Advertising and Promotion

Marketing public relations rarely stands alone. It is most effective when it works strategically with advertising and promotion to meet marketing goals. MPR is used both to complement and supplement advertising. It can extend the advertising message by delivering different but complementary messages to the same mass audience. It can also complement advertising in mass media by reaching discrete or specialized demographic, psychographic, ethnic, or regional audiences with specifically targeted messages. On other occasions, MPR might complement consumer advertising by influencing influentials who in turn influence the consumer.

Alternatively, MPR can be used to supplement the advertising campaign by carrying the same message to the same or different markets. By using a variety of media not included in the ad budget, MPR can extend the reach of advertising and make it work harder.

MPR can also be used to test marketing and positioning concepts. Public relations pioneered the fitness walking concept that became The Rockport Company's total marketing thrust and the basis of its advertising. Likewise, Campbell Soup Company developed the healthful eating concept as a public relations program before it became the national advertising campaign.

ADVERTISING MAKES NEWS

Sometimes the advertising campaign is in itself strong enough to make news. Mary Wells Lawrence understood this and created her pattern-breaking, newsmaking campaigns in the 1970s with that in mind. Her brightly painted Braniff airliners grabbed attention in ads and in the news media and were the talk of the industry. In the absence of real product news, a newsy advertising campaign may be equally effective in generating media coverage.

The trend accelerated in the 1980s. Commercials have been run in TV newscasts reporting on the cola wars, beer wars, the burger wars, and even the bank-card wars, garnering valuable free air-time in the process. Philip Dusenberry, chairman of the giant BBDO advertising agency, told *The New York Times* that "when you get this type of publicity, it's like somebody coming along and handing you a whole pile of money you didn't have." Dusenberry said the advertising:

> takes on more value because it's being mentioned in a non-advertising context. You're not thrown into that cluttered commercial pod. Your commercial is being voiced over by the local announcer. Anytime you release a new advertising campaign, you would be wise to bring in your PR people and ask: "Is there anything in this that can stretch it beyond our media expenditure?"[1]

Apple Computer's startling *1984* commercial which introduced the Macintosh Computer, ran only once on network TV, during the Super Bowl telecast on January 22, 1984. But once was enough to generate far more in pre- and post-publicity than the equivalent cost of producing and airing the extravagant Orwellian spot. The combination of the spot and the publicity about it sent droves of buyers into computer showrooms. MAC sales reached 72,000, surpassing Apple's most ambitious sales goals. *Advertising Age* named it the "TV Commercial of the Decade" and said that the spot "created a new genre of commercials—advertising as an event—and transformed the Super Bowl into a venue of choice for campaign launches."

Publicity about Diet Coke's first 3D television commercial, aired on the 1989 Super Bowl, was so effective that supermarkets gave away 22 million special 3D glasses before running out of stock. The promotion generated $65 million worth of publicity and was carried by 2,200 newspapers, 850 radio stations, and all 3 television networks. The spot and the publicity it generated produced a 23 percent increase in Diet Coke's case sales and raised advertising awareness 58 percent for the month. In 1990, Super Bowl advertisers paid $700,000 for 30 seconds. The new ads or campaigns introduced included the first commercials for the much publicized Gillette Sensor razor and "Bud Bowl II," a $2-million-plus video production that pitted teams of helmeted bottles of Bud and Bud Light battling before 30,000 cheering fans, in a series of 6 commercials with a secret surprise ending. Anticipation for the spots was built by a publicity blitz in the nation's news media. A lead article in the *Chicago Tribune* titled "Bud Bowl's Back, Talking Tradition at Age II" was typical.

One of the most talked about advertising campaigns of recent years was the introduction of the Infiniti by Nissan Motor Corporation. The Japanese-style image campaign featured plants, rocks, and clouds but never a car. The showroom was the only place where car buyers could actually see what an Infiniti looked like. Chuck Kushell, executive vice president of Hill, Holiday, Cosmopulous, Infiniti's agency, acknowledged advertising's limitations and told *Advertising Age* that "advertising is nowhere near as good as word of mouth or public relations."

In an article called "Free Association: More marketers seek out media exposure to enhance their traditional paid campaigns," *Advertising Age* reported:

> The TV commercial—once the ultimate form of advertising—is just the beginning these days. Increasingly, advertisers are augmenting traditional media schedules with additional exposures, the so-called "free media." . . . Public relations agencies are telling clients that such exposure is as much as four times as valuable as equivalent paid time. . . . Amid concern about the escalating cost of TV time as viewership fragments and clutter cuts an ad's impact, more advertisers are exploring free media possibilities.
>
> To some extent, the trend is a result of the growth of PR to equal stature with advertising in the marketing communications mix. But it also suggests marketers are re-examining media advertising's value and return on investment. Does a 30-second spot really deliver a message or does it just provide impressions? If the goal is impressions, there are less expensive ways to deliver them. Advertisers know what they are and PR agencies are learning how to value them.[2]

THE COLA WARS MEET THE PRESS

Advertising Age points to the experience of Pepsi-Cola Company, which generated $12 million in free media in 1988 through publicity generated by their use of newsworthy celebrities, including Michael Jackson and Madonna, in commercials. According to the article, Pepsi-Cola learned that free media greatly expands the value of advertising when Michael Jackson's hair was accidentally set on fire during the filming of a Pepsi commercial. The incident was reported by television news, complete with outtakes. Many stations showed the completed commercial as a news item before it was ever aired as paid advertising. As a result, the company is coordinating advertising and publicity more closely than ever before.

Trying to repeat the PR success of its Michael Jackson commercial, Pepsi-Cola's publicity machine generated great anticipation for Madonna's "Like a Prayer" commercial. Unfortunately, viewers confused the spot with a sexually explicit Madonna video using the same music. After running it twice, Pepsi was forced to drop the spot because of a threatened consumer boycott. The cost of the spot was reported to be $10 million, but it attracted more exposure through news coverage than in paid time. As a result, consumer awareness of Pepsi advertising rose even though the spot was not on the air.

A *New York Times* article, "Star Wars in Cola Advertising," points out that many of the current Pepsi-Cola and Coca-Cola commercials "present themselves as one-minute movies, rock concerts, or music videos" and that in some of them "the soft drink is scarcely mentioned or even seen." Since there is very little product differentiation in the cola wars, both companies have turned to celebrities to identify their products with youth and glamour. It is Pepsi's Michael Jackson and Madonna vs. Coke's Whitney Houston and George Michael.

Randall Rothenberg, advertising columnist of the *Times,* notes that:

> Advertisers are increasingly using their commercials not for the tried-and-true purposes of showcasing products or appealing to consumers' emotions, but to generate controversy that they hope will translate into free air time and press clippings. The strategy, perfected by political media consultants in the 1980's, has now become a standard act in the repertoire of product and service marketers.

He points out that:

> Celebrity endorsements, an advertising staple since the 1920's, has become a main weapon in the "Cola Wars" between Pepsi and Coca-Cola because such endorsements receive a barrage of news coverage. That coverage has resulted largely from the growing number of television news programs. News is an inexpensive form of programming but it's insatiable maw needs filling.[3]

COUNTER REVOLUTION

Sometimes newsworthy advertising backfires. When Nike wanted to revitalize interest in its Nike-Air Cushioning System, it created a campaign called "Revolution in Motion," featuring the original sound track from the Beatles' song "Revolution." Because this was the first time any Beatles recording had been licensed for use in a television commercial, it made big news. National and local TV coverage usually ran the entire commercial, and the campaign even generated a full-page story in *TIME* with a color picture of the product. Unfortunately, 1960s rock 'n' roll enthusiasts and Beatles fans found the commercial use of a classic and the distortion of its revolutionary theme offensive and the commercial did not last.

Arch competitor Reebok took its lumps when a commercial showing two men bungee jumping from a bridge caused an outcry of public indignation and had to be withdrawn. In the spot, the jumper wearing the Reeboks dangles safely from an elastic cord while the other jumper, wearing another brand of shoes, slips out of them to meet his fate.

NO EXCUSES FOR PUBLICITY-PRODUCING ADS

An executive of No Excuses jeans told a CNN reporter that the company was "put on the map" by the publicity it obtained by hiring notorious celebrities to appear in commercials.

First up was a commercial featuring model Donna Rice, who had earlier made headlines as the playmate of then presidential candidate Gary Hart. Three years later, it was that other Other Woman, Donald Trump's friend Marla Maples. Scores of newspapers and television stations reported that the company had signed Ms. Maples for a commercial.

The making of the commercial was the subject of a front-page color picture in New York's *Newsday* and a four-page color layout in *Entertainment Weekly*. In the spot, Ms. Maples, wearing size 5 No Excuses jeans, delivers a message about cleaning up the environment and tosses tabloids that had given her a hard time into the trash.

No Excuses issued a press release declaring that two networks had turned down the ad but *The Wall Street Journal* found that the company hadn't bought any network time in the first place and concluded that the media had been manipulated.

George Lois, whose agency created the ad, told the *Journal* that "if we don't run one commercial, it still looks like we spent $50 million." The veteran adman asked, "How do you buy the publicity we're talking about?" Neil Cole, president of New Retail Concepts, the company that makes No Excuses jeans, said, "without the free publicity, I would be lost in a jungle of TV advertising." He asserted that the more publicity the company got, the less air time it would have to buy, saving money for the shareholders.

GOING TO THE WALL

A world event of great significance provided the setting for instant newsmaking commercials produced by three American advertisers in

December 1989. Within weeks after East Germany made its dramatic decision to open the Berlin Wall, Pepsi-Cola, AT&T, and quite unexpectedly Quintessence, a Chicago-based cosmetics marketer, all shot commercials at the Wall. AT&T's commercial featured interviews with Germans telling what they were doing and how they felt when they heard the news about the opening of the Wall and how they shared the good news with family and friends around the world by telephone.

Quintessence, a small advertiser by comparison, achieved the greatest media coverage for its spot. Victor Zast, senior vice president of corporate marketing, told *The Wall Street Journal* that he hoped the commercial would create brand awareness of the Quintessence name and its products, which were listed on the screen. He said, "This is nothing more than a Peace-on-Earth message from a company trying to do something a little differently."[4] He might have added "from a company that understood the news value of being the first and the most unlikely company to shoot a 'noncommercial' commercial at the Berlin Wall." A video news release on the filming of the commercial was transmitted by satellite and reached 2 million viewers on 20 television stations.

"KLEENEX SAYS BLESS YOU" AWARDS

In addition to utilizing advertising spokespersons, marketing public relations can reinforce advertising by incorporating advertising themes, provided that the theme can be meaningfully translated in a way that is palatable to the media.

One product that makes effective use of its advertising theme line in a public relations program is Kleenex Brand Facial Tissues. Company research showing that the Kleenex trademark is associated by the consumer with comfort and caring led to the creation of an advertising campaign that identifies the product with values and occasions that are important to consumers' lives. The theme line is "Kleenex Says Bless You." The lyric of the commercial created by Foote, Cone & Belding goes like this:

> We've shared your joys
> We've dried your tears
> We've touched your life
> Through all these years
> Kleenex Says Bless You.

It was appropriate for a public relations program to celebrate this sentiment with the "Kleenex Says Bless You" Awards. The awards were designed to draw attention to the type of heart-warming good deeds that represent the American spirit at its best. The program was created by

Golin/Harris for Kimberly-Clark Corporation, makers of Kleenex brand products. It honors individuals, both high- and low-profile achievers, whose initiative or bravery made a difference in their communities. The winners range from celebrities like actor Paul Newman, who founded a camp for kids with potentially fatal diseases, and singer Dionne Warwick, who organized a memorable four-day New York City benefit for AIDS education and pediatric AIDS care, to a Chicago woman who founded Mothers Against Gangs when her own son was killed and a Minnesota ten-year-old who wrote *My Book for Kids with Cansur*.

Nominations are solicited from editors of local newspapers across the country who are asked to submit stories and pictures from their papers to support their nominations. The top ten honorees are flown to Washington to receive their awards, and a $2,000 donation is made in their name to the charitable organization of each honoree's choice. The awards are presented appropriately on Valentine's Day at the National Press Club by NBC weatherman Willard Scott who reports on the event on the "Today" show.

WHERE'S THE CAP'N?

MPR can be particularly effective when it is integrated strategically with both advertising and sales promotion. Cap'n Crunch is a case in point. In 1985 when the Quaker Oats Company brand group wanted to create a "Who killed J.R. for nine-year-olds," they struck on the idea of removing the Cap'n from the cereal box he had occupied for 23 years, as shown in Figure 8–1. Those who correctly identified his whereabouts were offered a share in a $1 million reward.

"Where's the Cap'n?" was an integrated advertising–sales promotion–public relations campaign that worked. More than a quarter-million kids recovered Crunch Squad Detective Kits from cereal boxes or wrote in for them. The Saturday-morning-cartoon-time animated commercials were supplemented by a variety of nontraditional public relations programs developed by Golin/Harris and directed to target audiences, including kids, teens, college students, and young adults. A syndicated radio series, a video news series, and news bulletins reported news of the Cap'n's disappearance to the media. Radio was used to promote live searches staged at major amusement parks and events at museums, parades, and other kid events. Crunch marketing executives were booked on local kids' shows where they provided clues to where the Cap'n could be found and gave away branded prizes.

Disk jockeys were enlisted to deliver clues about the Cap'n's whereabouts and played a "Where's the Cap'n?" record that used the theme line (and product plug) 25 times. A music video, one of the first to

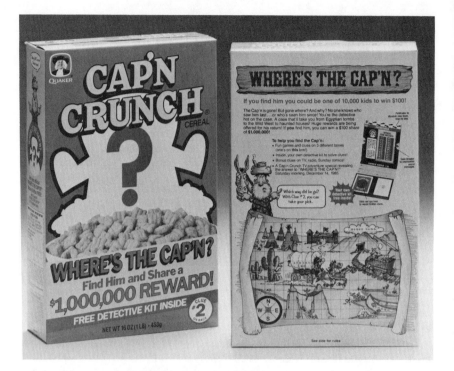

FIGURE 8–1 "Where's the Cap'n?" revitalized interest in Quaker Oats' Cap'n Crunch cereal in 1985. The Cap'n's picture was removed from cereal boxes, and 10,000 kids who correctly identified his whereabouts shared in a $1-million reward. MPR, promotion, and advertising worked together to make this program successful.

tie in with a branded product, was produced with rock musician Rick Derringer. The video, which ran on music video shows, featured children dressed as pop stars repeating the question, "Where's the Cap'n?" The music was also featured by the Stanford University Marching Band in a halftime salute to Cap'n Crunch, a cereal that enjoys great popularity among college students who grew up eating it. Students on other major campuses were encouraged to develop events. They formed an Eta Kappa Crunch chapter, held Cap'n vigils, circulated petitions, and organized flash-card sections at football games.

As a result of this integrated program, the brand regained top-of-mind awareness among its target audiences and achieved record sales by the time the mystery was solved four months later when a special two-minute Saturday-morning-cartoon segment revealed the Cap'n's location. The contest attracted 280,000 entries. More than 150 million consumer impressions were generated through publicity in national media like the popular syndicated "Entertainment Tonight" TV show, which ran the entire "Where's the Cap'n" video, and "Saturday Night Live," which joined the search with an irreverent sketch.

AND WHO'S MIKEY?

Quaker Oats Company repeated its successful mix of advertising, promotion, and marketing public relations by conducting another search, this one for the living actor who appeared as "Mikey" in a favorite old television commercial for Life Cereal. Hill & Knowlton found the full-grown "Mikey," an actor named John Gilchrist, and hid him from the media for the duration of the promotion. Consumers were invited to guess which of the 20 photos on the back of the box was the grown-up "Mikey." Supported by an effective public relations program, the search for "Mikey" inspired 750,000 Life Cereal buyers to send in their guesses. Despite the small sweepstakes prizes, 100 awards of $100 each, it was the largest coupon response Quaker ever had.

PROMOTIONAL FIREWORKS

One of the nation's leading sales-promotion firms, Einson Freeman, recognizing the topspin that marketing public relations can add to a strong promotion, has designed a number of notable programs that successfully integrate promotional vehicles and publicity.

Jeffrey K. McElnea, president of Einson Freeman, believes that:

> event marketing can pay out in a big way by moving products off the shelf and into the hearts, minds, and shopping carts of target audiences. But only if it's done correctly. Ideally, a marketing event should be fully integrated with a product's marketing mix including advertising, public relations and sales. It should reinforce and enhance a brand's image. It should be big enough to attract enormous attention—sometimes even national attention. But it should be small enough to capture the local spirit of the town or city in which the event is taking place. A marketing event should be meaningful to the intended audience. It should be sufficiently exciting and different and compelling to motivate consumers and attract their participation.[5]

Einson Freeman developed Wisk Bright Nights '87 to help Lever Brothers' Wisk maintain its number-one position in the liquid laundry detergent category, to promote the product's new formula, and to celebrate Wisk's 30th anniversary. Wisk Bright Nights was an integrated trade-and-consumer promotion/public relations program. It was the first national fireworks tour ever held in the United States. Fireworks shows in 23 cities across the country, tied in with local festivals, fairs, municipal celebrations, or special events, such as Philadelphia's "We the People 200 Constitution" festivities and Chicago's Venetian Night.

Each show consisted of a 24-minute fireworks display that included a special "Ring Around the Sky" fireworks effect symbolizing the famous "Ring Around the Collar" advertising theme. The fireworks were choreographed to a musical retrospective of 30 years of rock 'n' roll, commemorating Wisk's 30th anniversary. The display was designed by the famous Grucci family whose members served as Wisk spokespeople for television, radio, and newspaper interviews in each Wisk Bright Nights city.

Consumer-promotion elements included radio simulcasts of the fireworks program, local radio and newspaper advertising, free-standing inserts (FSIs) offering high-value coupons, and a consumer sweepstakes offering a chance to win a trip to the International Fireworks Competition in Monte Carlo. In addition to trade allowances, Lever Brothers held VIP parties for retail supermarket buyers and their families at the site of each show.

The Wisk Bright Nights '87 program was the most successful event promotion in Lever Brother's history. It helped enable the brand not only to maintain its category leadership but to set new sales records for the year, despite increased competition from new products. The fireworks shows attracted 3 million people, and the media relations program conducted by Ogilvy & Mather Public Relations generated over 175 million impressions through national and local TV, print, and radio media.

PART II

USING MARKETING PUBLIC RELATIONS

9

Winning Consumer Trust

Public relations is the only management function that is uniquely able to build consumer trust. It is simplistic but axiomatic that people patronize companies they know, like, and trust.

As veteran Cleveland public relations counselor Davis Young puts it:

> Public relations relates to enhancing perceptions of trust. That's our business—getting people to have trust in products, services, other people, companies, institutions, governments and so on. Nobody really makes important decisions in this life without having some measure of trust. If ours is a business that influences decision making, then enhancing trust gets to the real core of public relations. . . . The only real objective of a communications program is to enhance trust—trust in a product, trust in a service, trust in the integrity of a company, trust in its quality and its service. . . . That is the first commandment of communications in the nineties. The winners will earn that trust. The losers will be perceived as unworthy of trust.[1]

Consumer trust must be earned over time. Direct involvement with consumers, both as individuals and as members of their communities, is required. Companies that earn consumer trust must be more than accessible. They must be involved with consumers. They must be responsive to consumer concerns, provide help to consumers in terms of information and service, and proactively participate in programs that benefit the community.

GIVING SOMETHING BACK

There has been no bigger winner in earning consumer trust than Mc-Donald's Corporation. It is no coincidence. From the beginning, founder

Ray Kroc believed that McDonald's should be committed to giving something back to the society from which the company derives its profits and putting something back into the local communities where it does business. He knew instinctively that good citizenship is good public relations and that good public relations is good for business.

To McDonald's, marketing public relations and community relations are inseparable, if not synonymous. From day one, McDonald's discovered that community involvement was a far more efficient and affordable form of promotion than advertising. In *McDonald's: Behind the Arches,* John F. Love points out that:

> For a drive-in chain looking to appeal to a family market and seeking respectability in an industry burdened with a questionable reputation, the community involvement by local operators produced the type of image-producing publicity that McDonald's needed. Yet, their early community service had a single motivation: to sell hamburgers.

Subsequently, according to Love, "community relations work has become one of the most powerful weapons in McDonald's impressive marketing arsenal."[2]

Al Golin, who has been public relations counsel to McDonald's for more than 30 years, says that with McDonald's spending more than $1 billion worldwide on advertising and promotion, the company no longer needs to participate in community involvement to generate awareness. Today, the purposes of McDonald's commitment to community relations are to reinforce its leadership position in the fast-service field and to generate the trust of its customers.

Golin explains,

> The essence of McDonald's is the individual, locally operated restaurant. Each restaurant's management and employees have an important stake in the community or neighborhood where they are located. They owe their success and their jobs to the patronage of their neighbors. Therefore, it makes sense that McDonald's has an unusually strong commitment to being a leader in community citizenship in each restaurant's trading area. There is a tradition of personal local involvement in community service that extends throughout the McDonald's organization. Whatever the project, it must always deliver a tangible benefit to the community. That must come before any publicity can be generated. . . .
>
> Positive community involvement is basic to McDonald's way of doing business. It is a reinvestment in the future of the community and, therefore, a reinvestment in the business. . . .
>
> Community relations is both an opportunity and an obligation. The opportunity is to establish a partnership and build trust among those who use the company's products and services. The obligation is to be a

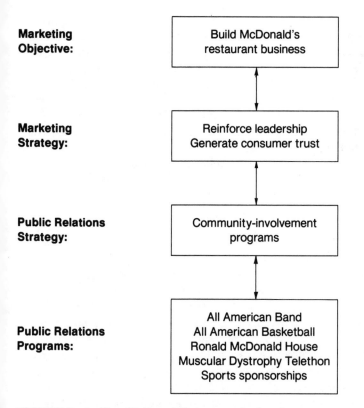

Marketing Objective:	Build McDonald's restaurant business
Marketing Strategy:	Reinforce leadership Generate consumer trust
Public Relations Strategy:	Community-involvement programs
Public Relations Programs:	All American Band All American Basketball Ronald McDonald House Muscular Dystrophy Telethon Sports sponsorships

FIGURE 9–1 How McDonald's community involvement programs serve the company's marketing objectives.

responsible corporate citizen, with the understanding that there, in fact, exists a moral obligation for a business to give something back to the society from which it derives a profit.[3]

McDonald's Charles Rubner believes that in the cluttered, competitive quick-service-restaurant market, McDonald's is the only company that has a distinctive difference. Rubner told the PRSA–AMA "Allies in Megamarketing" Conference:

> We believe that our distinctive difference, beyond our food and service, is our image and community involvement—and that is what helps distinguish us from the pack. In an industry where the perception of real product and service differences is becoming narrower and obscure, we believe that, more and more, it is the way people feel about you, and the trust they have in you that sets you apart from and above the rest. That's certainly true at McDonald's.

Rubner said that McDonald's marketing and public relations efforts team up to give the company an identity and leadership edge which few companies in any industry can match. He noted that all of the company's communications efforts have the common purpose of increasing its food sales but they also have a common goal: to preserve, protect, and enhance McDonald's image and reputation in the marketplace. Advertising, promotion, and public relations programs give McDonald's a day-to-day presence in customers' lives, a presence that builds preference for McDonald's.[4]

Figure 9-1 shows how public relations programs at McDonald's involve the company in local communities wherever it does business, thereby generating consumer trust and patronage.

MCDONALD'S TRUST BANK

The dedication to giving something back is accepted by McDonald's as an article of faith. It is expressed in what the company calls its "trust bank" philosophy. McDonald's believes that its community involvement results in "deposits" of trust from its customers. The accumulation of these deposits builds consumer confidence, and that trust is especially important when the company has to make a "withdrawal" from the trust bank—when the company is faced with a tough or sensitive situation, such as the tragic incident at San Ysidro, California.

On July 18, 1984, a crazed gunman walked into a McDonald's in this poor, Mexican-American-border community and opened fire on McDonald's customers, crew, and passersby. Before he was killed by a police sharpshooter, he had taken the lives of 21 innocent people.

McDonald's reaction to the mass murder was swift and decisive. The company suspended its national advertising for several days. It contributed $1 million to the survivors' fund organized by Joan Kroc, Ray Kroc's widow, who herself donated $100,000. Then a team of McDonald's senior officials, including communications vice president Dick Starmann and public relations counselor Al Golin, flew to San Ysidro to attend the funerals and to meet with community leaders, including the spiritual leader of the Catholic community. The decision was made to close the store inconspicuously but permanently. Five weeks later, after discussion with community leaders, McDonald's donated the property to the people of San Ysidro, who turned it into a park.

In *McDonald's: Behind the Arches,* author John Love describes the aftermath: "While it had not sought favorable publicity on San Ysidro, McDonald's handling of the crisis generated hundreds of positive letters to the chain. It also produced scores of complimentary newspaper editorials. Even in the minds of San Ysidro residents, McDonald's had succeeded in separating its image from the memory of the worst tragedy in the community's history" (p. 382).

Because of its deposits over the years in the trust bank, the company was given credit by the media for doing the right thing. An editorial in the *Philadelphia Inquirer* offers proof positive of the viability of the trust-bank concept:

> America's business giants, often with justification, have been accused of corporate insensitivity. Critics complain that many corporations think of profits but rarely of people.
>
> A number of companies clearly don't fit that negative description. One of them is McDonald's.
>
> In the wake of the terrible attack at one of the fast-food chain's 7,000 restaurants last week, in which 21 people died and 19 were wounded, McDonald's responded to public concerns by agreeing to close the restaurant in San Ysidro, California.
>
> In addition, the corporation, along with many of its franchisees, donated $1 million to aid in the psychological rehabilitation of those who survived the shootings. McDonald's also will aid the families of the victims and a number of the restaurant's youthful employees who lived through the 90-minute ordeal. Several area people, deeply shaken by the shooting, and police personnel traumatized by the unprecedented bloody massacre will receive assistance from the McDonald's fund.
>
> In the aftermath of such unspeakable tragedies, those who perform swiftly and selflessly on behalf of the community too often go unnoticed. But the world's number-one fast-food-restaurant chain has long been responsive to community needs. McDonald's sensitive response in such an unusual situation should be applauded widely.[5]

MPR AS A POSITIONING STRATEGY

A dedication to consumer service is one of the surest ways to engender consumer trust. That means providing consumers not only with quality products, but with helpful ideas, information, and answers.

Kenneth Lightcap, vice president of corporate communications of Reebok International, believes that MPR should be used by companies as a positioning tool, to gain "share of mind" with consumers and other publics over time. In Lightcap's view, a gradual buildup of impressions forms a lasting impression that causes consumers to value the company's products and be more receptive to product publicity. "The one-two punch of public relations in the marketing sense is to position first, followed by or in some cases simultaneously with product publicity—then advertising. This sequence is important, because to move first with advertising is to pay dearly for stealing your own thunder."[6]

Lightcap cites the success of companies that have provided meaningful, useful information to consumers and by so doing have gained their trust. By positioning themselves as knowledgeable experts who care about and want to help consumers, these companies have established themselves as leaders and have earned consumer loyalty and trust. Through their consistent, service-based PR efforts, Pillsbury has become synonymous with baking and The Rockport Company with walking.

The Pillsbury Bake-Off

In February 1990, 100 regional finalists competed for $126,000 in prize money at the 34th Pillsbury Bake-Off contest (see Figure 9–2). Since the first "Grand Recipe Hunt and Baking Contest" was held at New York's Waldorf-Astoria Hotel in 1949, with former First Lady Eleanor Roosevelt as guest of honor (Figure 9–3), the nationwide event has become an American institution and has made Pillsbury synonymous with baking.

FIGURE 9–2 Thousands of men, women, and children have participated in the Pillsbury Bake-Off, which has become the premier contest to select the nation's best nonprofessional cooks. Over the years, more than $2 million in prize money has been awarded for recipes, many of which are now classics.

FIGURE 9-3 Eleanor Roosevelt was guest of honor at the first Grand Recipe Hunt and Baking Contest in 1949. From left to right are Phillip Pillsbury, then president of Pillsbury; Mrs. Roosevelt; Art Linkletter, master of ceremonies; and finalist Laura Rott, whose cookie recipe earned her $10,000. The contest name was later shortened to the Pillsbury Bake-Off.

This event has been highly publicized through the years. At the first event, a *LIFE* magazine photographer captured a picture of a finalist dropping her cake upside down. Decades later, on February 29, 1988, a *Newsweek* headline proclaimed "They're Cooking for Cash: A Major Culinary Contest Shows How America Eats," and the story described how "very few food ideas hit American homes with the speed and thoroughness of Bake-Off recipes, which begin to appear in daily newspapers as soon as the winners are announced."

Newsweek reported that Pillsbury can tell that people start making the recipes right away because of immediate sales of products used by the winners. One year, a Chicago supermarket chain sold in two weeks a half-year supply of the Pillsbury's lemon frosting mix used in the winning recipe.

Pillsbury has changed the Bake-Off rules and categories over the years, to reflect both trends in American cooking habits and the development of new products. In 1949, all recipes submitted had to contain Pillsbury flour. Later, categories covering nutritious and ethnic recipes were added. In 1988, the name of the event became the Bake-Off Cooking and Baking Contest, to acknowledge the addition of recipes using Green Giant canned and frozen vegetables.

Finalists are selected from tens of thousands of entries received between June and October. After several rounds of screening, more than 1,500 selected recipes are prepared for taste panels of Pillsbury home economists. The 100 finalists are called in December and told that they have been selected for the February trip to the contest site and the opportunity to compete for cash prizes and national recognition, that is, publicity for their outstanding cooking skills.

On February 20, 1990, Linda Rashman of Petaluma, California, the grand prize winner of that year's Pillsbury Bake-Off, was pictured in *The New York Times* with her blueberry poppy seed brunch cake. The accompanying story was headlined "At the Super Bowl of Bake-Offs a Dream Can Be Worth $40,000." The article commented that while the company will not divulge the cost of the Bake-Off, "it appears to be worth every penny." Gary Klingl, president of the Pillsbury's Green Giant division, explained why. He told the *Times* that "an analysis of newspapers and magazines showed that the publicity pays for the contest."

Rockport Writes the Book on Walking

Anticipating the walking trend of the 1980s, The Rockport Company preempted the competition not only by designing the first shoes especially for fitness walking but also by becoming the experts in walking and by communicating that expertise to opinion leaders and consumers. Using walking as its innovative leadership position, the company became known as "The Walking Shoe Company."

ADWEEK credits Rockport's public relations firm, Cone Communications, with "taking the lead in developing the 'big idea' for the product's positioning in the marketplace." Advertising's role, *ADWEEK* said, is to follow through as a sales support mechanism.

The first step in the MPR program to elevate the commonplace activity of walking into a legitimate form of aerobic exercise was to gain the endorsement of the American Podiatric Medical Association. The next year, the company updated and rewrote an earlier book and retitled it *Rockport's Complete Book of Exercise Walking*. Dr. James Rippe, a cardiologist and director of the Exercise Physiology Laboratory at the University of Massachusetts Medical Center, was engaged as medical spokesperson and director of scientific research.

The company also developed Rob Sweetgall's "50/50 Walk for the Health of It," a year-long solo walk throughout the United States to educate Americans on the health benefits of walking. Sweetgall, who lost several members of his family to heart disease and wanted to promote the health benefits of walking, covered 50 states in 50 weeks, an 11,208-mile walk that generated more than 300 media interviews and a half-billion favorable media impressions of walking. Sweetgall and Dr. Rippe then authored *Rockport's Fitness Walking*, which presented a walking program to improve heart and health. The book sold more than 75,000 copies.

In 1986, the company's scientific research culminated with the announcement of the formation of the Rockport Walking Institute (RWI), the nation's first organization dedicated to research and education on walking. RWI's 30-member Scientific Advisory Board of leading exercise physiologists act as regional spokespersons and opinion leaders regarding Rockport Walking research. The RWI is the vehicle for distribution of information to consumers, retailers, and the media through books, films, pamphlets, and a speakers bureau.

Out of the RWI came the Rockport Fitness Walking Test, the first physical fitness test designed to determine a person's level of cardiopulmonary fitness based on walking. The test was introduced to the media at a New York YMCA, where reporters, wearing Rockport ProWalkers, were able to take the test on the Y's indoor track. To explain how to take the test, Rockport published a booklet and a four-minute video for retailers, walking clubs, health organizations, and hospitals. The test was widely publicized; a single appearance on "Good Morning America" generated 60,000 booklet requests. The test has since become a benchmark for determining physical fitness. More than a million copies have been distributed nationwide.

The next year, Rockport developed a program and book specifically targeted for the women's market. The company subsequently expanded the fitness-walking program by sponsoring a "Walk with Your Doc" program, with Dr. Art Ulene of the "Today Show," and a Walk Leader program complete with a 150-page manual, clinics in cities in major markets, and its own awards program.

Rockport recently combined fitness walking with a low-fat diet and proper nutrition in a life-style program for the 1990s. The new book, *The Rockport Walking Program*, written by Dr. Rippe and Dr. Anne Ward, includes a 30-day, step-by-step plan of low-fat menus, recipes, and daily walking programs.

The work of the Rockport Walking Institute is cross-marketed in the company's advertising. A recent ad states: "Rockport has literally written the book on walking. In fact, three books, four video tapes, and seven abstracts that were accepted by the American College of Sports Medicine." Its current advertising theme is "Rockports Make You Feel Like Walking."

10

Introducing New Products

Marketing public relations can be used effectively throughout a product's life cycle, but its best known use has been and continues to be in the introduction of new products. Most modern marketers understand that the announcement of a new product offers a unique opportunity for obtaining publicity and for dramatizing the product. The introduction comes only once in the product's life cycle, and the opportunity to make the most of it must be seized. Marketers also understand that the news of the new product must precede the advertising break. Once the advertising is seen by the consumer, the product is no longer news to the media. The operative word is *new* because *new* means "news." The business of the news media is to cover the news and the business of marketing public relations planners is to orchestrate plans that persuade media gatekeepers to make room for new-product news, despite its commerciality.

Products that are newsworthy to the media and of high interest to the consumer (reporters are consumers, too) have the best potential for maximum exposure. This chapter relates some outstanding examples of the successful use of MPR to introduce such products as cars, computers, pharmaceuticals, foods and beverages, and toys and games.

THE MAKING OF THE MUSTANG

About the time I entered the public relations business, a then little-known businessman, Lee Iacocca, appeared on the covers of *TIME* and *Newsweek* in the same week. The cover stories, of course, were no coincidence. They launched a carefully orchestrated, national, media-relations campaign to introduce Ford's Mustang before the car was advertised or seen in the showroom. In *Iacocca*, his mega-best-seller, Lee Iacocca describes the key role public relations played in launching the Mustang

114

Age—and, not so incidentally, Mr. Iacocca himself, as an American business leader cum celebrity.

He relates how the introduction of the Mustang was conceived three years before the car was designed. The target date was the opening of the New York World's Fair in April 1964. As Iacocca puts it:

> It was the ideal place to launch our car. Although new models are traditionally introduced in the fall, we had in mind a product so exciting and so different that we would dare to bring it out in the middle of the season. Only the World's Fair had enough scale and drama for the car of our dreams.[1]

I recall standing in the long line at the World's Fair, waiting to enter the Ford Pavilion. What made the wait well worth it was the opportunity to ride through the Ford exhibit in the new Mustang. Six million visitors gawked as the procession of brightly painted, sporty cars from Ford passed by. The Mustang became the talk of the Fair.

Ford had produced a minimum number of 8,000 Mustangs so that every Ford dealer would have at least one in his showroom when the car was officially launched.

Then the media relations campaign began. Here is how Iacocca describes it:

> We promoted the Mustang to the hilt. We invited the editors of college newspapers to Dearborn, and we gave them a Mustang to drive for a few weeks. Four days before the car was officially launched, a hundred members of the press participated in a giant seventy-car Mustang rally from New York to Dearborn, and the cars demonstrated their reliability by breezing through the seven-hundred-mile trip without any problems. The press recorded its enthusiasm in a massive and lyrical outpouring of words and photographs that appeared prominently in hundreds of magazines and newspapers.
>
> On April 17, Ford dealerships everywhere were mobbed with customers. In Chicago, one dealer had to lock his showroom doors because the crowd outside was so large. A dealer in Pittsburgh reported that the crush of customers was so thick he couldn't get his Mustang off the wash rack. In Detroit, another dealer said that so many people who had come to see the Mustang had arrived in sports cars that his parking lot looked like a foreign car rally.
>
> The Mustang was destined to be an incredible hit. During the first weekend it was on sale, an unprecedented four million people visited Ford dealerships. The car's public reception was exceeding our wildest hopes.
>
> The press played an important role in creating this excitement. Due to the tireless efforts of Walter Murphy in public relations, the Mustang was featured simultaneously on the covers of both *TIME* and *Newsweek*. This was an astounding publicity coup for a new commercial project. Both

magazines sensed we had a winner, and their added publicity during the very week of the Mustang's introduction helped make their prediction a self-fulfilling prophecy. I'm convinced that TIME and Newsweek alone led to the sale of an extra 100,000 cars.

The twin cover stories had the effect of two gigantic commercials. After telling its readers that my name "rhymes with try-a-Coke-ah," TIME noted that "Iacocca has produced more than just another new car. With its long hood and short rear deck, its Ferrari flair and openmouthed air scoop, the Mustang resembles the European racing cars that American sports-car buffs find so appealing. Yet Iacocca has made the Mustang's design so flexible, its price so reasonable and its options so numerous that its potential appeal reaches toward two-thirds of all U.S. car buyers. Priced as low as $2,368 and able to accommodate a small family in its four seats, the Mustang seems destined to be a sort of Model A of sports cars—for the masses as well as the buffs." I couldn't have said it better myself.

The automotive press was no less enthusiastic. "A market which had been looking for a car has it now," began the story in Car Life. Even Consumer Reports, generally no great fan of Detroit, noted the Mustang's "almost complete absence of poor fit and sloppy workmanship in a car being built at a hell-for-leather pace."

We also ran hard-hitting national promotion programs. We displayed Mustangs in fifteen of the country's busiest airports and in the lobbies of two hundred Holiday Inns from coast to coast. At the University of Michigan football games, we contracted for several acres of space in the parking lot and put up huge signs that said: "Mustang Corral."

After only a few weeks it became clear to me that we had to open up a second plant. The initial assumption had been that the Mustang would sell seventy-five thousand units during the first year. But the projections kept growing, and before the car was introduced we were planning on sales of two hundred thousand. To build even that many cars, we had to convince top management to convert a second plant in San Jose, California, into producing more Mustangs.

I had a target in mind for the first year. During its first year, the Falcon had sold a record 417,174 cars, and that was the figure I wanted to beat. We had a slogan: "417 by 4/17"—the Mustang's birthday. Late in the evening of April 16, 1965, a young Californian bought a sporty red Mustang convertible. He had just purchased the 418,812th Mustang, and we finished our first year with a new record.[2]

Twenty-five years later, Lee Iacocca had long since departed from Ford but Mustangs were still sought-after collectibles, bringing resale prices as high as $20,000. On the 25th anniversary of the Mustang, Ford's New York district sales office threw an anniversary party at the Flushing Meadows site of the 1964 World's Fair. About 250 vintage Mustang owners parked their cars around the still-standing Unisphere. The event also drew car dealers, road ralliers, restoration specialists, and members of regional chapters of the some 2,000 Mustang clubs in the United States.

In honor of the occasion, a "thundering herd" of nearly 40 European-owned Ford Mustangs participated in an American Pony Drive. The cars, co-driven by 100 Mustangers from 3 European countries, covered more than 7,000 miles in their 2-month-long odyssey. The vintage Mustangs, owned by the proud European drivers, ranged from mint-condition 1965 models to the more powerful pony cars of the early 1970s. The American Pony Drive route passed through 17 states, with stops in 25 cities. The Europeans were joined enroute by up to 1,000 North American Mustang car-club members who accompanied the caravan on portions of the drive. Mustang car clubs hosted car shows and social events in each city where the Pony Drive made an overnight stop.

A large contingent of Mustang car-club members and fans joined the caravan in Las Vegas to head west to Los Angeles for the "Fabulous Fords Forever" classic car show at Knott's Berry Farm in Anaheim, California, where 2,000 classic and vintage Ford cars were displayed. Ford Chairman Donald E. Petersen, the owner of a 1965 Mustang, was on hand there to greet the European and North American Mustangers.

From Los Angeles the trail headed north and east to Dearborn, Michigan, for a visit to Ford World Headquarters and a tour of the Dearborn Assembly Plant, the only Ford plant that has built Mustangs over the entire 25-year history of the car.

The anniversary video news release was one of the most popular of 1989, airing on 98 stations plus "ABC World Tonight," "CBS This Morning," CNBC, CNN, and FNN.

FORD DOES IT AGAIN

Twenty-two years later, a new generation of leaders at Ford borrowed the lessons learned from the introduction of the Mustang and proved again the value of a carefully orchestrated, pull-out-the-stops public relations effort. The occasion was the introduction of the Ford Taurus and Mercury Sable automobiles. The results were: the most successful new-model launch since the Mustang, and the transformation of the image of Ford, which had suffered in the intervening two decades, from an also-ran to the innovative trend setter of American car makers.

The Taurus introduction was proof-positive of the power of public relations to generate marketplace excitement and sales success. Before the market introduction, Ford had written more than 146,000 dealers' orders worth $1.5 billion for the Taurus and Sable. Over 20,000 of those were actual customer orders.

Implementation of the public relations plan began nearly a year before the cars were to actually reach the market. Ford decided to throw a splashy Hollywood preview of the cars on January 29, 1985. With the

Chicago Auto Show scheduled to be held only ten days later, the wisdom of the pre-preview in Hollywood was questioned.

But Ford went ahead with the Hollywood-preview plan and hired Rogers & Cowan, an entertainment–PR firm, to stage the event. Because California is the nation's trend setter in new consumer products, Ford believed that an initial burst of enthusiasm on the West Coast would carry over to Chicago. The media were intrigued with the uniqueness of an automobile preview in Hollywood, and Ford upheld the spirit of glitz and glamour.

The actual unveiling took place on an MGM sound stage after a full day of activities planned for a select group of invited guests, including Hollywood celebrities, reporters, columnists, editors, and broadcasters from 370 news and business organizations. Major portions of the program were transmitted over Ford's nationwide Employee Communications Network; video coverage was provided by satellite to commercial television stations across the country.

Technical exhibits were set up in three Los Angeles-area hotels in addition to the sound stage. A formal press conference started the day, and Ford experts from every department were made available for informal media interviews on technical matters. Emphasizing the corporate commitment to this project, then-Chairman Philip Caldwell, President Don Petersen, and the heads of both the engineering and design teams responsible for the autos participated and were available to reporters.

The media response qualified this "premiere" as a glowing success. *USA TODAY* reported, "The Hollywood setting for Ford's preview is appropriate. In recent years, Ford has staged the kind of turnaround that usually happens only in the movies." Shortly after the event, David Scott, who was then director of public affairs at Ford North America, reported that the media gave "nothing but outstanding reviews on the program."

A week later, the cars were shown to the general public for the first time at the Chicago Auto Show. Ford held a news conference before the show opened. The result was widespread national coverage by the wire services and networks, including a piece on the "CBS Evening News" with Dan Rather. In the months that followed, both the trade and consumer press published and broadcast story after story praising the Taurus and congratulating Ford on its comeback.

During the year following the Hollywood kickoff, Ford hosted media events for some 1,500 representatives of trade and consumer press; 350 reporters were given the opportunity to test drive the new cars. No media blitz had ever been undertaken for the introduction of a new automobile so far in advance of its actual market release.

Another innovative approach to promoting the Taurus and Sable was the invention of a simple and effective program called "caravan." Two working models of the automobiles were trucked around the country for live showings at Ford facilities and supplier plants. This tour gave Ford employees and suppliers the opportunity to preview the autos, and it created media events in small, out-of-the-way communities that would never normally be targeted for this type of attention. The grass-roots "caravan" program generated enormous pre-product-launch good-will and publicity in local communities and greatly increased product awareness.

Finally, Ford broke all the rules by officially unveiling the vehicles on December 26, 1985. Since the two weeks following Christmas tend to be a slow advertising period, Ford took advantage by staging an all-out advertising and publicity blitz.

The combined total of advance orders and first-quarter sales exhausted planned production for the first two quarters. Projections were for 190,000 car sales through September; by the end of March, Ford had already sold 170,000 Tauruses and Sables. The success of Ford's year-long public relations campaign can be documented not only by its advance orders, but also through awareness studies conducted by the company. Before national advertising broke, Taurus awareness was an impressive 35 percent, with Sable around 25 percent. By the time of its public release, one out of every three American drivers was aware of the Taurus.

Motor Trend named the Taurus "Car of the Year" in North America in January 1986. In second place was the Sable, and *Motor Trend* exclaimed that these two cars "ran away from the rest of the competition." By the end of 1986, just one year after the public had access to it, the Taurus had become the best-selling mid-size car in the United States.

The use of MPR to garner headlines is alive and well in the 1990s. When Ford launched the 1991 Escort, *USA TODAY* reported that "Ford sent its shock troops across the USA to Escort media orgies in 30 cities." A Ford spokesperson called it "a throwback to the old days when you used to launch the cars with a lot of hoopla, passion and drama."[3]

General Motors Chairman Roger Smith, still suffering from the publicity fallout unleashed by the film *Roger and Me*, took the opposite approach. On the day before his retirement in 1990, he personally drove the first Saturn off the assembly line and achieved high visibility for the long-awaited car, which was his pet personal project, despite banning the media from the event. The video news releases, press releases, and pictures released by General Motors were widely used by the media.

MPR AND THE WALKMAN

MPR played a major role in the introduction of consumer electronics products in the 1980s. The list begins with personal computers, but includes such conspicuous successes as VCRs, camcorders, compact discs and CD players, cellular telephones, telephone-answering machines, fax machines, and the Sony Walkman and Watchman. All of them made news not only when they were introduced but also when their widespread use was reported.

In the consumer electronics field, there is no greater worldwide-success story than the Sony Walkman. The marketing executive responsible for the Walkman told *Advertising Age* that, "Worldwide Walkman fever was created through our public relations efforts rather than our advertising." Indeed, Sony launched its worldwide marketing campaign in 1979 without the benefit of consumer advertising.

The product was positioned as a powerful, portable, high-quality-sound-producing, personal-entertainment vehicle. Sony first aroused public interest by giving Walkmans to Japan's leading musicians, teen idols, and magazine editors. They were seen everywhere wearing a Walkman months before the product was introduced to consumers. An introductory press event in Tokyo's equivalent of Central Park featured a chorus of teenagers skating to the music on their Walkmans.

In the United States, the name Walkman was timely, coinciding as it did with the boom in walking, running, and jogging for which it became standard equipment.

Geltzer & Company conducted a multifaceted public relations program that promoted the new "stereo on the go" as a Christmas gift item. The imaginative publicity campaign included conducting silent disco contests for "movers and shakers" who danced to the music on their Walkmans and providing to newspapers photos of office workers walking to work, wearing their Walkmans, during a New York subway strike. Another effective technique was to place the Walkman in photography for advertising of designer products like Christian Dior sheets and Gloria Vanderbilt fashions.

The massive publicity was heard around the world and the product was a walkaway success despite its high initial price (around $200 in the United States). But no one could have foreseen that within 10 years, 50 million would be sold. The Walkman not only ushered in the era of the personal stereo, but was responsible for igniting the growth of prerecorded audio cassettes, 450 million of which were sold in 1988.

MPR AND HIGH TECH

The electronics industry is now the fastest growing and largest manufacturing segment in the United States. *Public Relations Journal* says that "rapid expansion, along with the far-reaching implications of new technology for all businesses and for our individual life-styles have made high tech one of the most fertile and challenging specialties for public relations practitioners."

High-tech public relations is one of the fastest-growing segments of marketing public relations because it supports a high-news, high-interest industry. Its growth has been fueled by the incredible number of new products that come to market each year. High-tech public relations specialists have two jobs: to translate technical language so that it can be understood by the products' end users and to make one company's product stand out from the rest. That means devising messages that will attract both media attention and buyer interest.

Andy Miller, head of Boston-based Miller Communications, one of the leading high-tech public relations firms, says that his job is "taking a new product and getting to the heart of what it means for the market, for society, for the economy. That means looking at the implications of technology and then getting the media and the public excited about those implications."

In 1982, Miller was approached by a venture capitalist for help in launching a new company called Gateway Technology. According to *Public Relations Journal,* the firm had 10 employees, $1.5 million in venture capital, and a portable computer it had developed to compete with IBM. Miller persuaded his new client to introduce its computer to the media in New York two weeks before COMDEX, the major trade show in the industry, was to be held in Las Vegas. As a result, the company, now called Compaq Computer Corporation, effectively positioned its product on the news-making concept of IBM-software compatibility, attracted dealers, and began its meteoric rise. To introduce Compaq products to the mass market for home use, Miller went beyond the technology media and placed computers in the hands of consumer publications, emphasizing graduation- and Christmas-gift issues.

Miller continued to generate headlines for the company. In 1989, his firm introduced the COMPAQ LTE line, the first notebook-sized computers to offer full PC functionality. The new computers were heralded at a New York press conference as being "so light and so compact that they redefine portability in personal computing."

High-tech companies have often sought thematic locations to launch their new products. "Harmony in Technology and Music" was the theme of a Control Data press conference at a new-age jazz club in New York's Greenwich Village. NCR might have been stretching a point when it introduced its 9800 at the Guggenheim Museum as "an effective way to emphasize the product's own architecture."

Out of the Big Blue

When IBM introduced its new generation of personal-computing products and programs—the IBM Personal System/(PS/2)—worldwide in 1987, it pulled out all the stops.

The company described the PS/2 as representing "the broadest range of compatible personal-computing systems ever offered." This statement was documented in a 100-plus-page press kit that included 9 press releases and 8 fact sheets, plus photos, illustrations, and price sheets.

Here is how *TIME* described the launch in an article titled, "Into the Wild Blue Yonder":

> It was an impressive debut, even by the standards of Big Blue. Some 2,000 computer dealers from across the country gathered in Miami Beach last week for a Beach Boys concert, the premiere of new print and TV commercials reuniting members of the M*A*S*H cast, and, most important, an elaborate presentation beamed live to 20,000 customers, analysts, employees and reporters nationwide. Before the spectacle ended, the world's biggest computer company had set a new standard against which personal computers will be measured for years to come.[4]

A cover story in *USA TODAY* described the festivities this way:

> Computer generated rock-beat music filled the huge Theater for the Performing Arts. Laser lights danced about the stage. Two thousand wide-eyed IBM Corp. dealers craned to get a peek at the four boxes on the stage. The tension mounted in New York and 70 other USA cities as 20,000 IBM customers and computer-industry watchers monitored the action via satellite and closed-circuit TV. This was the moment the computer world was waiting for. IBM was about to chart a new course in personal-computer history.[5]

The PC/2 family of computers was described by the company as "the next generation in personal computing." Perhaps they were also engaging in the next generation of marketing public relations. The PS/2 gala linked all of IBMs "publics" in a dramatic response to mounting competition from low-cost domestic and Asian computers.

What's Next?

The two-covers-in-one-week feat accomplished by Lee Iacocca in 1964 when the Mustang was introduced was duplicated 25 years later by Steven Jobs, the young computer wizard who had mastered the art of marketing public relations in an earlier life. Jobs, who helped shape the computer industry with the Apple II and Macintosh computers, was back with a new company and an amazing new computer. The event was celebrated by cover stories in both *Newsweek* and *Business Week* in their October 25, 1988, issues. *The New York Times* proclaimed "The Return of a Computer Star" in its "Business Day" and, nine months later, in its Sunday magazine, ran a six-page story on Jobs, complete with full-page color photo, when his new machine was shipped to retail stores.

The *Times* described the dramatic return of Steven Jobs and the San Francisco introduction of the NeXT computer this way:

> To a hushed crowd of 3,000 at Davies Symphony Hall here, Mr. Jobs introduced the machine—a black magnesium cube housing the electronics, accompanied by an optical disk storage device and a large black-and-white screen capable of displaying photographic quality images.
>
> Mr. Jobs is known for his dramatic product introductions and he and his company took advantage of intense interest in the computer industry about both him and his new machine. He stood alone on a dark stage with just the computer and a vase of flowers, a huge screen behind him, and took the machine through its paces. He demonstrated how it could record and send voice messages, play music with the quality of a compact disc and instantly retrieve quotations from the complete works of Shakespeare stored on its optical disk. After the two-hour demonstration, capped by a duet featuring the machine and violinist for the San Francisco Symphony, the audience gave Mr. Jobs a standing ovation.[6]

The Wall Street Journal, in a front-page story, described how Jobs, "the P.T. Barnum of the computer industry," introduced "his sleek personal workstation for university students and educators with all the subtlety of a Hollywood premiere" and "worked the crowd like an entertainer."

Steve Jobs had made the introduction of his NeXT computer one of the biggest business stories of the year. Fifteen months later, he was making a few headlines of a different sort. "Job's New Computer Off to a Sluggish Start" reported *The New York Times*. "Slow Start for NeXT Doesn't Worry Jobs" said *The Wall Street Journal*. Jobs returned to the same symphony hall in San Francisco two years after the introduction of the black cube to unveil a faster and less expensive version of the NeXt personal computer, capturing more national headlines and reviving interest in his faltering line.

GLOBAL MPR: THE SENSOR RAZOR

Three months before the product was shipped to stores throughout the world, the Gillette Sensor razor was named one of 1989's Products of the Year by *FORTUNE* magazine. The media introduction of the Sensor was also one of the MPR programs of the year, an outstanding example of the role of public relations in "pull" marketing and one of the best demonstrations of the trend toward globalization in both marketing and marketing public relations.

The Gillette North Atlantic Shaving Group launched the Gillette Sensor on the same day in 19 countries throughout Western Europe and North America. With a marketing budget of $175 million, it was the largest product launch ever undertaken by Gillette and one of the largest new-product introductions in the history of the shaving industry.

In its press kit, the company described the Sensor shaving system as "the most revolutionary breakthrough in shaving in a generation." Gillette also pointed out that its multinational, multimedia marketing campaign was equally revolutionary. The company said its program was designed to "use advertising, display, sales promotion, and public relations to synergistically create a communications explosion generating unprecedented excitement and demand from consumers and the trade."

The Omnicom PR Network introduced the product to the business and trade media simultaneously in each of the 19 North Atlantic countries on October 3, 1989. Major press conferences were held in New York, London, Paris, Milan, Barcelona, and Dusseldorf. In addition, media briefings were held in Canada, Ireland, Iceland, Belgium, The Netherlands, Denmark, Norway, Finland, Sweden, Switzerland, Austria, Portugal, and Greece.

To coordinate this cohesive and simultaneous launch, all press-kit materials were written and designed under North Atlantic coordination (handled by the New York office of Porter/Novelli) and distributed to each of the participating Omnicom PR Network agencies. The content of the conferences, including all audio-visual materials, was developed centrally and adapted appropriately for each country's individual needs.

Media coverage throughout the world was outstanding, especially for a product category that would not normally be plotted on the Harris Grid as being high-interest. More than 85 journalists and reporters representing national and international business and trade media attended the New York press conference. The results were front-page features in numerous business sections, including *The New York Times* ("Gillette's Challenge to the Disposables") and *USA TODAY* ("Man's Best Shave Ever"), and unprecedented coverage for a new product in all three newsweeklies. A photo of the president of the Gillette North Atlantic Shaving Group holding the product was distributed over the Associated Press wire to newspapers throughout the United States.

The October launch focused mainly on business and trade media because the product was not to be advertised until the 1990 Super Bowl telecast and was not to become available at retail until the first quarter of 1990. The prelaunch publicity and advertising payoff were so effective that stores sold out of Sensors, and Gillette scaled back the $110 million advertising budget. Within six months, Gillette had shipped 17 million Sensor razors, double the company's sales forecasts. Prudential-Bache analyst David Shore called the Sensor "the single most successful consumer non-durable product introduction in the history of the planet."[7]

PHARMACEUTICAL MPR

Another hot area of marketing public relations is the new specialty of pharmaceutical PR. The emphasis that pharmaceutical marketers are placing on public relations has led to the formation of firms specializing in pharmaceutical programming and of medical divisions within major public relations firms. These firms conduct programs for prescription drugs and for the increasing number of products that are moving from prescription to over-the-counter.

John Bryer, president of Lexis Pharmaceuticals and long an innovator in drug marketing, pioneered rebates, consumer advertising, and the use of public relations when as president of Boots Pharmaceuticals he introduced Rufen, an ibuprofen equivalent of Motrin. He took the then-novel step of engaging a PR firm, Golin/Harris, to take his message directly to consumers, asking them to ask their doctor about Rufen. After obtaining national publicity, including full-page stories in the newsweeklies, Bryer became his own spokesperson on a tour of major markets where his interviews and personal sales calls caused local drug-chain buyers to stock Rufen, a new product from a little known company in the United States.

MPR also played a key role in the "ibuprofen wars" with the successful launch of Whitehall Laboratories' Advil. When the Food and Drug Administration approved an ibuprofen dosage for OTC sale, Advil and Bristol-Myers' Nuprin were introduced simultaneously. Daniel J. Edelman Inc. sprang into action "literally within minutes" after approval, transmitting an Advil video news release that detailed the benefits of the new brand. The public relations program was supported by the immediate establishment of an Advil Medical Advisory Board. The product story was carried to the consumer by an appropriate celebrity spokesperson, veteran baseball-pitching-great Nolan Ryan, who endorsed Advil as his pain medicine of choice and told broadcast- and print-media audiences how the product fits his personal fitness program. Ryan stars in a 30-minute video distributed to junior and senior high schools, to provide young athletes with information on sports conditioning programs, sports nutrition, injury prevention, and treatment, while establishing loyalty to Advil at an early age.

The first American headache art exhibition, "Through the Looking Glass," sponsored by Sandoz Pharmaceuticals for Boston's Headache Research Center was the grand prize winner in *Relate* magazine's first public relations Creative Awards competition in 1990. The exhibit and the publicity it generated benefited Sandoz, one of the leaders in severe headache treatment, and the Center, which had to add two full-time physicians to its clinical staff to accommodate a 36 percent increase in new patients.

PR, Promotion, and Scientific Exchange

When CBS's "60 Minutes" ran a segment on Ortho Pharmaceutical Corporation's Retin-A, it attributed the spectacular sales success to "one of the most sophisticated public relations campaigns ever launched by a drug company." The influential investigative program raised the larger issue of the "commercialization of science," especially with regard to the use of paid medical consultants as spokespersons and the practice of announcing product-benefit claims to media before they are presented to the scientific community or approved by the Food and Drug Administration (FDA).

The specific claim that Retin-A helps remove wrinkles from aging skin was made by the chairman of the Department of Dermatology at the prestigious University of Michigan Medical School at a January 1988 news conference. The doctor, a consultant to Ortho, reported the results of a study of the product's efficacy on 30 people and showed slides as evidence of how well the product had worked on the 30 subjects. The story made big national news, appeared on the nightly news of all three networks, and became the front-page headline story of USA TODAY. A month prior to the national announcement of the study, other university dermatologists who consult with Ortho were booked to discuss the wrinkle-removing properties of Retin-A on television and radio, and in newspaper interviews in major markets. Stories about the study also appeared in medical publications including the Journal of the American Medical Association. The immediate effect of the announcement was a rise of five points on the common stock of Ortho's parent company, Johnson & Johnson, on the New York Stock Exchange. Investor confidence was well placed. Sales of Retin-A tripled, reaching $60 million.

"60 Minutes" reported that the National Institutes of Health then asked independent medical authorities to determine whether there was sufficient reliable evidence that Retin-A works on aging skin. Retin-A had previously received FDA approval for use with acne. The program added that, two years after the successful New York news conference, the company had also applied for FDA approval of its antiwrinkle claims. An FDA spokesperson interviewed on the program expressed concern about the appropriateness of using a press conference to exchange scientific information and said the government was trying to determine whether Ortho's public relations campaign constituted promotion and therefore should be regulated under the current FDA definition.

Newsweek, in a follow-up story, said that Retin-A had ushered in the era of "cosmeceuticals." The magazine said Johnson & Johnson "used public relations to go around the doctor to the consumer, and the consumer came back asking for the prescription. . . ." The implications hold widespread significance for the practice of medical public relations. All pharmaceutical companies employ recognized medical specialists to consult on products and rely on their third-party endorsement to gain acceptance in the medical community. Increasingly, these consultants have been used to explain product benefits to the public as well as the profession. While the Retin-A situation is unique in that the specific benefit claim had not been approved by the FDA prior to its public announcement, the public relations programs for virtually all pharmaceuticals are based on the endorsement of medical authorities.

Mickey's Drug

An FDA official told *The Wall Street Journal* that the agency needs to look at "the whole area of companies going directly to consumers" and "putting their message out around the usual methods." The FDA was particularly upset when former New York Yankee slugger Mickey Mantle appeared in person and on a video news release for Voltaren, a Ciba-Geigy arthritis drug he said helped his arthritic knees.

Mantle's talk-show appearances included an interview on NBC's "Today Show," which sent scores of patients into their physicians' offices asking for "Mickey's drug." A few days later the show's medical reporter, Dr. Art Ulene, corrected the earlier report. He said that Voltaren was no more effective than many other arthritis drugs already on the market and that the only reason Mantle had felt such benefits was that it was the first time he had taken any arthritis medication. He added that Mantle's "enthusiasm for Voltaren is understandable, especially since he is a paid spokesperson for the company that makes the drug."

The Promise of Prozac

The antidepressant Prozac was introduced by Eli Lilly in 1987 and, according to *TIME* magazine, "surged to star status, thanks to skillful promotion, glowing word of mouth among doctors and heavy media attention including cover stories in *Newsweek* and *New York*."

The *Newsweek* cover on March 26, 1990, was a painting of an oversized Prozac capsule floating over a surrealistic landscape. It proclaimed Prozac "A Breakthrough Drug for Depression." The article, "The Promise of Prozac," said it "is easier to prescribe and has fewer side effects—and that makes patients and doctors happy."

Prozak became the leader in its category and had achieved annual sales of $500 million by 1990. Then reports were published stating that the drug could cause some users to feel suicidal. This unfavorable publicity led to a backlash in the medical community and among users of the drug. Prozac thus became both the beneficiary and the victim of excessive publicity.

FOOD AND BEVERAGE MPR

Marketing public relations has been widely and successfully used to introduce new food products for years. Charles Lubin, founder of the Kitchens of Sara Lee, said that, in the early years, "public relations was worth 100 times the advertising" in telling the Sara Lee stories to consumers and the trade. He credited a *Wall Street Journal* article with causing an immediate demand for the product from food chains across the country. Stories in *LIFE, TIME,* and *Newsweek* and in newspaper food sections whetted consumers' appetites for Sara Lee frozen baked goods.

I have personally been involved in the launch of dozens of food products from Sara Lee, Kraft, Armour, Campbell, and others. The introductions usually included a media event that allowed the editors to sample the new product or an attention-getting way to bring the product to the editor. Three recent Golin/Harris product introductions illustrate the variety of techniques now being used by MPR people to gain editorial attention and interest for new products:

- ○ To introduce Campbell's new dry soup mixes, Campbell called on pop artist Andy Warhol, who had achieved fame in the 1960s with his paintings of Campbell Soup cans. Warhol was commissioned to paint a portrait of "Campbell Soup Box," the package for the new line of soup mixes. The painting was unveiled at a media event at New York's Whitney Museum of American Art and later displayed as part of a traveling "Soup Is Good Food Art Exhibit." Consumers saw the art and sampled the soup at locations ranging from art galleries to high-traffic locations like New York's Penn Station and Boston's Faneuil Hall. Warhol and his new soup art were featured on network television and radio and in newspapers, which ran "Warhol and Campbell's Team Up" AP stories.
- ○ To introduce McDonald's salads, an "edible press kit" was sent to food editors across the country. The kit was an insulated cooler containing press releases and photos, nutrition information about McDonald's salads, and two to four salads, complete with napkins and eating utensils. Over 2,800 edible press kits were delivered to media in test markets alone (many of them by vegetable-costumed kids) before the product went national.

○ To introduce its new Dorito Lights, Frito-Lay shipped complimentary bags of its new low-oil, cholesterol-free chips via Federal Express to accountants in 40 markets on April 14, 1990, the eve of National Tax Crunch Time, inviting them to take a break from number crunching. Frito-Lay's marketing director told the media that the company wanted to use nontraditional methods of marketing that would be completely unique, capture consumer attention, and excite the sales force.

Perrier Creates a Market

The bottled-water market, a $1.7 billion business in 1988, was virtually nonexistent a decade earlier when Great Waters of France introduced Perrier to the United States. The timing could not have been better. Americans were becoming health and fitness conscious and looking for food and beverage products that were good for them. The marketing problem for Perrier was to transform its product from "The Snob's Drink" to a mass-marketed product "while still maintaining its cachet," according to Stan Bratskier, whose Rand Public Relations played a key role in accomplishing that trick. The top public relations priorities were to get the word out about the product to consumers and to try to convince them to part with a dollar for a bottle of water.

The press was skeptical about the product and its natural-carbonation story; so a press tour to the source at Vergeze, France, was arranged. Twenty American food-and-beverage writers, joined by reporters from the Paris Bureau of major U.S. publications, tasted waters from the spring, toured the bottling plant with Perrier's president, and washed down lavish French meals with Perrier.

Here's how Bratskier described the premiere Perrier press tour:

At the Perrier spring, we arranged for construction of a plexiglass dome, so that reporters could see the water bubbling naturally from the center of the earth. We mapped out a plant tour, appointed spokespeople to describe Perrier's history, production and prospects, and orchestrated a series of dinners and parties that not only provided entertainment, but also established a tone and style for the product.

We decided that only reporters who had decision-making power could join us; so if we were successful in telling the story, editors would have the authority to report on it. We compressed the trip into three and one-half days, and insisted that all reporters who went with us returned with us, as well. This eliminated many of the "junketing" aspects of the trip and communicated the feeling that there was a real story here, albeit a delightful one. We worked closely with each editor traveling with us to learn of his or her story needs and, subsequently, to create a tour that satisfied as many of those needs as possible.[8]

After the reporters' return, publicity extolling the product began to appear. An article by *New York Times* reporter Jim Clarity emptied Manhattan grocers' shelves of Perrier instantaneously.

Perrier also took advantage of the new interest in fitness by becoming one of the first companies to sponsor road races and marathons. Hundreds of runners were seen in person and on television holding the distinctive green Perrier bottles after a race, helping Perrier gain a reputation as the refreshment to drink after exercising.

Perrier's reputation was further enhanced when it was seen being served at better bars and restaurants. When customers saw or read about others drinking it in chic places, they wanted to buy some and serve it at home.

When Perrier suspended production in 1990 because some product had been found to be contaminated by benzene, *The New York Times* reported in a front-page story that "the news hit with a shock because Perrier has become more than a mere product in the American marketplace. The tony little green bottles of French sparkling water, which sell for up to $3.50 in restaurants, have become the most vivid symbol of the status minded and health-conscious lifestyle of the baby-boomer generation."[9]

The *Chicago Tribune* commented that "the re-call's aftermath will be an even greater challenge for its public relations muscle than its introduction in this country 12 years ago when Perrier virtually created the $2 billion bottled water market."[10]

The company took the unusual step of hiring Burson-Marsteller, a public relations firm, to assess the damage and create an interim ad campaign. At a news conference held at the French Consulate in New York, Roland V. Davis, president and chief executive of Perrier Group of America, introduced the campaign's theme, "Perrier. Worth Waiting For." The print ads created by Burson state "The problem has been fixed. It was never a health or safety problem. But for a product known for purity, it was definitely a mistake."

Inside Public Relations, a trade journal, remarked that "while Perrier may not dominate the market as it has been in the past, the swift and complete recall of its product, the concern it displayed for public sensitivity and good launch PR should ensure a successful return to the shelves."

Coke: Diet, New, and Classic

Coca-Cola pulled out all the stops when it introduced Diet Coke in 1982. The company hosted an intimate party for 6,000 of its best friends at New York's Radio City Music Hall to introduce the product. Among the friends assembled were representatives from the major media who reported the festivities to consumers in the daily newspapers and the nightly news. To make the most of the first new product ever to use the Coca-Cola name, the company staged a gala featuring a 40-piece band, the Rockettes, and cabaret singer Bobby Short, but the real star of the show was a 14-foot Diet Coke can rising from the orchestra pit on cue. The company liked the venue so well that the Radio City premiere was featured in the initial Diet Coke commercial. This may have been the first time that a media event was filmed for a commercial to dramatize the news of the announcement of a new product.

Brian Dyson, then president of Coca-Cola USA, told the media:

> We believe Diet Coke will be the most significant beverage marketing activity of the Coca-Cola Co. in the 1980s, and it might well be the most important new soft drink brand for the entire industry.

He was right. Diet Coke soon became not only the nation's leading diet soft drink, but also the biggest new soft drink introduction of the 1980s. It is now the nation's third-largest-selling soft drink. The editors of *Advertising Age* selected Diet Coke the "Brand of the Decade."

Of course, the company achieved even greater attention on April 23, 1985, when press and security analysts were summoned to a press conference to hear "the most important announcement in the company's ninety-nine-year history." Hundreds of reporters and analysts attending in a theater at Lincoln Center, and hundreds more reached by a satellite hookup, learned about the reformulation of Coca-Cola. Media headlines made the world aware of the "new Coke" overnight, touching off an immediate and intense negative reaction. The "new Coke," the now legendary product failure, reminded people how much they loved the old Coke and put it back on top. Donald Keough, Coca-Cola's president, said that "all the time and money and skill poured into market research on the new Coca-Cola could not measure or reveal the deep and abiding emotional attachment to original Coca-Cola."

"Some critic," he said, "will say Coca-Cola made a marketing mistake. Some cynic will say that we planned the whole thing for the publicity value. The truth is that we are not that dumb and we are not that smart."

In March 1990, the company made the surprising announcement that it would reintroduce "new Coke" in test markets with a new package and a new name: Coke II. *The Wall Street Journal,* calling it "the new new Coke," pointed out that "almost five years after its now infamous new Coke debacle, Coca-Cola Co. is taking the troubled product, renaming and repositioning it with the hope of keeping the drink alive—and perhaps this time converting Pepsi fans." The move led an industry observer to comment, "The cold war may thaw but the cola wars—never."

The Simple Pleasures of Simplesse

In 1988, the NutraSweet Company caused a major media stir when it announced the development of Simplesse, the first all-natural substitute for fat. The company staged a "mega media event" at which reporters sampled chocolate ice cream and salad dressing made with Simplesse. The event was reported on the evening news by Dan Rather (CBS), Peter Jennings (ABC), and Tom Brokaw (NBC) and was featured prominently in newsweeklies and newspapers everywhere. The coverage was so extensive that the product achieved a remarkable 30 percent awareness overnight. However, the good news was tempered by questions from ABC's "Nightline" and others who believed the product required approval of the Food and Drug Administration (FDA) even though it is made from egg white and milk.

Two years later, the FDA approved Simplesse for use in frozen dessert products. A *New York Times* front-page story reported that the approval "opened the door for a new class of reduced-fat food products that may revolutionize the American diet."

NutraSweet, one of several companies experimenting with fat substitutes (others include Procter & Gamble, Kraft, General Foods, Unilever, Frito-Lay, and Best Foods), got the jump on the competition and was ready to make the most of the announcement. The company immediately called a news conference at New York's Pierre Hotel to announce its plans to begin national sales of Simple Pleasures, a frozen dessert made with Simplesse, pictured in Figure 10–1. The product was so well received that the company doubled its plant capacity in the first three months.

ADWEEK's *Marketing Week* reported NutraSweet was "savoring the moment":

> It was clear that the company had been preparing for this occasion for a long time. It had only gotten FDA approval to market Simplesse that morning but by mid-afternoon the company's public relations machine had pulled together a most elaborate press conference—complete with old-time ice cream shoppe, product samples and giveaways galore.[11]

The company had prepared the media by providing advance samplings of the ice-cream-like dessert. The verdict, as reported on the day of the announcement by newspaper food writers, TV reporters, and consumers, was a classic case of third-party endorsement. *The Chicago Tribune* said it is "virtually indistinguishable from the real thing; some even go so far as to compare the taste to the so-called 'superpremium' ice creams that are extra high in butterfat."

NutraSweet said that its dessert product was only the beginning for Simplesse. The company said it could be substituted in a wide variety of products that have a high content of fat and is seeking FDA approval of its

FIGURE 10–1 NutraSweet made big news in 1990 when the U.S. Food and Drug Administration approved Simplesse, the first all-natural fat substitute. The company was ready with a "scoop" for the media, a ready-to-market ice-cream-like dessert called Simple Pleasures. They staged an instant press conference complete with an old-fashioned ice cream shoppe where reporters could sample the confection.

use in mayonnaise, salad dressing, sour cream, yogurt, coffee creamer, soft cheeses, butter, and margarine.

The hastily called news conference played to an SRO crowd of reporters and nine camera crews. The news, featured on both the evening news and morning shows on all networks, was so widely reported that it became the subject of a "Tonight Show" monologue and a "Saturday Night Live" sketch. NutraSweet stopped counting media impressions at 1 billion.

The result was to excite both the trade and the consumer. The product demand outstripped supply for Simple Pleasures before any advertising had run for the product.

TOYS AND GAMES

There is little built-in consumer or media interest in the hundreds of toys that are introduced every year. There are no toy buffs, just toy-buying parents and toy-receiving children. There are no consumer publications devoted to toys as there are to cars and computers. Still, over the years, some of the most remarkable marketing public relations successes have been for toys and games. MPR played a key role in introducing the toy industry's most enduring toys for boys (G.I. Joe) and girls (Barbie) and keeping them high on the best-seller list for over a quarter-century.

The annual New York Toy Fair in the spring of 1959 was the scene of the introduction of a product concept that was to become one of the marketing phenomena of the next three decades—Barbie, the Teen-Age Fashion Doll. Few could envision at the time that this new doll would become the hub of a world of toys, costumes, games, and many other products.

Publicity was designed to carry the Barbie message to parents as well as children and to enhance Mattel's advertising campaign. The public relations effort on behalf of Barbie became one of the most extensive for any single product in toy history. In the first year, Barbie was depicted in a four-page layout in *LIFE*, featured in *Readers Digest*, and chronicled by syndicated columnists. She became a guest star on network variety shows and the object of business stories in *The Wall Street Journal*.

In addition to the publicity in newspapers, magazines, radio and television, a major public relations vehicle was The Barbie Fan Club. Barbie, for all her popularity, was not without detractors; some contended that the fashion doll, with her ever expanding wardrobe, tended to promote materialism to young girls. Sensitive to this criticism, Mattel executives sought to counter the arguments. The Barbie Fan Club established a line of direct communication with Mattel's young customers and their parents.

In 1965, over 100,000 letters were written to Barbie, all of them personally answered by the doll's friends at Mattel and its PR firm, Harshe Rotman & Druck. Hedda Hopper noted in her syndicated column that the Barbie doll's fan mail exceeded that of almost all established motion picture stars. Today, The Barbie Fan Club has 650,000 members who still receive Barbie magazines.

Barbie and her friends, including long-time boyfriend Ken, continue to be one of the toy industry's most perennially popular products. Today, 90 percent of little girls in the United States between ages 4 and 10 own a Barbie. More than 500 million have been sold, including 21 million in 1988, her best year ever. Sales of the Barbie line of clothes, cars, pets, and friends accounted for 45 percent of Mattel's total revenue that year.

In 1990, *The Wall Street Journal* proclaimed, "Barbie, the world's best-selling plastic playmate, isn't just a doll anymore. It's now Barbie, the 'lifestyle.'" The company, continuing to rely on MPR, announced its plans to extend Barbie beyond the toy category to "bring the product to life for real live girls." Retailers were introduced to the Barbie Style line of girl-sized costumes, Barbie bedsheets, stationery, backpacks, and a line of trading cards featuring Barbie through the years. The line extension even included a limited-edition Barbie dressed in a Bob Mackie designer gown selling for $120. Barbie had come a long way since 1959, and the company predicted that with heavy international marketing she might become a "billion dollar baby" in the mid-1990s.

Like Barbie, Hasbro Inc.'s G.I. Joe has maintained his popularity through the years, in contrast to the typical hot toys of the 1960s whose life cycle rarely exceeded three years. G.I. Joe, who enlisted in 1964, lost popularity in the 1970s when anti-war sentiment was high, took a "furlough" in 1978, and returned in 1982 as an action adventurer fighting terrorists. In 1988, 24 years after his introduction, sales were $200 million, which ranked G.I. Joe among the year's best selling toys.

The company used some typical public relations comparisons in announcing their famous character's sales success over a quarter-century. They revealed that 200 million toys had been sold ("enough for every man, woman, and child in the United States and Europe") and that 100 million of Joe's tanks, trucks, and planes had been sold, generating more than $1.2 billion in retail sales ("equivalent to the annual defense budget of Austria").

Oh, You Beautiful Dolls

That was the title of a six-page cover story in Newsweek on the hottest toy of the 1980s. The article was the culmination of a six-month MPR effort that was largely responsible for what has become known as the Cabbage Patch Kids "phenomenon."

The skillfully planned MPR program, combined with an enormously appealing product concept, made it mandatory for every kid in America to have (or rather to "adopt") at least one of these homely, cuddly dolls. Modern technology made it possible for every child to become a parent to a doll that was uniquely his or her own. Described by Newsweek as "the first toy of the post-industrial age," each one-of-a-kind Cabbage Patch Kid came off a computer-controlled assembly line with a different combination of hair and skin color, clothing, type of mouth, dimples and freckles, and sex. Each was packaged in a see-through box so kids could pick the Kid of their choice. Perhaps most importantly, each came with a name and adoption papers.

The public relations program designed by Richard Weiner and his staff depended heavily on research and the advice of child psychologists and educators, who advised that the dolls' appearance brought out the nurturing instinct in kids. The Director of the Psychology of Parenthood Program at New York University worked with the public relations firm to develop a "Cabbage Patch Kids Parenting Guide," which accompanied each doll. This piece won the hearts of the kids and the minds of parents and influentials and gave legitimacy to the value of the adoption idea.

The incredible success of this MPR program is a testimony to the value of research and advanced planning. Toy buyers were introduced to the Kids at the New York Toy Fair. Coleco's showroom was converted into a replica of Babyland General Hospital, generating an avalanche of trade publicity that helped stimulate the interest of the consumer media. The consumer media relations effort was launched at a New York press conference in June, even though the Kids would not be available in stores until the Christmas shopping season. Two hundred reporters attended, including magazine writers who needed the long lead time to feature the dolls in their Christmas gift-suggestion stories.

The New York press event at the Manhattan Laboratory Museum was duplicated in Atlanta and Boston. Pupils from selected local schools were invited and toy buyers attended the press event with their own children. Each event featured a "mass adoption" by the children present.

In the fall, Cabbage Patch spokespersons hit the road for a fifteen-city media tour, extolling the dolls' virtues and showing them off on TV interview shows. Interviews were also arranged with newspapers and on newscasts; talk-radio listeners were permitted to call in with their questions.

A doll sent to Jane Pauley, then host of the "Today Show," who was at home expecting a baby, resulted in a five-minute segment on the show and started the national publicity ball rolling. The other two networks followed with their own stories. In the end, "the Cabbage Patch Kids were on every TV station, in every major newspaper and general interest magazine in the United States and not just once," according to Dick Weiner. "Everybody in the United States, whether or not they were parents, knew about the Cabbage Patch Kids."

The mad rush for dolls at stores throughout the country could have resulted in a negative backlash had Coleco not pulled its advertising and had the story not been tempered by the PR decision to give away dolls to hospitals and other charities. A wire picture of First Lady Nancy Reagan presenting Cabbage Patch Kids to two Korean children who were heart patients at a Long Island, New York, hospital was seen throughout the world.

The result: $600 million in sales of the dolls in 1985. The success of the Cabbage Patch Kids became a PR classic because it was primarily PR-driven. In contrast to conventional toy-marketing wisdom, advertising played only a supporting role.

Post script: In 1989, Hasbro acquired the line from Coleco and announced that it was planning "a giant reintroduction" of the Kids, in hopes of restoring them to their former glory. At year end, *USA TODAY* reported that "Cabbage Patch Is Blooming Again":

> With nurturing from new parent Hasbro Inc., the Kids are making a comeback. Hasbro says they're coming back to stay. Its strategy: escape the boom-and-bust cycle that can kill trendy toys and turn Cabbage Patch

dolls into consistent, steady sellers that Hasbro chairman Alan Hassenfeld says, "have the potential to be here 10 years down the road."[12]

The Pursuit of Trivia

Like Cabbage Patch Kids, the marketing campaign for Trivial Pursuit, the hottest game of the 1980s, relied almost entirely on public relations. Like the Kids, the program involved an imaginative campaign to excite toy buyers and consumers.

Selchow & Righter Company, makers of Trivial Pursuit, decided not to run advertising for the introduction and did not advertise until late in the year, when the ad space that was committed to was no longer needed. The intent was to create word-of-mouth advertising through the adroit use of public relations.

A first step was to send all living celebrities mentioned in the game copies of the card on which their name appeared. Word-of-mouth began in California and moved east to other celebrity centers like New York, Chicago, and Washington. Another tactic used by the public relations firm, Pezzano & Co., was to send Trivial Pursuit games to disk jockeys at radio stations throughout the country, with the suggestion that they be given away to listeners who correctly answered trivia questions from the game. The game's Canadian creators were booked as guests of talk shows on more than 125 stations. Finally, the PR program involved raising money for Easter Seals by scheduling Trivial Pursuit parties in 80 U.S. cities in November, a month before the Christmas selling season.

In the first year alone, Trivial Pursuit sold 22 million games, a result achieved almost exclusively through the use of MPR.

Fresh from the Sewer: Teenage Mutant Ninja Turtles

Teenage Mutant Ninja Turtles was just one of thousands of toys introduced at New York's Toy Fair in 1988. Turtle Raphael is shown in Figure 10–2. The action-figure line by Playmate Toys had to compete in an overcrowded field of boys' action toys, and the company needed a way to separate its product from the pack and draw buyers to the showroom. It was decided that the Turtles should literally fight for attention. Two professional stuntmen costumed as Turtle characters staged karate-chopping "hand-to-claw" combat inside the Toy Fair buildings and outside for local television crews. The next day, a newspaper boy delivered a special newspaper to buyers explaining that the Turtles had saved the Toy Fair from villains. Then, in keeping with the product's story line (the Turtles grew up in the sewers of New York), the city's Department of

FIGURE 10–2 Raphael, one of the wildly successful line of Teenage Mutant Ninja Turtle action figures from Playmate Toys, and star of the runaway movie hit. Publicity fueled the "Turtlemania" phenomenon.

Environmental Protection bestowed them with the "Key to the Sewer" for their meritorious deeds at the Toy Fair.

A second strategy to heighten buyer interest was to gain and merchandise media exposure during the show. On the opening day of the Toy Fair, thousands of copies of *USA TODAY* with a cover story on Ninja Turtles were distributed to the buyers. Titled "Who Is that Masked Reptile?," the story featured a four-color illustration of the Turtles, labeling them "loony enough to be a hit." The Keys-to-the-Sewer presentation was covered by the New York newspapers, ABC, and "Entertainment Tonight."

The public relations program engineered for Playmate by Berkhemer & Kline Golin/Harris not only brought buyers to the showroom but caused such demand for the product that the company had to increase its production. The media effort resulted in long-lead Christmas features in newspapers and on radio and television. A UPI "What's Hot" story was carried in hundreds of newspapers, and a two-page "Trends" story ran in *People* magazine ("Just when you thought we were out of superheroes, along comes Teenage Mutant Ninja Turtles"). Bucking the toy-industry slump, Teenage Mutant Ninja Turtles became an instant best-seller, outselling the perennial category leader G.I. Joe and ranking among the top ten of all toys of the year.

A year later, the Turtles were still on top. *The Wall Street Journal* featured a drawing of a Teenage Mutant Ninja Turtle on its front page, in its December 1989 Christmas-toy-industry roundup story. The paper reported that "retailers snickered two years ago when they saw the characters," but "ever since, the pizza-eating humanoid turtles have been one of the hottest new toys." Another *Journal* story predicted that the Turtle toys "are expected to lead the North Pole parades in units sold this Christmas." In 1989, Playmate sold $100 million worth of Turtle figures and accessories, making it the leading action-figure line and the third-hottest-selling toy line behind only Nintendo and Barbie.

At the 1990 Toy Fair, Playmate continued its wacky MPR strategy by staging a Turtles-on-Ice presentation in Central Park, followed by a "Meet the Mutants" session for kids. *The New York Times* ran a picture of Turtles Raphael and Donatello and reported that "a brigade of giant turtles fielded by Playmate Toys added to the traditional tumult of the toy fair with their high visibility around town; they went ice skating in Central Park on Sunday and, on the opening morning of the fair, they paraded from the Toy Center on lower Fifth Avenue to the New York Stock Exchange on Wall Street."[13]

THAT'S ENTERTAINMENT

There has long been a symbiotic relationship between the entertainment and media industries. Stories about movies, TV, and live entertainment sell magazines and newspapers and attract viewers. The entertainment industry responds by providing a never-ending parade of stars to interview and products to publicize. I wrote my master's dissertation on how the old Hollywood studios used publicity to sell a picture and make a star. Today's more sophisticated producers use every tool in the marketing book to bring consumers to the box office. Probably in no industry is the success or failure of a marketing program registered so quickly and decisively. If the prepublicity, advertising, and promotion do not spell instant box office, the product will be pulled and shelved after a few weeks with only a dim hope of resurrection through movie video release and cable showing.

The "hype" is not enough to save a dog, but it did wonders for a rabbit and a bat in the 1980s and a band of pizza-eating turtles who are ushering in the 1990s. The hottest film of the summer of 1988 was *Who Framed Roger Rabbit?*, which combined live action and animation with every famous cartoon character plus two new stars, Roger and Jessica Rabbit. The mighty promotion hand of Walt Disney Productions, the best in the business, was apparent in a campaign that made Roger the must-see film of the year. The biggest box-office hit of 1988 ($184 million in ticket sales) had advance orders of $180 million for the video cassette when it was released in October 1989.

Roger, like the following year's biggest box-office star *Batman*, was featured on the cover of *Newsweek* and other national magazines, and scenes from the film were previewed not only on syndicated TV shows like "Sneak Preview" and Siskel and Ebert's "At the Movies," but on hundreds of local news shows as well.

The *Newsweek* cover story in June described the early marketing decisions that detonated Batmania:

> The filmmakers cut a trailer and persuaded Warners to screen it in Los Angeles. It was a hit, even among 300 Bat-fans who showed up for the late show. When the trailer went into general release at Christmas, word of mouth spread among the fans. Retailers began to see a bump in interest. Warners' in-house merchandising arm began to sprinkle just enough movie-licensed goods into the marketplace—apparel, hats, and pens—to freshen buyers' interest. "By the start of the year," says Rob Friedman, Warner's president of worldwide advertising and publicity, "there was a feeding frenzy that we took advantage of, and to a certain extent fueled."

The article pointed out that Warners was pinning its hopes on a blockbuster campaign for *Batman*. [14] Work it did. Just six weeks later, in a follow-up story called "Boffo Box Office Big Boost to Biz," *Newsweek* pointed out that Batman was breaking all records:

> Logic and common sense cannot begin to explain the phenomenon of *Batman*, a merchandising, musical and motion picture grand-slam of unprecedented proportions. Quite simply, it is a movie that every kid in the world—and a good many adults—would be ashamed not to have seen. . . . Obviously Warners did a bang-up job of creating an "event" mentality though many people in the business thought the pre-release hype could boomerang, and half the people who looked at the wordless logo couldn't even see the bat." [15]

Batman became Hollywood's fifth biggest all-time top money-maker, with initial-release revenue topping $250 million and the sale of *Batman* spinoff goods doubling that figure.

Upon the release of the home video (which includes a Diet Coke *Batman* commercial), *The New York Times* commented:

> "Can somebody tell me," the Joker wonders, "what kind of a world we live in where a man dressed up as a bat gets all my press?" Press, of course, is the operative word when you talk about *Batman,* which owes so much of its monstrous success to a public relations and merchandising sideshow.[16]

A video news release showing Batman, the Joker, and the Batmobile delivering the first shipment of the cassette to a video store on Hollywood's Sunset Strip ran in TV news in all of the nation's top 30 markets.

Teenage Mutant Ninja Turtles, the live-action movie based on the popular animated TV series based on the aforementioned Playmate action-figure toys of the same name, racked up $25 million in its first weekend at the box office. This occasioned a spate of publicity, including a five-page layout in *Entertainment Weekly* (despite a grade of F from its own reviewer), a *TIME* magazine piece, "Lean, Green and on the Screen," and a two-page article in *Newsweek* called "Ninja Turtle Power." The magazine said it was the second-biggest cinematic debut in U.S. history after *Batman,* and *The Wall Street Journal* pointed out that it was "the largest non-summer, non-Thanksgiving-weekend opening of a movie ever."

The movie is just one of 600 Turtle products including everything from videos of the cartoon show to Turtle comic books, pajamas, toothbrushes, bedspreads, sleeping bags, blimps, beach balls, and breakfast cereals, as well as the action figures kids cannot live without—a quarter-of-a-billion-dollar business *before* the movie! Within a month after release of the movie, sales of Ninja Turtle goods had exceeded $650 million. In the fall of 1990, Pizza Hut Inc. sponsored a 40-city "Coming Out of Their Shells" rock concert tour with musicians appearing as singing, pizza-eating turtles.

THE DISNEY MAGIC

The world of Walt Disney has long been known for its masterful use of public relations in marketing its films, characters, and theme parks. The company's publicity and promotion armada was so effective that an amazing 100 percent of the moviegoing public was aware of the existence of Disney's movie *Dick Tracy* before it opened in the summer of 1990. The most lucrative debut of any Disney film ever was fueled by the sale of some 600 Dick Tracy products, including the detective's famous two-way wristwatch and a T-shirt that entitled its wearer to admission to the film on opening night. Disneyland and Walt Disney World featured Dick Tracy musical stage shows and opened stores selling only Dick Tracy merchandise. Pop idol Madonna, who played Breathless Mahoney in the movie, released a new album called "I'm Breathless" simultaneously and, in a much publicized concert tour timed to the release of the film, featured a production number in which she danced with a male chorus line of Dick Tracy-costumed dancers.

The film's producer, director, and star, Warren Beatty, known for never giving interviews, talked to Barbara Walters about the film on her Oscar night ABC Special, and followed this "exclusive" with an endless series of interviews including *Newsweek, Entertainment Weekly, Premier, Rolling Stone, Us, The Los Angeles Times, The Detroit Free Press, USA TODAY,* Liz Smith's column, Roger Ebert's column, "Arsenio Hall," "Prime Time Live," "ABC's 20/20," "Larry King," "Late Night with David Letterman," and "Donahue." He described himself to Phil Donahue as a "publicity machine."

Among Disney's newest new products is the Disney–MGM Studios Theme Park, a 135-acre spectacular in Walt Disney World in Orlando. The park opened in May 1989, with festivities that out-Disneyed anything the entertainment giant had done before. Here is how *TIME* described the doings:

> What movie extravaganza has a cast of 2,000 including Warren Beatty, Bill Cosby, Bette Midler, Robin Williams, Walter Cronkite, Chevy Chase, Martin Short, David Letterman, Mel Gibson, Pee-Wee Herman and George Lucas? Features an earthquake, a shipwreck, a giant bee, several gunfights and a zillion other acts of harmless mayhem? Costs about $500 million to produce? And with gobs of charm, sly wit and relentless good cheer brings off the film magician's trick of making make-believe believable?
>
> Answer: The Disney–MGM Studios Theme Park. With a lavishness the Sultan of Brunei might envy, Disney threw himself a premiere party last weekend and invited a few friends: Audrey Hepburn, George Burns, Willie Nelson, Kevin Costner, the Pointer Sisters, Buffalo Bob Smith and 6,000 journalists. The do, trumpeted in by an NBC special, was Disney's way of telling Hollywood, "Hey, guys, the magic is back. And we brought it. To Florida."[17]

TIME reported that "Disney–MGM Studios marries movies to theme parks with the astuteness of Hollywood's hottest studio and the spell of a professional dream weaver."

The Grand Opening weekend began with the dedication on Friday of the Backstage Studio Tour by Bette Midler and Disney Chairman Michael Eisner. Saturday featured live performances by George Burns and Willie Nelson, a Disney extravaganza with production numbers by 800 singers and dancers, and spectacular fireworks. On Sunday evening, stars of classic TV shows, including Buffalo Bob, Art Linkletter, Imogene Coca, and that original Mouseketeer Annette Funicello, were honored at the Official Commemoration of the 50th Anniversary of Television Broadcasting. The gates were opened to guests by Eisner, Bob Hope, and Mickey and Minnie Mouse and the official first visitors, a family from York, Pennsylvania, were welcomed to the park.

The reporters did their job well. Here are rave reviews on the opening:

"If you like movies, you'll love Disney's newest theme park."—*Miami Herald*

"It is spectacular. . . . It's all part of Disney and it's all fun. . . . It's all done so well."—NBC's "Today Show"

"Disney's creation is a re-creation of the Golden Age of Hollywood."—"ABC Evening News"

". . . fulfills Walt Disney's wildest dreams."—*Newsweek*

"Take it from a movie critic who mistrusts superlatives: The Disney–MGM Studios Theme Park is a winner."—New York *Newsday*

"Hollywood has been transported to Florida."—"Entertainment Tonight"

"As one family last week strolled down Hollywood Boulevard toward the exit, a Disney policeman stopped them and wrote out a summons because they pleaded guilty to 'having too much fun.' Hey, everybody at Disney–MGM Studios Theme Park, you're under arrest!"—*TIME*

11

New News about Old Products

The role of marketing public relations in introducing new products is widely accepted by marketers, and it is almost always an integral part of the total introductory marketing effort. Its use in growing brands, sustaining mature brands, and supporting declining brands is less universally understood. In fact, public relations programs can and do support products in every phase of the product life cycle. While MPR may lack the ability of reminder advertising to reach the consumer with measured frequency, it can often surpass advertising with its greater reach. Advertising media budgets for many old products are reduced or eliminated altogether when the company puts its advertising muscle behind new product entries. As a result, many marketers rely on promotion techniques, like couponing and free standing inserts (FSI), whose immediate sales impact is measurable but whose long-term effect on the brand franchise may be detrimental.

Marketing public relations, on the other hand, provides marketers with the opportunity to extend the reach of advertising and to capitalize on the credibility factor to build brand loyalty. As a result, the role of MPR in relaunching, revitalizing, repositioning, and sustaining mature and even declining brands may be ultimately of even greater value to the company than the quick and dramatic hit that can be achieved in publicizing new products. Maintaining and building the brand franchise is a role for which marketing public relations is particularly well suited because of the variety of tools and tactics that it can apply.

HOW IBM USES PR THROUGH PRODUCT LIFE CYCLES

IBM points out that in a market-driven company, marketing does not focus solely on product launches but on strategies and programs for the entire product life cycle. IBM also believes that communications and other marketing efforts can forestall the "decline" stage by revitalizing interest in the product among prospects and channels.

In the introductory stage, the marketing objective is to create product awareness and trial.

In the growth stage, it is to maximize market share.

In the maturity stage, it is to reduce expenditure and milk the brand.

The company believes that media relations should be used throughout the product life cycle for:

○ Spotlighting newsworthy events or high-interest subjects

○ Positioning products prior to launch

○ Launching products

○ Keeping the product and category in the public eye through postlaunch publicity

○ Reaching markets that are knowledgeable about category benefits

○ Repositioning mature products

○ Defending products that have image problems

○ Influencing specific target groups.

PROMOTING NEW BENEFITS

One of the best ways to make old products newsworthy is to discover and promote new uses or new consumer benefits. This chapter explores how MPR is used by major marketers and trade associations to generate new news about old products to keep them top of mind and relevant to consumers' changing needs and expectations.

America's preoccupation with health and fitness is a continuing trend. Faith Popcorn, futurist and founder of Brain Reserve, has categorized this trend as "Staying Alive." According to Popcorn, this desire for good health and longevity has created a new way of life—a need to understand the direct benefits of what one eats and drinks, a fear of illness, and the motivation to stay fit.

Marketers have responded by creating a plethora of new products, like cereals with psyllium, fat substitutes, and an endless parade of reduced-calorie, reduced-sugar, reduced-fat, reduced-cholesterol, and "lite" flanker versions of old products. Marketers have also made a major effort to look for new benefits for their old established products. They may have been there all the time. Kraft promotes Philadelphia Cream

Cheese: "as always, half the calories of butter or margarine." Others have publicized research that documents the new health benefits for their products. Some of this research is based on existing data. Other companies and trade associations have commissioned researchers to study the health benefits of their products or have capitalized on independent research that reports news favorable to their products.

Arm & Hammer Baking Soda has been particularly skillful in finding new uses for a product that has been on the market for over a century. In the 1970s, Arm & Hammer Baking Soda achieved a remarkable 74 percent increase in volume when its use as a refrigerator deodorizer was publicized to the consumer. This was followed a few years later by a successful promotion of its use as a freezer deodorizer. Arm & Hammer now owns a remarkable 85 percent of the baking soda business and has built on the consumer awareness and acceptance of its brand name by introducing a series of products, including a detergent and a dentifrice, under the Arm & Hammer label.

Aspirin: The Miracle Drug

In 1986, Alka-Seltzer, which contains aspirin for pain relief and an antacid for upset stomach, publicized a study that showed that one Alka-Seltzer tablet a day reduced by 51 percent the incidence of MI (myocardial infarction, or heart attack) in patients with unstable angina.

Another study showed that second heart attacks were reduced by 21 percent and overall mortality of 15 percent as a result of taking aspirin. This widely publicized study caused many doctors to recommend an aspirin every other day to help heart-attack victims prevent a replay.

Then, a study published in the *New England Journal of Medicine* in 1988 revealed that aspirin can help prevent first heart attacks. In the study, more than 22,000 physicians over the age of 40 took one Bufferin (buffered aspirin) every other day while another group of physicians took placebos or fake aspirin. At the end of 57 months, those healthy men taking aspirin had 47 percent fewer heart attacks. Dr. Charles Hennekens of Harvard Medical School told *Newsweek* that "the extremely beneficial" effect of aspirin was so apparent that doctors monitoring the trial recommended that it be stopped and those volunteers getting the placebo be informed so they could take aspirin if they wished.

Newsweek featured an aspirin tablet on its February 8, 1988, cover with a story titled, "What You Should Know About Heart Attacks: The Aspirin Breakthrough" and published "A User's Guide to Taking Aspirin." Within hours after the news of the *New England Journal of Medicine* story was reported by the news media, one aspirin maker beamed a video news release to hundreds of television stations by satellite uplink. Bufferin, Anacin, and Bayer flooded magazines and television with advertising identifying their products with cardiovascular health. Bayer even issued a "calendar pak" reminding users to take a tablet every other day. Sales of aspirin increased 25 to 30 percent in the month following the publicity.

Six months later, the aspirin tablet was pictured on the cover of *Business Week* under a bold-type headline, "Miracle Drug." This article was occasioned by yet another study on aspirin and heart attacks published in the respected British medical journal *Lancet*. In this study, 17,000 heart-attack patients were given aspirin alone or in combination with a clot-dissolving enzyme. The combination cut mortality by 50 percent, 22 points higher than the enzyme alone. Aspirin alone reduced deaths by 21 percent when given within 24 hours.

The article also reported on some PR activities aspirin makers had undertaken to link their brands with good health. "Bayer adopted an entire town in West Virginia called, not coincidentally, Wellsburg, where it is trying to raise the town's cardiovascular health through education, diet, and exercise. Bristol-Myers even distributes a cookbook with foods that are healthy."

New studies continue to document the health benefits of this 90-year-old product. One study, for example, showed that women at high risk for pregnancy-induced hypertension can lower their risk by taking children's doses of aspirin. As *Business Week* proclaimed, "researchers are finding a cornucopia of exciting new uses for this old standby. It might even help in combating AIDS."[1]

A *TIME* magazine story in April 1990 heralded "A New Role for the Wonder Drug." It said that "the ubiquitous little pill that seems to be good for everything from headaches to menstrual cramps has done it again; its new role: preventing strokes." It reported on a new study in the *New England Journal of Medicine* that revealed that daily doses of aspirin or the blood-thinning medication warfarin could sharply curtail the risk of stroke in patients suffering from fibrillation, a condition in which the heartbeat is rapid and irregular. The magazine pointed out that a million Americans who have this abnormality face five times the normal risk of stroke.

New News about Soup

There can be no question that marketing public relations provides the vital link to the consumer. The credibility of the news media coverage makes advertising claims believable and marketing programs successful.

Campbell's Soup has long been a staple in America's households. The average home has nine-plus cans of Campbell's soups on the shelf. The mission of the public relations program has been to motivate consumers to eat more soup more often. In marketing jargon, the objective is to increase per capita consumption of Campbell's soups. Although there

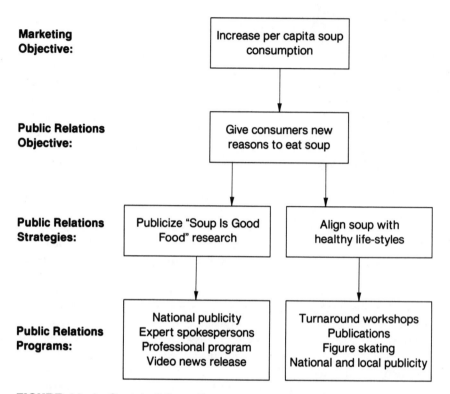

FIGURE 11-1 Campbell Soup Company used dual MPR strategies to increase soup consumption, providing consumers with good news about soup and sponsoring events that identified soup with good health.

have been some variations in programming, the company has adhered to a strategy of giving the consumer new reasons to buy and use more soup. Figure 11-1 illustrates how MPR strategies relate to Campbell's marketing objectives.

During the 1980s, the good news about soup relied heavily on research studies that underscored the benefits of the product as a healthful, good food that plays a significant role in the American diet. These studies documented the claim that soup is good food. They included:

  ○ A study conducted by the Applied Research Center at the University of Pennsylvania's Wharton School, showing that people who ate soup for lunch consumed fewer calories daily

  ○ Analysis of a government study showing that the healthiest people follow an eating pattern that includes more soup and dairy products, and fewer sugary foods

- A second government study showing that soup acts as a "dietary pacesetter" to help regulate caloric intake over the course of a day
- Nutrient analysis showing that, calorie for calorie, soups are more "nutrient dense" than other foods.

A wide spectrum of public relations techniques has been used to communicate the good news about soup. They include:

- The creation of The Turnaround Workshop, a program for health-care professionals, which stresses the role of soup in a healthy life-style
- The publication of research results in dietetic journals and medical publications
- Mass publicity in consumer print and broadcast media
- Distribution of a *Reader's Digest* reprint at point-of-sale in supermarket soup sections
- Media tours for expert academic spokespersons from the fields of nutrition and behavior modification
- Publication of a nutritionally sound soup diet that slows down caloric intake
- Celebrity media tours directed to target audiences, including black and Hispanic consumers
- Sponsorship of figure skating and other activities that align the product with a healthy, fit image
- Production and distribution of video news features on the fresh, quality ingredients that go into Campbell's Soup
- Creation of National Soup Month in January as a vehicle to communicate all the good news about soup.

The public relations campaign was the precursor of the company's successful "Soup is Good Food" advertising campaign. The first commercial in this campaign, in fact, featured a newsstand seller telling a customer the good news about soup that appeared in *Medical World News.* This underscored the value of implied editorial endorsement and the effective mutual reinforcement of advertising and public relations.

This integrated "Soup is Good Food" campaign was tested in California with such positive results that the program was taken national the next year. Campbell's marketing research showed that in markets where the advertising ran alone, there was no effect on sales, but where advertising and public relations were used together to tell the good-food story, there was a very significant increase in sales.

Repositioning Quaker Oats

In the mid-1980s, Quaker Oats Company initiated a series of MPR programs to promote the special health benefits of its longtime staple Quaker Oats, which it linked with new Quaker Oat Bran Cereal.

Quaker recognized the potential opportunity in the marketing of foods high in complex carbohydrates and dietary fiber. Quaker's research programs with university scientists revealed that oats are a particularly good source of water-soluble fiber, which is effective in reducing cholesterol and blood pressure and in regulating blood glucose. Quaker Oat Bran was shown to be an even more concentrated source of water-soluble fiber than oats. As such, oats and oat bran could be recommended within the total diet of individuals with high cholesterol levels or diabetes—and of anyone seeking a more healthy diet.

Quaker developed the Fiber Factor program to educate medical and health professionals and food-opinion leaders on the health benefits of oat fiber. A pioneer in the field of dietary fiber research was retained as the program's spokesperson. He conducted workshops on high-fiber diets for dieticians in major cities, presented his latest fiber-research findings at medical conventions across the country, and was the subject of media interviews on the health benefits of a high-fiber diet.

Quaker carried the story to the annual meeting of the American Dietetic Association, reaching 10,000 attending dieticians. The company produced a series of recipe pamphlets featuring Quaker Oats and Oat Bran for low-cholesterol, glucose-metabolism, low-sodium, weight-reduction, and healthy diets, which were made available in quantity to physicians and dieticians for patient use. They endorsed the information about the benefits of Quaker Oats and Oat Bran by distributing over 1.5 million of these recipe pamphlets to their patients in the first year.

The Fiber Factor program was introduced to food editors at a breakfast meeting on dietary fiber at the Newspaper Food Editors Conference. Quaker Oats and Oat Bran were featured on the menu and in the press kit, which generated feature stories in major market newspapers. Six million junior- and senior-high-school home economics students were reached through a lesson package. Finally, the Fiber Factor program was featured in a newsletter distributed by Quaker's Consumer Affairs Center to supermarket consumer affairs directors, another audience that is influential in reaching the consumer.

In 1988, Quaker updated the program to maximize consumer acceptance of the cholesterol-lowering benefits of oats and to position Quaker as the oats expert and source authority on cholesterol education. Scientific research supported Quaker's claim that the soluble fiber found in oats helps to reduce cholesterol when added to a fat-modified diet. The new program was focused on increasing consumer understanding of cholesterol as a major risk factor in coronary heart disease and on encouraging Americans to know their cholesterol level and take steps to reduce it through dietary management.

The public relations program supported the advertising slogan from Quaker's popular Wilford Brimley TV commercial, "It's the Right Thing to Do," through use of the theme, "Oats for Life . . . It's the Right Thing to Do." The principal vehicle used was a shopping-mall program staged in ten major markets. The Quaker exhibit included cholesterol screenings by certified technicians, cooking demonstrations of low-fat oat recipes conducted by a registered dietician, and interactive learning games, product coupons, and sweepstakes prizes. More than 75,000 consumers visiting the exhibit over its weekend runs received informational materials including an "Oat Meals!" recipe booklet and guidelines for following a low-cholesterol diet.

The Quaker program was a major stimulus to making the health benefits of oats one of the top news stories of 1988. However, in January 1990, the *New England Journal of Medicine* reported that oat bran has no greater cholesterol-lowering abilities than ordinary low-fiber wheat flour and cereal. The author of the study said, "There is nothing the matter with oat bran or oat meal. It's a fine food, but it's been overhyped."

The story was prominently featured in the nation's news media and was the subject of an entire "Nightline" program on the day the report was issued. *ADWEEKS's Marketing Week* commented on the quick reaction of both consumers and the media to the new information. *Business Week* said, "The media response was near hysteria."

Quaker quickly hopped to oat bran's defense. It said that the company had anticipated the study and challenged its methodology. A Quaker nutritionist said that "twenty-five years of research has established that oats and oat bran have important cholesterol-reducing benefits."

A few days later, the company ran full-page ads in seven newspapers across the country headlined "Quaker Oat Bran Can Help Reduce Cholesterol. Look at 27 Years of Research." The ad listed ten studies published in medical and nutrition journals from 1963 through 1988 and concluded that "these studies all suggest that Quaker Oat Bran can help reduce cholesterol above and beyond a low-fat diet alone." The ad, which Quaker said it ran in response to research it has done with people who have been making serious attempts to change their diets, offered readers, through the mail, more information and research results.

The company, which had enjoyed the benefits of positive publicity about oat bran for years, said it decided to run the ads because "the sheer amount of the media coverage and the one-sided aspect of it led us to believe that people need to be made aware of the fact that there is a solid body of research supporting oat bran."

Consumer expectations of oat bran as a panacea were dashed by the report, and sales of the company's hot oat bran cereal, which had peaked at $50 million, dropped 50 percent.

MPR FOR FOOD TRADE GROUPS

The strategy of generating new news about old products can be used effectively both by brands and by entire product categories. Many companies have joined with their competitors to support trade-group MPR programs that generically promote the benefits of entire product categories. The theory is that, if the category grows, there will be greater opportunity for brands to increase sales by running their own promotional and public relations campaigns to gain a greater share of a larger market.

Some of the most successful public relations campaigns have been those conducted by food trade associations and grower groups to keep their products in the news, top of mind, and relevant to consumers. One of the most successful of all food-trade-group programs has been conducted on behalf of the Florida Citrus Commission by Dudley-Anderson-Yutzy (now part of Ogilvy & Mather Public Relations) for more than 50 years, resulting in a more than 1,000 percent growth in Florida-orange consumption since the program began.

Some of these groups run advertising and public relations programs in tandem; but as advertising costs have risen, most have come to depend almost entirely on the power of public relations to carry news about their products to the consumer. These days a million dollars will not buy enough media time and space to sell a branded product, much less move the needle for an entire industry. But a million-dollar marketing public relations budget can buy a lot of awareness for the category. MPR programs are particularly effective because they are perceived by press and public as "noncommercial." Editors who resist using brand names have no problem running stories about California avocados, Idaho potatoes, or Florida oranges.

FACT and CFIC

I know from personal experience that these programs work, having supervised extensive MPR programs for the frozen- and canned-food industries. In the late 1970s, when the American Frozen Food Institute (AFFI) and the National Frozen Food Association formed a joint effort to promote the benefits of frozen foods, my firm created an industrywide information program called FACT, the Frozen Food Action Communications Team. Wearing my industry hat, I served as its executive director for five years. The mission of FACT was to correct misconceptions about the quality of frozen foods and to promote the acceptance and use of frozen foods for all meal occasions both at home and when eating out. Through broad educational initiatives and an immediate response program, FACT sought equal space and time to tell the positive story of frozens. The program was credited by *Frozen Food Age*, the industry's leading trade publication, with reversing a decline in frozen-food sales.

As the industry improved the quality of frozen foods and the attacks subsided, the AFFI was able to move from a defensive to a promotional position.

In 1985 the canned food industry followed suit. The National Food Processors Association joined forces with the American Iron and Steel Institute and the Can Manufacturers Association to launch a public relations program to revitalize consumer interest in canned foods. Golin/ Harris was retained to conduct the program and in turn created the Canned Food Information Council (CFIC) to serve as the industry's umbrella communication organization.

The public relations program established CFIC as the primary source of information on canned foods.

The program included an aggressive media relations campaign and the development of materials that positioned canned foods as contemporary, convenient, and elegant. One vehicle for communicating the upscale image of canned foods was a cookbook, *Carefree Cuisine*, comprised of fast, easy, low-calorie recipes. Another was to use CFIC spokespersons to appeal to target-market light users and provide them with gourmet canned-food recipes appropriate to their tastes and life-styles.

Canned Food Month was created as a news hook for publicity and in-store promotion. February was designated, because canned-food sales peak during this time of the year when much fresh produce is unavailable or expensive. Guideline kits for manufacturers, retailers, and brokers gave suggestions on how to run canned-food promotions and offered Canned Food Month point-of-sale material. Manufacturers were encouraged to offer their customers trade deals during February and to advertise their participation in Canned Food Month; retailers were urged to hold special sales, promotions, and displays and to run special newspaper advertising. *Woman's Day* has run a special Canned Food Month editorial and advertising section every year since the special month was created. An all-media publicity program has featured canned-food recipes, menu suggestions, nutritional information about canned foods, and governors' proclamations declaring February Canned Food Month in their states. Participation in Canned Food Month increases every year. In 1988, 73 retail chains, including Kroger and Safeway, the nation's two largest retailers, participated.

Ocean Spray Cranberries

Three decades ago, cranberries were practically wiped out as a viable consumer food product when the federal government issued a warning of a potential health threat associated with pesticides used on cranberries. The timing could not have been more damaging. The government warning was issued before Thanksgiving 1960. While the warning was later proven false and was withdrawn, the damage had been done to the cranberry industry. Ocean Spray, a cooperative of 600 cranberry and citrus growers, wanted to restore public confidence in cranberries as quickly as possible and turned to the public relations firm of Creamer Dickson Basford.

Ocean Spray's public relations program concentrated on correcting misconceptions about the safety of cranberries. The focus then shifted to eliminating the high degree of seasonality of cranberry products. As the seasonality valleys leveled out, the public relations program began to identify uses of cranberries in cooking. In recent years, the public relations program, still conducted by Creamer Dickson Basford, has focused on "mainstreaming" the cranberry into American everyday-food-and-beverage habits.

One particularly successful strategy has been to associate Ocean Spray with significant American culinary developments. Ocean-Spray-sponsored food-media events were created to draw attention to American food trends and leaders. These culinary extravaganzas, held every other year, highlight the brightest and best American chefs. During the past decade, the program has generated over 10 billion media impressions on the versatility of cranberries for year-round menus in newspapers, magazines, radio, and television.

Public relations continues to play a significant role in Ocean Spray's marketing efforts, both in terms of stimulating consumer interest in cranberries and cranberry-based products for everyday meals and refreshments and in introducing new products. An all-out trade, business, and consumer media effort for Ocean Spray's Paper Bottle™, the first aseptic packaging for juice drinks, resulted in over 5,500 separate stories in 1981. Within 10 months of the introduction, sales of their single-serving juices in the new packaging, stimulated by the PR media blitz, increased nearly 400 percent.

Public Relations and the Avocado

Of all the fruits and vegetables that appear on the shelves and bins of America's food markets, one of the most aggressively and innovatively promoted has been the California avocado.

Throughout its 25-year history, the California Avocado Commission, which represents the 6,000 avocado growers in California, has placed a high priority on public relations in its overall efforts to market avocados across the United States.

The public relations focus has shifted from creative campaigns that promoted avocados as a cosmetic skin treatment and taught people how to grow their indoor plants from avocado pits to an emphasis on nutrition. Avocados are misperceived by consumers to be high in calories, fat, and even cholesterol (which they do not contain). To overcome these challenges, the Commission has focused its efforts on communicating the dietary benefits of eating avocados.

To counteract the negative perception of fat and increase frequency of purchase among current users, the Avocado Commission's public relations agency, Berkhemer Kline Golin/Harris, created a program that promotes California avocados as an ideal baby food. Fat, especially the healthful monounsaturated variety contained in avocados, is essential to a baby's diet. Yet research discovered that pediatricians rarely suggest avocados to new mothers.

To create awareness of avocados as the perfect baby food, the firm published a brochure titled "Baby's Garden," about the benefits of feeding infants and toddlers fresh fruits and vegetables, including avocados. In addition to being the cornerstone of a national consumer information and publicity campaign, the brochure was offered to pediatricians nationwide for distribution to their patients.

The avocado nutritional message was also communicated by a well-known pediatrician who was featured as a spokesperson on a major market-media tour demonstrating the benefits of "healthy fats." An avocado baby-food-recipe contest was created in conjunction with *Baby Talk*, the nation's largest-circulation parenting magazine. These combined programs communicated the avocado-nutrition story to millions of parents and introduced a brand new consumer to the fruit.

The Commission also allied itself with the country's leading researcher in the study of monounsaturated fat. Using his research data, consumer-education materials were prepared, explaining the dietary benefits of monounsaturates, with information on foods like olive oil and avocados that are sources of this healthful fat. This positive message was communicated through media interviews and appearances at the Food Media Conference and the American Dietetic Association's annual meeting. The nutrition message is woven throughout all public relations communications, including quarterly recipe releases sent to newspaper and magazine food editors.

The California Avocado Commission has created high awareness and demand for the avocado through continued innovative, strategic public relations campaigns that, as part of the overall marketing program, have enabled their growers to maximize their profits despite fluctuations in yearly crop size.

Uniting Adult Peanut Lovers

The Peanut Advisory Board (PAB), a farmer-funded organization representing growers in Georgia, Alabama, and Florida, effectively uses marketing public relations to increase consumer demand for peanuts and peanut products. Peanut butter is particularly important since 50 percent of the peanuts grown are used in peanut butter.

A 1986 research study revealed that adults eat half of the 700 million pounds of peanut butter produced in this country annually. The three major peanut butter brands had virtually ignored this market, spending some $75 million in marketing directed primarily to children. PAB's public relations firm, Ketchum Public Relations, seized the opportunity to reach this untapped market and generate peanut butter publicity. They developed restaurant and hotel-chain promotions featuring upscale peanut butter menu items, conducted events for food editors to sample adult food made with peanut butter, and created the Adults Only Peanut Lovers Fan Club. An Adult Peanut Lovers Kit, including an official membership certificate, refrigerator magnet, button, bumper sticker, and newsletter was sent free to anyone who asked to join the club. Soon membership exceeded 25,000 adults who shared their peanut butter passion through letters published in the "Spread the News" newsletter.

It was decided to activate the membership by staging a Reunion at the Opryland USA Hotel in Nashville, Tennessee. Over 1,000 people attended the event. Comedian Soupy Sales, billed as "one of America's most celebrated nuts," served as master of ceremonies and acted as the peanut-butter-lover media spokesperson. The event included peanut butter samplings, a celebrity corner, cooking demonstrations, music, games, contests, and peanut butter trivia. Pre- and postpublicity, plus on-site media coverage, exceeded projections and delivered the message that adults are "stuck on" peanut butter.

The program effectively repositioned peanut butter as an adult food, contributing to a six-percent increase in peanut butter consumption. The effectiveness of this marketing public relations program was recognized by both the marketing and public relations industries.

Cooking with Catfish

Marketing public relations has played a key role in the economic development of the state of Mississippi by building demand for catfish and repositioning it as an upscale, tasty, and nutritious dish. The Catfish Institute was established in 1986 in Belzoni, Mississippi, to change the public reputation of catfish and distinguish commercially raised catfish from scavenger, river catfish. The public relations program was designed to sell the merits of "Mississippi Prime" catfish to the American people as a sweet-tasting, nutritious, low-calorie food that can be prepared in a variety of ways.

The program is targeted psychographically to "early adapters," consumers between 25 and 35 years old who are adventurous, trendsetting, and eager to try new foods. Other targets include professional cooks and chefs, restaurateurs, and opinion leaders. A number of high-impact supporting materials and events have been used in the program. A four-color cookbook, "Fishing for Compliments," featuring catfish appetizers, soups, stews, and main dishes was introduced at a gourmet luncheon held for leading food editors in a New York City loft apartment. The guests dined on recipes from the cookbook and were served smoked catfish and champagne in their offices.

A *Newsweek* reporter and photographer attended the luncheon. The resulting story, in the June 29, 1987, issue, was called "No Mud for the New Catfish: A Classic Southern Favorite Is Changing Its Image." The article declared that "the fish that can stand in for chicken is fast becoming a best-seller, with production more than doubling since 1983 to an estimated 250 million pounds in 1987." It also described how catfish, "one of the freshest fish available," are raised in fresh-water ponds and rushed to nearby processing plants. So impressed was the magazine that it ran a color photo of the luncheon plate with the caption "catfish chic."

The program utilized credible chefs, cooking authorities, and cookbook authors as spokespersons and distributed press kits and recipes throughout the year at special events. The first National Catfish Day was proclaimed jointly by President Reagan and the U.S. Congress on June 25, 1987. In 1988 and 1989, August was declared National Catfish Month. To celebrate, editors were supplied with product information and Mississippi Prime aprons and chefs' hats.

In the summer of 1989, the Catfish Institute issued its first membership cards to the Loyal Order of Catfish Lovers. Members receive a free subscription to *Mississippi Prime Times* and a "Honk If You Love Catfish" bumper sticker. And they automatically become eligible for an annual drawing for a trip for two to Belzoni, Mississippi, for the World Catfish Festival. They are polled to learn more about the heavy-user target market.

Mississippi catfish continues to receive widespread media coverage. In 1988, less than two years after the program was launched, *PR News* reported that it had generated more than two thousand "generous and highly favorable print and broadcast stories nationwide." According to the *Dallas Morning News* of June 25, 1989, the catfish program is "one of the most visible, entertaining, and successful campaigns in recent memory."

PETS ARE WONDERFUL—EXPANDING THE MARKET

In most instances, the objectives of the trade-group public relations programs are straightforward: to increase consumption by telling the positive product story; to increase "share of mind" awareness; and to give people persuasive reasons to try or to buy more of the promoted-product category.

The Pet Food Institute faced a different problem. Per-capita consumption of dog and cat food was steady, but there was a decline in pet ownership. The objective, therefore, was to increase the number of pets owned. By so doing, the market for the sale of pet food could be expanded. The underlying assumption was that as the market grew, each of the supporting manufacturers would share in a bigger pie. The industry is, of course, highly competitive, and the battle for market share is backed by multimillion-dollar brand-advertising campaigns.

The approach taken by the Pet Food Institute and its public relations counsel, Golin/Harris, was to address pet acquisition rather than sell pet food. The program, in fact, assiduously avoided even the most generic references to what to feed pets. The program was called Pets Are Wonderful (PAW), and its sponsor was a nonprofit public service organization called the Pets Are Wonderful Council.

The marketing objective of the Pet Food Institute was to sell more pet food by creating more canine and feline mouths to feed; the public relations objective was to persuade people to acquire a pet. The public relations strategy was to communicate the benefits of pet ownership to a principal target market of families with children at home (see Figure 11–2).

It was determined that these benefits are both rational and emotional. If the decision to acquire a pet were plotted on a grid, as shown in Figure 11–3, it would probably fall between a rational, thoughtful, considered decision and an emotional decision, where feelings make the difference. In either case, the decision to acquire a pet is a matter of high involvement.

The PR strategy was expressed this way: to communicate the joys and rewards of pet ownership.

Here are a few of the tactics that worked to communicate these messages. The joys of pet ownership (feeling benefits) were communicated through several projects:

- A traveling shopping-mall exhibit enabling prospective pet owners to see and touch animals from local shelters.
- "Most Wonderful Pet" contests in cities across the country showcased the importance of pets in their owners' lives.
- National PAW spokespersons, celebrity pet lovers like TV's Betty White, Sally Struthers, and Bill Cosby, appeared in Pets Are Wonderful PSAs and on national television.
- Media spokespersons brought lovable puppies and kittens from local shelters on television talk shows, inevitably resulting in a wave of adoptions.

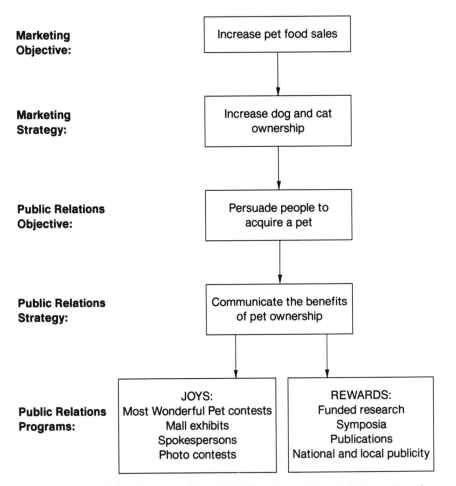

Marketing Objective:	Increase pet food sales
Marketing Strategy:	Increase dog and cat ownership
Public Relations Objective:	Persuade people to acquire a pet
Public Relations Strategy:	Communicate the benefits of pet ownership
Public Relations Programs:	JOYS: Most Wonderful Pet contests / Mall exhibits / Spokespersons / Photo contests — REWARDS: Funded research / Symposia / Publications / National and local publicity

FIGURE 11–2 The Pet Food Institute's "Pets Are Wonderful" public relations program was designed to expand the market for pet food.

The rewards (thinking benefits) of pet ownership were also communicated.

○ Research was funded in a new field of scientific study called the human/companion animal bond.

○ Papers presented at the Human/Companion Animal Bond Conference on such subjects as the importance of pets in teaching children responsibility, in lowering blood pressure, in helping heart-attack victims, and in providing companionship for the aged were widely publicized; exposure included a four-times-repeated segment on TV's top-rated "60 Minutes" called "Man's Best Medicine."

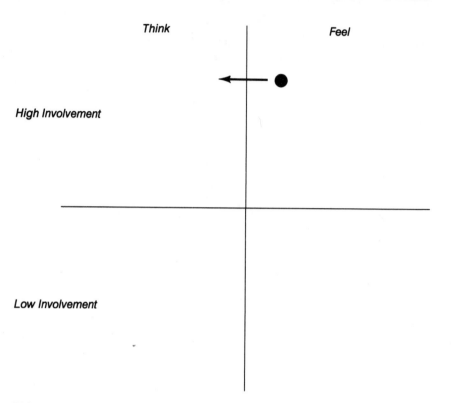

FIGURE 11–3   The pet-ownership decision grid.

- ○ A program directed to city dwellers communicated the ease of urban pet ownership.
- ○ A program directed to parents of latchkey children extolled the benefits of coming home from school to a loving pet rather than an empty house.

How do we know the program worked?

First, unlike many marketing communications programs, the public relations program stood alone. There were no advertising or sales promotion or direct marketing components to this program. Therefore, measurable results could be directly attributable to public relations.

Second, the program had a built-in research program from the outset. Again, this is unlike many PR programs where a limited budget must be devoted entirely to implementation. PAW employed several research methods. Focus groups were held to determine consumers' views about pet ownership. Media analysis was used to track publicity regionally and measure the incidence of positive, negative, and neutral publicity about pets. The media plan was revised quarterly to overlay certain messages in specific geographic areas. A benchmark national-attitude survey was conducted to determine attitudes toward pet ownership and compare them with subsequent studies reflecting attitude change in specific areas addressed by the program.

Finally, a national survey on the incidence of pet ownership was conducted annually among 7,500 households nationwide. It revealed that in 1986 dog ownership increased, marking the first reversal of a 10-year decline.

Another vital, albeit less tangible, measurement of program success is client satisfaction. The Board of the Pet Food Institute took the unprecedented step of passing a resolution stating that during its first six years the Pets Are Wonderful program had met its objectives of "improving the attitudes toward and incidence of pet ownership."[2]

12

Celebrating Special Occasions

In the absence of product news, marketing public relations can effectively focus attention on products by celebrating what I call a Special Occasion. Some of these company occasions may be true milestones—a 25th, 50th, or even 100th product birthday—or a company may create a reason to celebrate and roll out the public relations artillery. Product anniversaries provide a versatile platform for revitalizing interest in old products.

In celebration of the 25th anniversary of Procter & Gamble's Mr. Clean in 1984, Burson-Marsteller staged a birthday party for the media, conducted a search for Mr. Clean's look-alike, and sent him on a media tour in a high-tech street sweeper dubbed the "Mr. Clean Machine."

In 1989, two perennially popular toys, Mattel's Barbie and Hasbro's G.I. Joe, celebrated big birthdays. Barbie's 30th was marked by a black-tie gala at New York's Lincoln Center. Seven hundred toy buyers (and media) attending Barbie's "pink jubilee" drank pink drinks, ate pink food, and had their pictures taken with a life-size Barbie cutout. Hasbro said it would not hold a celebration of Joe's 25th in deference to critics who charge him with being the embodiment of militant maleness. Instead, the company sponsored a "Great American Hero" contest for kids who perform heroic deeds.

To celebrate the 50th birthday of Bugs Bunny, Warner Brothers ran 32-page special advertising sections in *TIME, LIFE, People,* and *Entertainment Weekly,* filled with features and ads for Bugs goods. Other events marking this special occasion included a $300,000 float in the Macy's Thanksgiving Day Parade, the release of the first Bugs theatrical short in 26 years, a prime-time CBS birthday special, a commemorative video cassette, an art book, and a traveling exhibit of vintage animation art, as well as special events at Six Flags amusement parks across the country and live appearances of America's favorite rabbit at major league baseball games throughout the season.

MCDONALD'S SPECIAL OCCASIONS

Golin/Harris has spent the better part of three decades looking for opportunities to focus attention on McDonald's special occasions. McDonald's signs have reminded us through the years of the millions and billions of hamburgers served, so the serving of the 50 billionth in 1984 was a natural. However, this milestone might well have gone unnoticed by the consumer and unnoted in history had it not been decided to make it a special occasion.

The 50 Billionth Hamburger

The occasion was announced locally in the then 6,500 McDonald's restaurants, and every patron was given a coupon for a free hamburger. A "900" number was activated two weeks before the event to "count up" to 50 billion, with the numbers updated daily on chalkboards in every restaurant. On the big day, the McDonald's All-American High School Band played a medley of music from McDonald's commercials while a new McDonald's grill was rolled onto the stage of New York's Grand Hyatt Hotel. There, McDonald USA President Ed Rensi, a onetime McDonald's grillman, cooked and served the 50 billionth hamburger to Dick McDonald, one of the brothers who started the original company and sold it to Ray Kroc.

United Press International reported, "It was an event on 42nd Street. McDonald's served its 50-billionth hamburger and pulled out all the nostalgia stops. There was all the New York media from TV to print to radio. The still photographers alone could bring tears to a PR man's eye."

The occasion proved to be nostalgic for local reporters and TV newscasters across the nation. Many of them covered the story line at a local McDonald's and recalled the McDonald's of their youth. Wire-service stories ran in papers throughout the country. Nationally, the story not only ran on network news but was raised as a social milestone and topic worthy of discussion by columnist George Will on ABC's "This Week with David Brinkley." Johnny Carson liked the story so well that he included it in his monologues for a week, using "Fascinating McFacts" such as how much catsup and how many french fries, pickles, and onions were consumed with the 50 billion burgers and how well an original 1965 McDonald's investor would have done after all the stock splits, stock dividends, and appreciation. In all, some 120 media representatives reported the news around the world, achieving some 300 million impressions.

The 10,000th Restaurant

McDonald's did it again four years later when it opened its 10,000th McDonald's restaurant. In 1978, the company had opened number 5,000 in Japan. McDonald's celebrated its 25th anniversary and opened its 6,000th restaurant in Munich, Germany, and its 9,000th in Sydney, Australia.

The 10,000th was opened in Dale City, Virginia, near Washington in April 1988. The press received an invitation in a box labeled "Open Carefully: Party in Progress." It contained balloons, confetti, a reporter's notebook with "10,000 and Growing" graphics, and a pop-up invitation depicting McDonald's restaurants through the years.

The media were invited to join the celebration of "a spectacular, one-of-a-kind event; one that will lift your spirits and your sights as number 10,000 is revealed." This was the release of thousands of multicolored balloons that had completely covered the 4,700-square-foot restaurant. The ribbon-cutting and balloon-release ceremony officiated by Fred Turner, McDonald's chairman, Mike Quinlan, president, and, of course, Ronald McDonald accompanied by the McDonald's All-American High School Band, was transmitted by satellite to 6,000 franchises and to employees, suppliers, and media around the world.

The press-kit cover was a three-dimensional hologram (also used as the cover of the company's annual report) celebrating the growth of McDonald's from the corporation's first restaurant in 1955 to number 10,000. It depicted a McDonald's restaurant with "Over 10,000 opened" on the familiar sign, replacing the number of hamburgers served.

The opening made national news on network shows like "Good Morning America," "CBS This Morning" and PBS's "Nightly News Report" and provided the occasion for another panel discussion on "This Week with David Brinkley" initiated by McDonald's enthusiast George Will. A video news release of the event was satellited to media throughout the world. In addition to coverage in 45 major U.S. TV markets, news of the opening of McDonald's 10,000th restaurant reached 23 countries. Modern technology enabled the coverage in countries like Korea, Japan, and Brazil to be satellited back to Washington and edited overnight for showing at McDonald's national owner-operator meeting there the next day.

McDonald's in Moscow

Al Golin said, "In my 32 years of involvement, this had to be the biggest single media event in McDonald's history and probably the broadest positive exposure any company in the world has ever received, from the

TV, radio, and print coverage in North America to front pages and news-casts in Japan, Europe, and the rest of the world."

He said the massive media coverage showcased "the McDonald's Magic," a rare combination of a friendly sense of humor, having fun while running a very successful business, plus these elements, which the media found irresistible:

- The McDonald's Free Enterprise Story: the dramatic contrast to the Soviet system
- The Crew Story: the training, work ethic, and clean-cut crew that was a welcome change from the typical Russian experience
- The Quality Story: helping Russian farmers grow potatoes and raise cattle and building a state-of-the-art food plant
- The McDonald's Leadership Story: how McDonald's patience, perseverance, and insistence on doing things the McDonald's way made Moscow possible

The publicity effort that culminated opening day was launched two and a half years earlier in 1988 when a press conference was called to announce the signing of the joint agreement between McDonald's Restaurants of Canada and the Food Service Administration of the Moscow City Council. The next major news break was a sign-raising ceremony marking the beginning of construction. The summer before the grand opening, the laying of the cornerstone of the food-production plant, the largest in Eastern Europe, made news and gave McDonald's an opportunity to tell its quality story. A human face was put on the story when the Russian managers came to McDonald's Oak Brook, Illinois, headquarters to be trained at Hamburger University. Toronto's annual Santa Claus Parade, featuring a spectacular Soviet Children's Fund float followed by the McDonald's float with Prime Minister Brian Mulroney aboard, was televised in Russia as well as North America. The final preopening publicity hit was the announcement that 27,000 Moscovites had applied for 600 jobs at McDonald's. The countdown had begun.

For thirteen months, public relations staffers from Continental Golin/Harris, headed by president Chris Bunting, commuted between Toronto and Moscow. Someone was there all the time. Explaining McDonald's to the Soviet media was a formidable job since the concept was brand new and culturally alien and since they had no business vocabulary.

The opening occurred at 2:00 A.M. Toronto time, and the agency team worked around the clock and without sleep for two days to make sure that someone was always accessible to respond to reporters, whatever the hour. Despite the obstacles, opening-day coverage was staggering: 175 reporters attended the preopening briefing in Moscow, 250 toured the food plant and restaurant the day before the opening, and 400 correspondents covered the grand opening event. "NBC Nightly News" reported, "The grand opening hype was as foreign to Moscow as the hamburger."

ABC could not wait for the restaurant to open. Six days earlier, Diane Sawyer reported on this "cultural milestone" on a 10-minute "Prime Time" segment called "Golden Arches in Red Square." She described the "superhuman persistence" of George Cohon, President of McDonald's of Canada, who negotiated his way through a maze of Soviet officials for 14 years before realizing his dream.

On the day of the opening, she revisited the store on "ABC World News Tonight," reporting that the restaurant had served 30,000 Moscovites, twice the number predicted by Cohon, and that the restaurant was receiving rave reviews. CBS anchor Dan Rather, reporting from outside McDonald's, said that "the gloom of these dark days in Moscow is mixed with some golden light from the West." He said people are used to standing in lines in Moscow for everything, including Lenin's tomb, and "couldn't wait to see an American hero." "NBC Nightly News" reported that the grand opening had set an all-time record, breaking the previous record of 9,000 served at McDonald's in Budapest.

The three networks' morning shows also reported live from Pushkin Square. "Good Morning America's" Joan Lunden said McDonald's was attracting "just as much attention in Moscow as Gorbachev" who, it was rumored, might be resigning his leadership of the Communist party. Lunden and "The Today Show's" Deborah Norville interviewed George Cohon consecutively from the store by satellite. "CBS Morning News" reported that the world's biggest country now had the world's biggest McDonald's: seating capacity 700 inside and 200 outside. "It might not turn the Soviet capital into McMoscow but it will bring Soviet kids closer to hamburger heaven."

The story was major news throughout the world. British television rhapsodized that "thousands of Russians were queuing up for the ultimate happiness symbol" and, as shown in Figure 12–1, they had "now had their first taste of glasnost literally."

The print media were equally effusive. *TIME* magazine ran a full-page story on the preparations for the opening, telling how Soviet crew kids were being trained to smile and greet customers. Three days before the opening, *The New York Times* ran a Sunday front-page story calling the opening a "triumph of capitalist determination." *The Los Angeles Times* ran a color picture of the lines waiting to get into McDonald's with a story titled "1st Beeg Mak Attack Leaves Moscow Agog." Seventeen separate wire-service stories and first-hand reports appeared in thousands of

FIGURE 12-1 A Moscovite enjoys a "milk cocktail" on opening day of McDonald's at Pushkin Square. Thirty thousand Russians were served. The opening of the world's largest McDonald's received massive media coverage from TV, radio, and newspapers throughout the world.

newspapers throughout the world. Editorial cartoonists portrayed Gorbachev as a McDonald's crew person and raised Ronald McDonald to the pantheon of Soviet heroes alongside Marx and Lenin.

Canadian Broadcasting Company called McDonald's Moscow opening the public relations coup of the decade. Rob Wilson of CBC reported:

> Despite the fact that the '90s are barely a month old, I think we've already witnessed the public relations coup of the decade. What I'm talking about of course is the arrival of the Big Mac attack in Moscow, the heart of the USSR. It was an event that had to be seen to be believed—tens of thousands of sober Moscovites waiting patiently outside the world's largest McDonald's franchise, all for a taste of something as humdrum as a hamburger, french fries and a soft drink. If someone had written this up as science fiction scenario ten years ago, they would have been laughed out of town. But there it was on TV screens around the world, live in some cases. Every newspaper carried an item and so did every radio station. It was dynamite public relations, the sort of PR exposure that McDonald's could never have bought even if it wanted to. I mean, the whole story unfolded over several weeks of news reports usually tied in with the dramatic political changes of Mikhail Gorbachev's perestroika. One minute we see Gorbachev pledging to support democratic movements in Czechoslovakia, the next moment we're seeing McDonald's training its Russian sales clerks to smile. The USSR supports the overthrow of a Stalinist tyrant in Romania but then we see that McDonald's has introduced special potatoes and beef cattle to Russia so that hamburgers and fries will taste the same as everywhere else. . . . The beauty of the whole process for McDonald's, was the re-emphasis of its corporate good-guy role, a role that it's extremely careful to maintain. In Moscow they put smiles on the faces of normally surly sales clerks. They brought in whole new technologies and farming practices. They gave the Russian people a new cultural icon, albeit a western one. And all of this serves to reinforce the company's corporate citizenship around the world—the Ronald McDonald House, the fact that they switched to CFC-free packaging, the idea that the company does, just like its ads say, do it all for you. The point of course is that McDonald's really isn't in the hamburger and fries business, it's in the good-guy business— its food, after all, is hardly a gourmet taste sensation. But its restaurants are always clean, the food is never likely to give you botulism and the staff will always smile. They sell happiness, and thanks to brilliant marketing, they sell lots of it.[1]

When McDonald's premiered a 60-second commercial, "Magic in Moscow," using footage shot at the opening, *Chicago Tribune* columnist George Lazarus commented, "There's been so much hype behind McDonald's Moscow opening, perhaps Big Mac addicts may be wondering if the hamburger chain still calls Oak Brook [Illinois] its headquarters."

No wonder. After a month in business in Moscow, George Cohon reappeared on "Good Morning America" with this good news—McDonald's had already sold over a million hamburgers there and was serving not 30,000 but up to 50,000 Moscovites daily.

SPECIAL DISNEY OCCASIONS

Just as the Walt Disney Company puts a full-court MPR press behind the introduction of every "new product," that is, the opening of every new film or theme-park attraction, the company never lets a special occasion go by without a special celebration.

When Walt Disney World was 15 years old in 1987, the company set out to stage "the largest gathering of press representatives ever assembled." More than 10,000 reporters, editors, columnists, publishers, disc jockeys, program directors, producers, and anchors appeared in Orlando to be greeted by Mickey Mouse, entertained by Dolly Parton, and inspired by Warren E. Burger, the retiring Chief Justice of the United States Supreme Court, who took advantage of the occasion to extol another significant birthday, the Bicentennial of the U.S. Constitution.

Disney CEO Michael Eisner unabashedly called the event "a marriage between the Disney company and the media." Over the weekend, crews from local radio and TV stations celebrated the nuptials by broadcasting more than 1,000 hours of coverage to all parts of the country. Even the big-city papers and the TV networks that ban press junkets paid their way to cover the story of how the story was being covered by their journalistic brethren.

Mickey Mouse's Birthday Parties

In the company's 1988 annual report, Eisner wrote: "I finally found somebody who celebrates his birthday more often than my 10-year-old son, Anders, but somebody out-partied him: Mickey Mouse."

He was referring to Mickey's 60th birthday, but even in the days before Eisner, Disney was making Mickey's big birthdays major publicity and promotional occasions. For his 50th in 1978, Mickey celebrated with a national coast-to-coast whistle-stop train tour commemorating Walt Disney's creation of Mickey on a 1928 train ride from New York to Los Angeles. This 50th-birthday tour reversed the itinerary. After a special ceremony in which Mickey became the first animated character to receive a star on Hollywood's Walk of Fame at Mann's Chinese Theater, 500 celebrities and reporters saw him off at a bon voyage party at Los Angeles's Union Station.

The tour covered 57 cities in 18 states and ended in New York City, where Mickey attended the installation of a bronze plaque in the lobby of the Broadway theater where he made his 1928 screen debut. Along the way, he attended such well-publicized events as a party honoring him at the Chicago International Film Festival and a birthday party at the White House hosted by Amy Carter, daughter of the President.

Mickey celebrated his 60th birthday during 1988, and as Eisner reported, "The year was filled from one end to the other with memorable events marking the milestone." Mickey seemed to be everywhere: at the United Nations where he was honored as Emissary of Good Will to the world; in commemorative supplements in *TIME, FORTUNE,* and *People* magazines; and dancing with New York Mayor Ed Koch in lower Manhattan and with Mischa the Bear in Red Square. A "Little Mouse on the Prairie" silhouette planted in an Iowa cornfield was seen by millions of people passing over on transcontinental flights. A video news release featuring the first visit of Mickey Mouse to Red Square was one of the top ten VNRs of the year, seen by 56.7 million TV viewers.

The culmination of this special year took place at both U.S. theme parks on Mickey's actual birthday, November 18. Associated Press reported from Florida:

> Some kids tweaked Mickey's nose Friday and others sang "It's a Small World" in Russian, German or English when more than 4,000 children joined to celebrate the 60th birthday of the famous Walt Disney mouse. Shortly after noon, specially invited children—many of them poor or from foster homes—from 116 U.S. cities and several nations assembled in groups of 10 to 100 for a Main Street Parade from Cinderella's Castle to town square in the Magic Kingdom. Friday's festivities also included a global sing-along of the "Mickey Mouse Club March," the famous theme song that spells out Mickey's name. Disney said radio stations on every continent and at the North and South Poles played the nine-line classic at 9:50 A.M. EST. Disney also threw a similar party for an equal number of children at Disneyland.
>
> To celebrate the event, a permanent new attraction, Mickey's Birthdayland, was opened on a three-acre site at Disney World's Magic Kingdom. Guests ride Mickey's Birthday Express on a grand circle trip around the park to Birthdayland, which features shows, attractions, games, music and [a spot] where they can pose for pictures with Mickey and other Disney characters. The Disney licensing division took advantage of the occasion by producing special products from souvenirs to jewel-studded Mickey and Minnie gold watches priced from $6,000 to $36,000.[2]

Mickey had come a long way from his 1928 debut in *Steamboat Willie,* the first cartoon with synchronized sound.

Disneyland's 35th

Disney's most recent special occasion was a year-long celebration of the 35th anniversary of Disneyland in 1990. The celebration was inaugurated in January with extravaganzas on both coasts; expansions at Disneyland and Walt Disney World in Florida were announced.

Also announced were a schedule of TV events including a live seven-minute Disneyland show preceding the network telecast of the Rose Bowl, a special anniversary edition of NBC's "Magical World of Disney," and a one-hour retrospective called "The Disneyland Story" on the Disney Channel.

On Main Street of Disneyland, the event was celebrated daily with the biggest parade and street show in park history, with a new feature added: 45-foot-high Disney character balloons. An assemblage called "Magical Memories" comprising 3,000 items of Disney memorabilia was posted in the promenade of the famed park. A new GEO automobile was to be given away daily at the park, together with 400,000 other gifts during the course of the year. In addition, Disneyland ran a special auction of hundreds of props, costumes, and other artifacts with the profits going to a children's charity. The year's events also included the premier of a preseason college football matchup called the Disneyland Pigskin Classic. As the company's annual report put it, "Only Disneyland could throw a party this big."

BH&G'S NATIONAL FAMILY REUNION WEEKEND

Better Homes & Gardens magazine created a special occasion that was celebrated nationally and did much to reposition the magazine as a contemporary, upbeat resource for today's active families.

Research showed that *BH&G* had an old-fashioned reputation as a "shelter" book and that the public associated the magazine almost entirely with recipes and home/garden features. The magazine wanted a way to communicate its new editorial mission ". . . to provide families with service in the form of ideas, help, information, and inspiration. . . ." Ketchum Public Relations devised the idea to further *BH&G*'s mission of serving families—a widescale family reunion celebration. The concept was tested with the *BH&G* Consumer Panel, a roster of 500 consumers maintained by *BH&G* on a year-long basis for such market research. The resulting data confirmed that there was strong interest in the topic and tremendous potential for media coverage. An audit of the news media, libraries, and genealogical organizations revealed that there was a lack of reunion advice for families. Based on these steps, *BH&G* embarked on a high-visibility reunion campaign for today's families.

Its focus was "National Family Reunion Weekend," August 1–3, 1986. The objectives were to increase visibility of *BH&G*, link the magazine with family reunions, and stimulate interest in reunions and *BH&G*-provided advice. "National Family Reunion Weekend" was comprised of seven inter-related elements implemented in ten markets selected as key to the *BH&G* ad-sales force.

Although there are many ways of signifying commemorative occasions, a Presidential proclamation is the most auspicious and most difficult to obtain. *BH&G* secured the endorsement of two Congressmen, two-thirds each of the House and the Senate, and, finally, the signature of the President. The Proclamation, declaring National Family Reunion Weekend, served as the news hook for a video news release called, "An American Tradition is Now Official." The VNR, featuring historic and modern-day footage of family reunions, was distributed to 200 stations nationwide.

In addition to the VNR, the media-relations effort centered around a ten-city media tour. To create a local-market hook for the media tour, mayoral proclamations declared the Weekend in the tour cities. Family Reunion Weekend radio promotions were run with stations in key *BH&G* markets. "My Family's a Winner!" T-shirts, family trips, family entertainment, and, of course, *BH&G* subscriptions were offered to listeners during the week before the Weekend.

BH&G's special occasion was successful in generating media coverage and involving *BH&G* with its target contemporary-family audience. Nearly 5,000 people wrote letters thanking *BH&G* for initiating the Weekend. The full press run of 15,000 booklets, the *BH&G* "Guide to Family Reunions," was depleted within two months. During July and August, *BH&G*'s overall media coverage had increased by nearly 20 percent and, more importantly, the number of impressions from family-related stories, as opposed to food or home/garden, nearly doubled.

NATIONAL SOUP MONTH

A number of leading companies have created special company-sponsored Weeks, Months, and Days to focus both media and trade attention on their product's category dominance and to preempt competitive brands.

In 1983, Golin/Harris Communications recommended that Campbell Soup Company declare the month of January, when soup consumption is highest, National Soup Month.

The program has continued to be a successful collaboration between the Soup Business Unit, Campbell's Communications Center, and the public relations firm. A variety of tactics have been utilized over the years, but the basic objective has remained the same: to keep soup top of mind and to increase soup purchases.

In the first year, National Soup Month was registered in Chase's Calendar of Events. Governors of 40 states where products used in Campbell's Soups are grown and where Campbell's plants are located signed proclamations declaring National Soup Month in their states. Also, it was determined that 1984 was the 80th birthday of the company's famous advertising characters, the Campbell Kids, so birthday parties were held for the media and Campbell employees.

The next year's celebration featured the first ever "Souper Waiters Race" to bring attention to the company's commitment to the "Year of Well-Being." The race, staged at New York's Bryant Park, was a half-mile run in which waiters and waitresses were required to carry a tray with a bowl full of hot tomato soup in one hand. To win, they had to have at least half of the soup left in the bowl when they crossed the finish line. The story attracted national media coverage. CNN ran a feature called, "Soup on the Fly." *The New York Times* carried pictures of the winning waiter and waitress in their sports section with a story headlined, "Well-Balanced Meal Is Moment of Glory." Several New York television stations ran the waiters' race as a weather story since the event was held on the coldest day of the winter.

The program was carried to the grassroots level during the next two years when a Campbell SoupMobile was created and sent on tour to further underscore the link between cold weather and soup's warming, nutritious properties. Free cups of soup were served to consumers in high-visibility downtown areas, to students on college campuses, to outdoor workers, and to the homeless. In each city, donations of cases of soup were made to deserving missions and shelters. Mayors or their representatives from human services departments appeared in each city to serve soup and commend Campbell Soup Company. Positive exposure was obtained because of the human interest/social responsibility news value of serving free soup to the needy and to city workers during the coldest month of the year. Mayoral appearances and proclamations enhanced the media coverage, which was extensive in all markets visited by the SoupMobile.

New news angles have been developed annually to maximize media exposure. In 1989, it was birthday time again for the Campbell Kids, their 85th. Other publicity was based on information from the company's market research department. One story revealed the 10 U.S. cities where Campbell's soups are most popular. Another listed the cities where each variety of soup ranked highest in per-capita consumption.

Television coverage has continued to be a focus of National Soup Month. Weathermen, from Willard Scott of NBC's "Today Show" to local forecasters, have encouraged viewers to celebrate National Soup Month and keep warm with a bowl of hot soup. David Letterman made soup a "Late Night" hit by featuring a "soup du jour" and the National Soup Month logo on his show every night throughout January. Campbell's celebrity spokesperson, Rita Moreno, told viewers of the "Tonight Show" that the healthiest Americans eat soup. In 1988, new technology made it possible for her to conduct a satellite media tour from her California home. From her kitchen, Ms. Moreno told the soup-is-good-food story and demonstrated soup recipes for local interviewers in 17 soup markets.

In 1990, Campbell's took the National Soup Month show on the road to Minneapolis, a leading city in tomato soup consumption, to celebrate the production of the 20-billionth can of Campbell's Tomato Soup. To mark this "milestone in Americana," Campbell convened an assemblage of celebrity spokespersons—Rita Moreno; singer Della Reese; actor Jack Scalia, who once worked in a Campbell plant; actress Marion Ross, the Mom of TV's "Happy Days"; and Olympic skater Jill Trenary—and had Robin Leach, host of "Lifestyles of the Rich and Famous," interview each about the role tomato soup played in his or her life. Some of the celebrities are shown toasting Campbell Soup in Figure 12–2. The festivities were transmitted by satellite to network and local TV, where coverage was extensive. The event was covered by 77 network-affiliated TV stations and such network and syndicated shows as "CBS This Morning," "The Home Show," "Live with Regis and Kathy Lee" and "Hard Copy." Four radio networks and National Public Radio fed the tour to their local affiliates. Wire-service stories were headlined "Rich and Famous from Leach in a Soup Line" and "M'm! Campbell Lauds Tomato Milestone."

Conceived as a PR program, National Soup Month has added such promotional elements as newspaper free-standing inserts, sweepstakes, cents-off coupons redeemable during January, and soup samplings, but it remains a PR-driven marketing program using print and broadcast media to raise soup awareness among target consumers.

In each year since it was launched, National Soup Month, a public relations concept supported at the trade level, has helped boost January soup sales to record highs, without increasing advertising spending above norms for the month.[3]

In its first year, Campbell recorded a 10 percent sales increase during National Soup Month, followed by a record 36 percent increase in 1985. This special occasion has continued to boost soup sales every January.

ZIPLOC SANDWICH DAY

DowBrands' Ziploc Brand Sandwich Bags created a special occasion called National Sandwich Day to differentiate its products from the

FIGURE 12–2 Campbell Soup Company celebrated the production of the 20 billionth can of Campbell's Tomato Soup with star-studded events hosted by Robin Leach of "Lifestyles of the Rich and Famous" TV fame. The author toasted the occasion with entertainers Della Reese and Rita Moreno.

competition and to establish Ziploc as the best product for carrying sandwiches.

The program is designed to convince sandwich-bag users that the Ziploc brand provides the food protection, versatility, and ease of use needed for all family-usage occasions. The program is directed both at mothers of young children and the children themselves. All publicity and information materials emphasize the product's benefits: a zipper closure that keeps food fresh and a pleated bottom that holds more.

November 3, the birthday of the Earl of Sandwich, the inventor of the sandwich, was selected as National Sandwich Day. This is a natural tie-in whose media appeal is evident. To reach schoolchildren in grades 1 to 6, DowBrands' public relations firm, Golin/Harris, annually produces a nutrition education unit that is inserted in leading magazines for elementary school teachers, such as *Instructor* and *Creative Classroom*. The material, "Two Slices of Bread and a Whole Lot More: The Earl of Sandwich's Guide to Nutrition," includes information and charts that illustrate why each of the four food groups is important, activity masters, games, and reproducible material for classroom use. To reach mothers, the unit includes a menu planner for the schoolchildren to take home and fill out with their parents. The benefits of Ziploc brand pleated sandwich bags in keeping foods fresh and locking in nutrients are presented to parents along with a free National Sandwich Day recipe booklet.

The material includes an announcement of the Ziploc Sandwich Bag National Sandwich Day Contest. Students are asked to create an original, nutritious sandwich and send the recipe to Ziploc for a chance to receive prizes and have their creation named "America's Favorite Sandwich." On National Sandwich Day, the media are invited to cover the judging by comedian Dom Deluise, Ziploc's advertising spokesperson, and a panel of children experts.

The Ziploc National Sandwich Day Contest involves thousands of schoolchildren and is broadcast to television stations across the country by a satellite feed. Since its inception, it has helped position Ziploc Sandwich bags as the authority on keeping foods fresh to both children who use sandwich bags and to parents who buy them.

13

Defending Products at Risk

Yesterday's marketing executives had it much easier. In a less hectic marketplace, there was time to build brand equity based on exclusive product benefits before a competitor could bring a me-too product to market. The placement of advertising in mass magazines and on network television assured efficient delivery of advertising messages to the right people in the right place at the right time. Consumers had not become consumerists. Management was under less pressure from the financial community and their shareholders to produce profits or else lose their jobs and maybe even the company itself in a hostile takeover. Today's marketing managers are forced to produce a better bottom line, quarter after quarter, month after month, before they move off the brand or out altogether.

To complicate life even more, they may be required to deal with any number of consumer concerns about their company's social responsibility and the efficacy of their products. In its January 29, 1990, issue, *PR News* said:

> It has become patently clear that activists representing almost every facet of life are not only increasing but also becoming skilled in the art of persuasion. Evident are articulate pleas from anti-abortion, anti-fur, anti-carcinogenic foods, anti-tobacco, anti-alcohol groups. Film stars with wide public followings are making public assertions that they would refuse to endorse what they considered harmful products.

Brain Reserve's Faith Popcorn labels the growing concern for the environment, the water, the fish, the ozone layer, and the garbage as S.O.S. (Save Our Society). She believes that consumers are looking at the ethics of the companies they do business with. They want to know what a company stands for as well as what its product can do for them.

The odds are increasing that young marketing executives will be faced with a threatening crisis situation sometime in their career.

An *ADWEEK's Marketing Week* 1990 cover story listed five products—aseptic juice boxes, microwaveable entrees, oil-based paints and solvents, disposable diapers, and blister packs—as "categories that will be in trouble within five years if marketers don't wake up." Some crisis situations like these develop over time. Others can strike without warning, putting the product and perhaps the company itself at risk. When disaster strikes, the best laid marketing plans can go awry.

How to deal with these problems is something they don't teach marketers at business schools—yet. That is why public relations is increasingly being called upon by corporations to identify emerging problems and corporate vulnerabilities, to prepare plans for crises that could occur, and to train executives how to respond when and if the need arises. A single incident, the Tylenol murders, raised the crisis consciousness of corporate America. Since that time, the need for crisis planning has become a universally accepted management responsibility and function and one of the fastest-growing areas of corporate public relations practice.

There is a growing body of crisis-communication knowledge and literature. It is not the purview of this book to discuss the wide spectrum of crises affecting business—AIDS in the workplace, industrial disasters like Union Carbide's tragic gas leak in Bhopāl, and the *Exxon Valdez* episode, which is certain to become the textbook example of poor crisis management. Rather, this chapter deals with issues and incidents that directly affect products and put them at risk.

In discussing R.J. Reynolds' withdrawal of its Uptown cigarettes and the FDA's and consumerists' attacks on the American Heart Association's Seal of Approval, Rinker Buck, editorial director of *ADWEEK's Marketing Week*, wrote:

> The most critical function PR can perform is assessing probable public reaction to a controversial launch or ad campaign. If experienced PR trouble shooters had been called in early to assess these projects, the outcome might have been very different. They might either have warned the companies off or suggested ways of making the programs more palatable to skeptical journalists and community leaders.[1]

THE TYLENOL TRAGEDY

Johnson & Johnson's handling of the Tylenol crisis has become a classic public relations case history. Although it has been widely told, it would be remiss not to include it in the present book because it is the penultimate example of the successful interaction of responsible management action, media relations, and marketing communications.

The Tylenol tragedy presented Johnson & Johnson with the greatest challenge in its 96-year history and was an event without precedent in American business, according to Lawrence G. Foster, J&J's corporate vice president for public relations.

The facts are well known. In September 1982, an unknown murderer contaminated Extra-Strength Tylenol capsules with cyanide and seven people died in the Chicago area. This was followed by a rash of reports of other illnesses and deaths implicating Tylenol. From the onset of the tragedy, the company cooperated fully with the media, answering literally thousands of calls openly with all information that was available. An entire lot of 93,000 bottles was immediately recalled, warnings were wired to doctors, hospitals, and distributors, and all Tylenol advertising was suspended.

Although the company was convinced that it was blameless, it recalled all Tylenol capsules nationally within the week and, through advertising and statements to the media, offered to exchange Tylenol capsules for tablets. The public relations effort restored confidence and trust in the Tylenol brand. J&J's chairman, James E. Burke, appeared on "Donahue," answering questions from the studio and viewing audience for an hour.

The company then agreed to allow "60 Minutes" to film its executive strategy sessions. Mike Wallace, known for his tough interviews, said,

> Only a few weeks ago many business experts were asserting that Tylenol was dead. Today they are beginning to hedge their bets—change their minds—for they have seen the men who run Johnson & Johnson use the facts, the media, and huge amounts of money, as in the recall ($100 million), in a way that confounded the crepehangers. Instead of stonewalling, Johnson & Johnson has been forthcoming and apparently has managed to avert disaster.

The Washington Post reported that, "Johnson & Johnson has effectively demonstrated how a major business ought to handle a disaster. . . . Johnson & Johnson has succeeded in portraying itself to the public as a company willing to do what's right regardless of cost."

Within two months, the product was reintroduced in triple-sealed, tamper-resistant packaging. At the recommendation of Burson-Marsteller, the news was communicated by means of a 30-city "Tylenol comeback" video news conference reaching representatives of over 600 news organizations by satellite. At the time of the murders, Tylenol was the leader of the OTC analgesic market with a 35-percent share. By the end of 1982, its share had declined to 18 percent. As a result of its actions and openness with the press and the public, the brand had recaptured 80 percent of its market share within a year of the tragedy.[2]

Then, incredibly, in February 1986, tragedy struck a second time when it was reported that a woman died in Yonkers, New York, after taking a capsule of Extra-Strength Tylenol. After additional poisoned Tylenol capsules were found, the company again suspended sale of its capsules; this time permanently. The company again went to the consumer, this time to offer to replace Tylenol capsules with Tylenol caplets, a solid form of the product, or a cash refund.

A front-page *New York Times* story described how Johnson's top management with its PR counsel acted "to control consumer reaction, exercise damage control, and make the best of a bad situation." By communicating openly and frequently with consumers through the news media and advertising, Tylenol survived its second life-and-death crisis with its credibility and integrity intact. And, remarkably, it allayed consumers' fears while simultaneously protecting its brand share. More than 95 percent of Tylenol users exchanged their capsules for caplets rather than cash.

James H. Dowling, president of Burson-Marsteller, who sat in on the J&J strategy sessions, said, "The great lesson here is that you can overcome bad news. You can win. You can come back."

KRAFT AND COKE PROMOTIONS BACKFIRE

Most marketers will not have to face life-and-death concerns like Tylenol, or health threats like those represented by the Dalkon Shield and Rely Tampons. They are more likely to deal with bottom-line-threatening marketing situations like the crisis that faced Kraft during the summer of 1989 and Coca-Cola the next summer. The public relations trade publication *O'Dwyer's PR Services Report* commented:

> For the second time this year, a large corporation has been unable to turn the tide of bad publicity stemming from a mistake. Like Exxon, Kraft stuck to a tight-lipped PR approach, ignoring Johnson & Johnson's open, informed and assertive handling of the Tylenol crisis in 1982, which PR people said helped defuse criticism and save the product[3]

The writer was referring to a foul-up of a regional promotion that made the national news agenda. Despite the small stakes and limited consequences, the incident at least temporarily damaged the well-earned reputation of one of the country's preeminent food marketers.

The incident revolved around a routine match-and-win game called "Ready to Roll." Consumers had to match right-side half pictures from a free-standing insert (FSI) in 13 Chicago and Houston newspapers with left-side half pictures from packages of specially marked Kraft singles, to make a complete picture of a prize. The game offered 8,000 packages of cheese, 500 skateboards, 100 bicycles, and a 1990 Dodge Caravan LE priced at $17,000. Due to a printer's error, virtually everyone won. When Kraft was flooded with calls from thousands of excited people claiming to be winners, Kraft immediately canceled the contest.

The abrupt cancellation created a national uproar. The story was carried on network news and in newspapers nationally. One of the "winners" appeared on ABC's "Nightline" demanding her van. Commentator Jeff Greenfield called for Kraft to make a large donation to Gamblers Anonymous for contributing to the corruption of the American dream.

Five days after the FSI appeared, Kraft announced its compromise. The company ran a full-page newspaper ad headlined "Ouch!" and agreed to give cash awards to consumers who sent in the matching game pieces: $250 for the Dodge Caravan; $50 for the bicycle; $25 for the skateboard; and $5 for the Kraft singles.

"The move was a few days late and many dollars short," according to public relations specialists interviewed by *The Chicago Tribune* in a story titled, "Experts offer Kraft lesson in 'crisis PR.'" In the article, Pat Jackson, public relations counselor and editor of *PR Reporter,* said, "The one thing that the public understands is that people screw up. Kraft should have gone majorly public. If they had carried it off with humility, they could have gotten the public on their side. Instead, this last-minute payoff doesn't take care of all the disgruntled people." Despite the small stakes and limited consequences, Kraft's mishandling of a regional promotion was compared to the *Exxon Valdez* public relations disaster.

While Kraft's "Ready to Roll" was a small-scale regional promotion, Coca-Cola's $100 million "Magic Summer '90" promotion was the company's largest ever for its flagship Coca-Cola Classic brand. The company planned to distribute 750,000 MagiCans containing pop-up cash and prize coupons during the summer of 1990. The company had distributed 200,000 when they began to receive complaints from customers who claimed that some of the cans didn't work and that others emitted a foul-smelling liquid that leaked from the inside lining of some Magi-Cans. The liquid had been put into the prize cans to give the same weight and feel as regular Coke cans. The company took out ads in newspapers in 50 major markets containing drawings of "properly working" and "malfunctioning" MagiCans. The ads explained that the liquid was harmless but should not be drunk.

A week later, the company abruptly canceled the promotion two months early. The MagiCan debacle was widely compared by the media with the failed introduction of New Coke. Journalists also questioned the practice of sending cash in MagiCans to reporters across the country, to announce the promotion.

BRITISH AIRWAYS' "GO FOR IT, AMERICA"

Coke's MagiCan mistake was a promotion that turned into a crisis; by contrast, British Airways' (BA) "Go for it, America" was a promotion that overcame a crisis. In 1986, because of terrorist threats at European airports, the U.S. retaliatory raid on Libya, and fears of fallout from the nuclear accident at Chernobyl, British Airways suffered a near-disastrous drop in seat reservations.

An action program was needed to achieve a turnaround in summer-season bookings, to bring them back to budgeted levels. The successful plan to reenthuse the American traveler to visit Britain was accomplished without any increase in the normal advertising/promotion/public relations budget.

Daniel J. Edelman Inc., BA's public relations firm, created "Go for it, America," a program that provided a dramatic and newsworthy event that turned media attention to the positive enjoyment and pleasure expectations of the tourist. "Go for it, America" was announced simultaneously at press conferences in 15 gateway cities in the United States by local BA station managers. They announced that on June 10, 1986, all 5,200 seats on 20 British Airways flights from each of the gateway cities would be given free to winners of a nationwide lottery and that a group of lottery winners would be invited to tea with British Prime Minister Margaret Thatcher. The blanket TV and newspaper coverage of the promotion in the United States and Britain was sustained for weeks preceding the departure as the entries poured in. BA's CEO toured major cities to meet travel agents and the media. Spectacular additional prizes like a Rolls Royce, a $150,000 Harrods shopping voucher, a portfolio of stocks, and a Concorde for a day were announced.

Finally, the winners of the lottery were announced. The departures from all 15 airports drew large crowds of reporters and TV crews, and special arrangements were made for crews and journalists to accompany each of the flights. Mrs. Thatcher's tea party for her American visitors at No. 10 Downing Street received extensive media coverage on both sides of the Atlantic.

The result of "Go for it, America" was that weekly booking levels increased 120 percent from an average of 8,000 a week before the promotion to 17,700, and load factors soon exceeded 1985 record levels. "Go for it, America" worked so well in restoring American travel on British Airways and turning around a damaging crisis in confidence that it was named one of the best promotions of the decade by *Promote* magazine.

THE SUZUKI SAMURAI

In the trade publication, *PR Today*, Paul Holmes wrote:

> If one were to make a list of the major business crises of the last few years one might start with the *Exxon Valdez* disaster, or the Union Carbide poison gas leak in Bhopāl, or with the recent scare over alar in apples. But somewhere on the list would be the 1988 attack by *Consumer Reports* magazine on the Suzuki Samurai. While the Samurai incident—it was the first time in ten years that *Consumer Reports* had determined a vehicle to be unacceptable and urged its recall—may have generated fewer headlines than the *Valdez* tragedy, it was far more damaging to Suzuki than the oil spill was to Exxon. At the time, the Samurai was the automaker's only U.S. product, and its withdrawal from the market could have meant the end of Suzuki in this country.[4]

American Suzuki Motor Corporation and its PR counsel, Rogers & Associates, learned that *Consumer Reports* had called a press conference just 12 hours before it was to occur. Rogers dispatched two staff members on the Los Angeles to New York red-eye to attend the conference at which *Consumer Reports* released its report, "The Suzuki Turns Over Too Easily" and showed films of the Samurai tipping over.

At the press conference, the Rogers staffers distributed a media alert to reporters advising them that a response would be made later in the day via satellite and wire services so that consumers could hear both sides of the story. Despite no prior knowledge of the nature of the *Consumer Reports* charges, a video response was prepared and transmitted by satellite three hours after the conference and in time to make the evening television news and the next morning's newspapers. Within 48 hours, the company and its PR firm had fielded calls from more than 1,200 reporters.

Since it was vital to communicate with employees and dealers, N. Douglas Mazza, Suzuki's general manager, transmitted his response by mailgram and a personal videotaped message.

A week after the *Consumer Reports* announcement, Suzuki held its own satellite news conference in Los Angeles, facilitating two-way communication with reporters in New York and Detroit. Mazza charged that the testing procedures used by *Consumer Reports* were biased and completely inaccurate. He said that the magazine's charges were "defamatory," that *Consumer Reports* had a responsibility to accurately and fairly report on products, and that "it has not done so as it relates to the Samurai." He said that Suzuki would not allow *Consumer Reports'* statements "that result from distorted testing and irresponsible reporting to go unchallenged."

He outlined to reporters the extensive tests that Samurai had undergone, which, he said, "prove conclusively that the Samurai is a safe, stable, and reliable vehicle." The head of the engineering consulting firm that had conducted the test participated in the satellite news conference. Suzuki also showed a video made by Transportation Research of Ohio, in which several light trucks and passenger vehicles were made to turn over in tests similar to those conducted by *Consumer Reports.* Mazza concluded that "if a driver wants to make a vehicle turn over, he can. In fact, under certain circumstances, any vehicle can be made to turn over—and *Consumer Reports* knows that." Mazza then engaged the press in a question-and-answer session that lasted over an hour.

While some believe that Suzuki's assault on *Consumer Reports* was excessive because of the publication's high degree of credibility with the public, the company believed it had been wronged and was in a fight for its life. The strategy worked. *The Los Angeles Times* reported that sales for the Samurai had been averaging about 6,000 vehicles a month but fell to about 1,000 in July when the *Consumer Reports* article appeared. Sales recovered to more than 12,000 units in August, after Suzuki launched its public relations counterattack and a heavy promotion and incentive program.

NUTRASWEET'S DEFENSE

From its beginnings a decade ago, the NutraSweet Company, a wholly owned subsidiary of Monsanto Company, recognized the need to inform and educate consumers about the taste and benefits of products sweetened with NutraSweet. A comprehensive public relations program has supported the company's mission to provide consumers with healthful and safe food choices.

Today, more than 3,000 foods and beverages around the world, including carbonated and powdered soft drinks, puddings, yogurts, and frozen novelties, are sweetened with NutraSweet brand sweetener. The company took responsibility for educating the public up front, eliminating the need for food and beverage manufacturers to explain the benefits of aspartame and the NutraSweet brand to their consumers.

It was not long before NutraSweet faced another critical communications challenge: to defend itself against claims from a few scientists who declared it unsafe. These charges were promulgated by the media, most prominently on a three-part series on "CBS Evening News" with Dan Rather reporting and on ABC's "Nightline." Local TV picked up 20-second sound bites of what NutraSweet called its critics' anecdotal claims. Consumer activists also picked up the issue, forming a group calling itself "Aspartame Victims and Their Friends." There were calls for a ban on the product and for Congressional hearings.

NutraSweet struck back by publicizing safety studies, conducted by prestigious universities, that refuted every allegation. The company inaugurated its own Scientific Good News Program and worked with the universities to disseminate information to publishers, editors, and reporters. Its primary message: Aspartame has been proven safe in over 100 scientific studies conducted over a 20-year period.

In August 1987, the University of Illinois College of Medicine announced that no link was found between consumption of high doses of aspartame and seizures. The nation's news media carried a Reuters report that a study of epileptic rats injected with varying doses of aspartame showed no ill effects even at the highest levels. *The New York Times* ran the Reuters story under the headline "New Findings Back Use of Sweetener."

A few months later, Harvard Medical School released the results of a study conducted by a research team headed by a world renowned expert on obesity. AP reported, "The popular sugar substitute NutraSweet doesn't destroy diets by making people eat more and it may even help women lose weight. The research found that women seemed better able to stick to low-calorie diets when they satisfied their cravings for sweets with sodas and snacks containing NutraSweet."

Then Duke University Medical Center issued a study refuting yet another charge against NutraSweet. The Duke study found that NutraSweet is no more likely to cause a headache than is a placebo. *USA Today* headlined its story "Headache? Not from NutraSweet." A 1988 University of Minnesota study found that fairly large amounts of aspartame can be safely consumed daily by most healthy people.

Wherever the critics were interviewed, NutraSweet sent Dr. Robert Moser, its Vice President for Health Communication and former Executive Vice President of the American College of Physicians, to respond, citing these and other reports that attested to NutraSweet's safety. Dr. Moser has conducted hundreds of interviews with local newspapers and television and radio stations, presenting NutraSweet's side of the story and offering NutraSweet literature to consumers. The result of this ongoing research and media-relations effort has been to silence critics, most of whom have gone on to other issues, and to reassure consumers, who continue to buy products sweetened with NutraSweet, and Equal, the company's tabletop sweetener.

FOODS UNDER ATTACK

Consumer concerns and media attention about food and product safety are not new. For decades, reports about the hazards of cholesterol, sugar, fats, caffeine, mercury, sodium, sulfite, nitrates, and other substances have been a staple of the American news agenda. Virtually all of these controversies evolve in the same way. A crisis or study raises a public issue. Aroused activist groups clamor for action, often calling for a ban or stricter regulation of the additive or product. The news media carry the story to consumers, raising their awareness and concern. Politicians take up the cause. Conflicting charges and counter charges are made and reported in the media. This may continue for years with no conclusive action taken. If action is taken, it can range from arbitrary labeling to the banning of particular substances and suspension of some products.

TIME and *Newsweek,* the two leading U.S. newsweeklies, often go to great lengths to avoid running cover stories on the same subject. Yet, on March 27, 1989, *Newsweek* ran a cover story called "How Safe Is Your Food?" and *Time's* cover headline was "Is Anything Safe?"

Both described how the discovery of two Chilean grapes found to have traces of cyanide triggered a panic. Coming as it did a week after the release of a controversial report linking an apple-ripening agent, Alar, with cancer in children, the episode focused attention on a variety of concerns that Americans have about many of the foods they eat.

Apples and Alar

The National Resources Defense Council (NRDC), a non-profit environmental group, orchestrated the release of its Alar report to achieve maximum impact. The story was leaked to *Newsweek* and CBS's "60 Minutes." A spokesperson for the group explained, "We deliberately chose '60 Minutes' because we wanted to reach the parents of young children. We talked to them and they said they would do it if they got an exclusive." The NRDC's public relations counsel added, "It was in the public interest to reach as many people as possible because we don't have the bucks."

On February 26, 1989, "60 Minutes" viewers heard reporter Ed Bradley declare:

> The most important cancer-causing agent in our food supply is a substance sprayed on apples to keep them on the trees longer and make

them look better. That's the conclusion of a number of scientific experts. And who is most at risk? Children who may someday develop cancer from this one chemical called daminozide. [trade name *Alar*]

The next day the report was officially released and was played as a major news story in the nation's news media, including the front page of *USA Today*. Actress Meryl Streep, NRDC's celebrity spokesperson, made an immediate round of appearances on nationally televised, big-audience talk shows: "Good Morning America," "Today Show," and "Donahue."

Significantly less media attention was paid to a report issued, the day after the "60 Minutes" exclusive, by the National Academy of Sciences, urging Americans to eat more fruits and vegetables as a way of cutting down on fat and decreasing the chance of heart disease.

The Alar scare planted the seeds of panic, causing apples to be removed by school districts in New York, Los Angeles, and Chicago, and forcing grocery stores throughout the country to post signs assuring consumers that their apples were not treated with Alar.

The apple industry launched an emergency counterattack. Hill & Knowlton mounted a public relations program for The Washington State Apple Commission to reassure consumers that apples were safe. H&K called on scientists outside the apple industry and government officials who emphasized that the danger from eating apples was minimal. The Commission, with the support of the International Apple Institute, ran ads in major daily newspapers under the headline, "Why an Apple a Day Is Still Healthy Advice." The ads asserted that a human being would have to eat 28,000 pounds of Alar-treated apples a day for 70 years to suffer the same Alar–cancer links as the mice used in NRDC's test.

Two weeks later, the U.S. Food and Drug Administration and the Environmental Protection Agency issued a joint pronouncement stating that apples were safe for children.

In the aftermath of the Alar blitz, the media began to express second thoughts about the coverage they had given to the story. *TIME* admitted that "The fruit frenzy taps into the media's fascination with harm with a personal angle," and that fruit had replaced other stories about a baby trapped in a well and an icebound whale.

The Chicago Tribune ran a story titled "How 'media stampede' spread apple panic," charging that the mix of one of America's most popular actresses (Meryl Streep), a television show ("60 Minutes"), tardy damage-control by government agencies, and a barrage of media reports that failed to give a balanced account could result in "panic on a national scale."

Writing in *The Wall Street Journal*, Hodding Carter, Jr., stated,

The Alar situation is a case study in the way today's journalism often makes the truth the first casualty of its most treasured conventions.

. . . The only problem was, and is, that a solid scientific case has yet to be made against Alar. Even if one had been made, the vast majority of all apples and apple derivatives have never been touched by Alar. And even those that were supposedly "contaminated" didn't rise to the risk levels detailed in the worst-case scenarios.

To all of which the media now says, in effect, "Oops, so sorry. We only report the news. We don't make it." Others, as the *Washington Post* reported this week, were a little more disturbed. The Food and Drug Administration commissioners lamented not having jumped "into it earlier. . . . If you can't get in within the first 24 hours, the story is lost." As the *Post*'s report put it, a complicated scientific issue came close to being decided not by solid evidence but by a frightened public acting on incomplete and often erroneous press reports.[5]

American Heart Association's HeartGuide Debacle

In early 1990, the American Heart Association (AHA) was ready to launch a program to put its seal of approval on products that met its guidelines for fats, cholesterol, and sodium. A bizarre controversy on the role of third parties who come between marketers and government broke out.

Because of public concerns about fats, cholesterol, and sodium, the AHA believed its HeartGuide program would be welcomed by consumers and marketers as well. But, as *ADWEEK's Marketing Week* reported, "The AHA couldn't have been more wrong." As the first HeartGuide approval ads began to appear, the acting director of the Food and Drug Administration (FDA) charged that a private organization had no mandate to get involved in consumer marketing and suggested that the FDA might take legal action against the AHA. Government pressure increased from the FDA, which threatened to seize products bearing the seal when it believed the label was misleading, and the Department of Agriculture, which banned the seal's use on meat and poultry products.

Two months after the HeartGuide program was announced, the American Heart Association announced that it was canceling its program. *The New York Times* commented in a front-page story that "the retreat by the Association appeared to signal the end of efforts by private organizations to rate the relative nutritional merits of various foods and left that burden to the Federal Government, which will now be under increased pressure to issue strong guidelines of its own."[6] Ironically, it was the inaction of the government that caused the American Heart Association to develop its seal-of-approval program.

Keebler Reformulates

Keebler Company was the first national snack-food manufacturer to reformulate its entire line in response to consumer concern about cholesterol. In

January 1989, Keebler announced that it would eliminate tropical oils and animal fats from all of its cookie, cracker, and snack-food products. Keebler said it would replace coconut, palm, and palm kernel oils as well as lard and beef fat with vegetable oils, such as soybean oil, which are lower in saturated fat. On advice of Keebler's public relations counsel, Golin/Harris Communications, the announcement was made two months prior to shipping the reformulated and repackaged Keebler products, pre-empting the competition.

Keebler also became the first major U.S. snack-food company to institute full-scale nutritional labeling on all its food products. Thomas M. Garvin, Keebler president and CEO, pointed out that the move was completely voluntary: "Consumers today want to know more about what they're eating, and we're happy to provide information on the package that will help them make smarter snack choices."

The announcement news release said that the consensus of authorities such as the U.S. Surgeon General and the American Heart Association is that Americans should reduce their consumption of certain vegetable oils high in saturated fats (the so-called tropical oils) because they cause the body to produce more cholesterol than it needs, contributing to the risk of heart disease. The release included an endorsement of Keebler's reformulation and move to nutritional labeling from Dr. Kenneth H. Cooper, author of the best-selling book *Controlling Cholesterol* and director of the Aerobics Center in Dallas.

A free booklet offering tips for adults and children on how to choose snacks that keep cholesterol levels in check was offered in national publicity and on a major market media tour by nutrition expert and dietician Patricia Baird. The booklet was also offered at the point of sale of Keebler products in supermarkets.

In an introduction to the booklet, titled "A Guide to Uncommonly Smart Snacking," Dr. Cooper wrote:

> The typical American diet, which is high in saturated fat, may contribute significantly to the development of cholesterol even at an early age. Generally, children eat large quantities of snack foods and are particularly vulnerable to the hidden fats found in these foods. If children consume snacks processed with large amounts of tropical oils, lard or beef fat, cholesterol problems can occur. It is for this reason that I compliment Keebler Company for its plan to reformulate its product lines so that no Keebler product will contain tropical oils or animal fats.

By becoming the first snack company to remove tropical oils from its products, Keebler beat the competition both in the marketplace and in the nation's news media. *USA Today* ran the story under the headline "Keebler lowers fat in snacks." Other stories had headlines like "Keebler puts its snacks on lower-cholesterol diet" and "Keebler joins crusade against cholesterol." Media coverage pointed out that Keebler food scientists had been working on the reformulation for over a year and that the company's action was not related to a national advertising campaign funded by an organization called National Heart Savers and its president, Phil Sokolof, an Omaha businessman and heart-attack patient.

Consumer reporter John Stossel demonstrated to host Joan Lunden on "Good Morning America" how tropical oils clog arteries and displayed the reformulated Keebler line.

MCDONALD'S AND THE ENVIRONMENT

Because of its omnipresence, McDonald's has become a lightning rod of sorts to anyone with a special interest or favorite cause. In the late 1980s, environmental issues began to draw more and more media attention. Over the years, the issue has moved from a concern about litter to rainforests to chlorofluorocarbons (CFCs). The newest focus is the question of solid wastes. While all packaging from all fast-food restaurants accounts for less than one percent of landfill, fast-food foam packaging is often portrayed as the cause of the solid-waste problem.

In an effort to be seen as part of the solution as opposed to part of the problem, McDonald's worked on pilot demonstration programs in New York, California, and Oregon. In 1989, the company announced that it and eight of the nation's largest plastics producers would set up a national program to recycle plastic hamburger containers and other packages. The $16 million program began in New England and was projected to extend into other sections of the country.

The New England program is the largest polystyrene recycling program ever undertaken. McDonald's customers of 450 restaurants in New England separate their polystyrene foam and other plastic packaging. McDonald's sends it to a major polystyrene recycling facility in Massachusetts.

At the announcement, the Regional Administrator of the Environmental Protection Agency said, "The program announced today is consistent with the U.S. EPA's efforts to encourage recycling and waste minimization. We hope that other large companies follow McDonald's lead to undertake similar programs."

The company issued its announcement in a press kit printed on recycled paper. A "backgrounder" on McDonald's and the Environment stated that the company was the first to announce a voluntary phaseout of potentially harmful CFCs and that by looking at ways to reduce the amount of packaging McDonald's uses, the company and its suppliers have eliminated tens of millions of pounds of McDonald's packaging. It also pointed out that:

o McDonald's is one of the nation's largest users of recycled paper products.
o The foam packaging used by McDonald's is 100 percent recyclable.
o In several restaurants, McDonald's has a number of customer-separation tests in place, as well as a recycling test program of its corrugated containers.

The company also stated that, despite a commonly held misconception, McDonald's foam packaging represents a miniscule amount of all garbage in a typical municipal sanitary landfill and that all quick-service restaurant packaging represents less than 1/4 of 1 percent of solid waste. It explained that McDonald's foam packaging is chemically inert and harmless.

Ed Rensi, president of McDonald's USA, said, "We've been committed to preserving the environment from the very beginning, when our founder, Ray Kroc, started the tradition of picking up litter in the communities around our restaurants. That commitment continues today with our efforts to find real solutions to the solid-waste problem in this country such as this recycling program."

In a feature story called "Environmentalism: The New Crusade," *FORTUNE* magazine predicted that it may be the biggest business issue of the 1990s and reported how "smart companies are tackling it." It cited:

> McDonald's, which produces hundreds of millions of pounds of paper and plastic waste annually, has become a crusading proponent of recycling, and aims to become one of America's leading educators about environmental issues. The company is embarking on a major educational campaign and is describing its efforts and explaining recycling on the paper liners on customers' trays, in advertising, in brochures it hands out in stores and in mailings to school teachers. That's a lot of describing and explaining: McDonald's serves 18 million customers in the U.S. each day, making the tray liners one of the largest of the nation's mass media.[7]

The company's 1989 annual report, printed on recycled paper generated from McDonald's operations throughout the world, was dedicated to a detailed discussion of solid waste management, resource conservation, recycling, and other environmental challenges facing the world.

On Earth Day 1990, Ed Rensi announced "McCycle USA," calling it the largest single commitment in history, by anyone, to buy and use recycled material. Under the plan, McDonald's will buy $100 million in recycled construction materials for use in construction, renovation, exteriors, furnishings, and equipment for its restaurants. The company said this represents one quarter of its annual budget for building or remodeling about 1,400 restaurants in the United States. To facilitate the program, McDonald's established a toll-free telephone line for suppliers and manufacturers to call for information on how to qualify for the program. Rensi told the media that the new market McDonald's was creating for recycled materials was in addition to the millions of dollars the company spends on recycled-paper products and that the company will expand its polystyrene recycling program as soon as more recycling outlets become available.

Just three months after reinforcing its commitment to using foam packaging, McDonald's abruptly announced that it would replace its "clamshell" hamburger box, symbol of America's fast-food culture, with paper packaging. The announcement was front-page news everywhere and was covered extensively by all networks' news programs.

The New York Times cover story of November 2, 1990, headlined "Packaging and Public Image: McDonald's Fills a Big Order," said the change shows how "public pressure can affect the decision-making process of a company, particularly one as concerned about its image as McDonald's."

Edward Rensi, president of McDonald's USA told the media, "our customers just don't feel good about it, so we're changing." Appearing with Rensi was Frederick D. Krupp, executive director of the Environmental Defense Fund, a public interest group that had formed a joint task force with McDonald's to study the solid waste problem. Krupp told the media, "We hope this marks the turning of the tide in our throwaway society. McDonald's is a trendsetter. They see the future as green."

14

Special-Events Marketing

Just as modern public relations has its origins in publicity, what we now call special events is a sophisticated extension of the press agent's stunt. A decade ago, special events were largely created and staged by publicity people. The modern concept of special-events marketing began in earnest in the early 1980s.

In a 1981 article in *Harvard Business Review,* public relations counselor Art Stevens described the process that "promotes products by linking them to events, issues, or ideas of inherent interest to consumers." He contrasted traditional product publicity, which focuses on the product's features and benefits, with event sponsorship, which he labeled "brandstanding:"

> By selecting or engineering links that connect the product or brand to an event of public interest or an area of public concern, brandstanding establishes a rapport between consumers and a product.

Stevens listed six characteristics of an effective brandstanding program.

1. The event or issue linked to a product must invite publicity. There must be sufficient newsworthiness or feature-story interest to ensure media coverage.
2. The people attracted must be users or potential users of the product.
3. There must be a meaningful or necessary link between the product and the event. The event can be linked to the effect of using the product, it can be associated with a range of concerns or interests, or it can require proof of purchase.

4. The link should be evident but not intrusive. The product must be treated as subservient to the event or issue.

5. A concurrent program of promotion must support the effort. Many companies take a marketing-team approach, combining advertising, dealer promotions, point-of-purchase, displays, and other methods of publicity with brandstanding. These techniques work together to produce interest, awareness of the link to the product, and product acceptance.

6. Follow-up evaluation of results is important. Brand managers who have extensive experience with brandstanding may be able to judge results while the promotion is taking place. Those who are not veterans, however, may want to use more objective means of evaluating results, such as analyzing sales figures or surveying participant and spectator attitudes.[1]

SPECIAL EVENTS BECOME BIG BUSINESS

While the term *brandstanding* has not come into general usage, Stevens's prediction that "over the next few years, special-event promotion will be the fastest-growing segment of corporate promotion" was on the money, literally.

Today, special events are big business. Fueled by the success of such mega-events of the 1980s as the 1984 Los Angeles Olympics, the Statue of Liberty Centennial, Hands Across America, and Live Aid, marketers have turned to special events of all descriptions to cut through mass-media clutter and gain greater brand awareness and loyalty. According to International Events Group, publishers of "Special Events Report," more than 3,700 companies spent $1.8 billion in fees alone in 1988, to sponsor special events. That does not include money spent on advertising, promotion, and public relations activities supporting these sponsorships. It has been estimated that total event expenditures of U.S. companies tops $3 billion annually. The field is growing at a rate of 30 to 40 percent in this country, a growth paralleled in Europe and Asia. Special events have become such important weapons in the marketing arsenal that more than 300 companies, led by the beer, soft-drink, cigarette, and automotive companies, have set up their own in-house special-events departments.[2]

The big sponsors are increasingly moving toward single sponsorships, or "sponsownership," a term coined by Paul Stanley of PS Productions. *ADWEEK's Marketing Week* points out that "in the current corporate climate, getting a return on an investment is a concept that every manager can grasp and event ownership can provide a mechanism for generating profit from the event itself while remaining true to marketing objectives." A sponsor who controls the talent can control location, promotion, and such MPR considerations as personal and media appearances.

The explosion of special events has spawned a growing number of companies specializing in creating and staging events. In the sports field, these companies include not only the "Big Three"—International Management Group (IMG), ProServ Inc., and Advantage International Inc.—but more than 500 smaller companies.

Advertising agencies that see themselves as full-service providers of communications services have set up their own special-events units. Backer Spielvogel Bates spun off a wholly owned subsidiary, Custom Event Marketing, in 1987. BBDO combines special-events marketing with sales promotion in a subsidiary named Promotion Dynamics Worldwide. Likewise, FCB/Impact combines promotion and events. These agencies see in special events not only an opportunity to sell programs to their advertising clients but to bring in new clients.

If sales promotion executive William A. Robinson is correct, "event marketing will offer a fantastic opportunity to harness, mature, and mold a bright new technique for the 21st century." The importance of special events raises the inevitable question "Whose turf is it, anyway?" Will it be the province of in-house company specialists, events-marketing firms, advertising agencies or public relations firms? The answer probably is— or will be—all of the above, until the time when companies find a way to integrate all of their marketing communications activities.

MPR AND SPECIAL EVENTS

A number of public relations firms have established special-events departments. Burson-Marsteller says its credentials in sports- and entertainment-event marketing are "among the best in the world," citing the company's efforts in staging the 1984 Olypmic Torch Relays, producing the 1988 Festival of Lights Celebration in Calgary, and managing communications for the Seoul Olympic Organizing Committee. Burson also conceived, managed, and promoted the Frank Sinatra/ Sammy Davis, Jr./Lisa Minnelli cross-country tour on behalf of its client, American Express. The agency supports not only sports-marketing and entertainment divisions but has become a partner in a number of event properties and has been developing diagnostic tools to help companies match their product or service category with an appropriate event. In 1990, Burson acquired Ohlmeyer Sports Marketing and combined it with its own sports and event specialists to form The

Sports Partners, Inc., a firm that develops sports strategies for corporate clients, sells sponsorships, negotiates and packages TV rights, and creates, manages, and markets events.

Today, public relations firms and internal PR departments are increasing their activity in the special-events arena in a number of ways:

- Producing events from beginning to end
- Evaluating available event vehicles
- Counseling management on the best vehicles reaching target markets
- Developing charitable-event tie-ins
- Optimizing brand identification at the event
- Creating promotional materials
- Entertaining trade guests
- Merchandising events to employees
- Arranging pre-event local promotion and publicity
- Maximizing on-site media coverage of the event

FRANKEL'S SPECIAL-EVENTS SCREENS

The importance of public relations in the special-events mix is noted by Bud Frankel, founder and president of Frankel & Co., one of the country's leading sales-promotion firms. Frankel says that finding the right "image and personality fit is clearly the first order of business. Once having done that, success begins and ends with clearly articulated objectives—real, quantifiable objectives stated in terms of audiences—such as consumer, trade, and sales force—advertising, promotion, public relations, and of course sales and profit."

The screens that Frankel applies to evaluate special events clearly indicate the value that public and media relations add to special events.[3]

- Are the venues appropriate and accessible? Are there adequate facilities such as stage, sound, TV, and media coverage?
- What signage is planned? Are there opportunities to identify involvement as a sponsor?
- Will there be hospitality opportunities for special customers?
- Will there be media coverage? Are the telephone and communications facilities acceptable?

o If there is TV coverage, how will a sign appear during the event? Are the camera angles consistent with the placement of sponsor identification?

o Can the sponsor use celebrities? Will they make personal appearances at the event, in other markets, and in the media?

o Will there be special PR opportunities? Can they be created?

o Are there limits to what can be communicated to the trade, the sales force, and the customer, as a result of the sponsorship?

o Can special awards be created and presented publicly at the event?

RMV, RV, SP, AND MPR

The thin line between sales promotion and public relations was underscored by Don Schultz, professor of advertising at Northwestern University's Medill School of Journalism, in *Marketing News:*

> Marketers must move away from the traditional definition of sales promotion toward a focus on brand loyalty and share and volume growth through the strategic use of long-term or a series of short-term programmed events.[4]

He proposed a new approach to sales promotion that embraces two new concepts, both of which strongly support MPR goals. Residual market value (RMV) involves the image-producing communication about the product or service that remains after the promotional event is over. Relationship value (RV) is defined as the bonds, actual and perceptual, that are created among the consumer, the marketer, and the brand.

Seen in this context, MRP, sales promotion, and event marketing are traveling the same road toward total marketing.

15

The Sports Marketing Boom

Sports sponsorship is by far the special-events category most favored by corporate America, and it continues to grow at 25 to 30 percent a year. It currently represents 80 percent of all sponsorships. More than 3,400 U.S. companies spent $1.35 billion to sponsor sporting events in 1987. *Sports Marketing News* estimates that total annual sports spending by companies exceeds $6 billion if event sponsorships, athlete-endorsement contracts, and commercial time sold within sports telecasts are included.

The biggest annual sports spenders of 1987, according to *Special Events Report* included Philip Morris ($85 million) and Anheuser-Busch ($50 million). That year, before the LBO, R.J.R. Nabisco, led by sports nut Ross Johnson, spent $58 million. (The star-struck Johnson created a stable of celebrity athletes called Team Nabisco and paid millions to Frank Gifford, Don Meredith, O.J. Simpson, Alex Webster, Jack Nicklaus, Ben Crenshaw, Fuzzy Zoeller, Bobby Orr, Don Mattingly, and Reggie Jackson for occasional personal appearances and has spent $10 million a year on the Dinah Shore Golf Classic.)

In a cover story in August 1987, *Business Week* exclaimed, "Nothing Sells Like Sports." According to the article:

> Advertisers are aiming to get more bang for their marketing bucks by sponsoring the event itself rather than by just buying 30 seconds of air time during a sports show. . . . Sports marketers are interested in creating stable, long-term marketing equities—the sort of image-building that comes from linking up with a popular sport in the consumer's mind. . . . Many marketers like sponsorship because it's a soft sell. Instead of trying to persuade a customer through a standard sales pitch, sports marketing associates the product with something the customer likes.[1]

Alan Friedman, editor of *Team Marketing Report,* says:

"Sports will continue to be a viable marketing tool for corporate marketers. Professional sports, with its high visibility ensured because of new network television deals, will continue to be attractive to marketers looking to reach the demographic group that sports fans represent. . . . [But] accountability will be the buzzword for sports sponsorship and sports marketing in the 1990s. Sports teams and event promoters will be under increased pressure to develop an accepted method for measuring sponsorship value.

MPR MOVES THE SPORTS-MARKETING NEEDLE

Recent research has shown that "editorial" coverage of a TV sports event can be as effective or more effective than running the sponsor's commercials.

Counselor Steve Lesnik, who operates one of the larger sports-marketing organizations in the country in addition to one of the fastest-growing PR firms, recently commissioned a research firm to conduct a four-city study to measure public attitudes regarding a company's sponsorship of a series of family-oriented sporting events. Questions were asked of two groups. One group had seen the event as it was shown on TV, including commercials. The people who had viewed the telecast saw the CEO present trophies and make a warm, engaging little talk; heard well-known, credible sports announcers mention the company's name repeatedly in association with the event; witnessed admired international superstars express gratitude to the company and its CEO; and saw the company's logo intimately associated with the event and celebrities. The second group had seen the TV show without commercials.

Lesnik said that the research found rather conclusively that viewers of the telecast were more likely to respond favorably to questions about the sponsoring company than nonviewers. But in addition, viewers of the telecast who had not seen the company's commercials in the program responded as favorably and in some cases more favorably than viewers seeing the program with commercials. Confidence in the company was about 45 percent higher for both viewers who had seen and who had not seen commercials in the program, compared with consumers who had not seen the show at all. Viewers of the program were also more likely to think the sponsor's product "is good for children," an important measure to the sponsor.

On both general and specific questions, viewers exhibited decidedly improved attitudes that were even better if they had not seen the commercials. Lesnik's conclusion: "This research refutes the old saw that event sponsorship just creates a warm and fuzzy plus or that advertising moves research needles and PR doesn't."

Barry Frank, senior corporate vice president of International Management Group and the country's leading authority on sports marketing, emphasizes the role of public relations in sports marketing:

> When a company spends hundreds of thousands or even millions of dollars to sponsor an event, it seems rather foolish to me not to spend the additional relatively small amount required to tell people you're doing so. Public relations is the final ingredient required to ensure the success of the buy; to fail to use PR seems kind of like buying a car without the engine: it still looks pretty but it won't go very far.

A CASE IN POINT: WHEATIES AND SPORTS SINCE 1933

The identification of sports with popular brand names, rediscovered in the 1980s, has been effectively used for decades. One of the pioneers was the association of Wheaties with baseball. In 1933, nine years after the cereal was first introduced by General Mills, Wheaties first ventured into the sports world as sponsor of play-by-play baseball broadcasts. That year, too, marked the creation of a slogan that became one of the most popular ever in advertising history: "Wheaties—The Breakfast of Champions."

Wheaties' baseball broadcasts were immensely popular throughout the 1930s. From one station they expanded to 95, spreading to teams and cities throughout the country. Athlete testimonials were a key part of the "Breakfast of Champions" broadcast package.

Wheaties sponsored the first televised commercial sports broadcast on August 29, 1939, when NBC presented a game between the Cincinnati Reds and the Brooklyn Dodgers for some 500 owners of television sets in New York City. Red Barber handled the commentary for the inaugural baseball broadcast.

Wheaties' broadcasts led to the film career of "Dutch" Reagan, a Des Moines, Iowa, sportscaster who made play-by-play recreations of Chicago Cubs games using telegraph reports. In 1937, Reagan was voted the most popular Wheaties announcer in the country and was rewarded with a trip to the Cubs' training camp in California. There he took a Warner Brothers screen test and subsequently became a popular film star. He later went into politics and was elected Governor of California and then the 40th president of the United States.

Wheaties' popularity boomed during the 1930s, and the cereal became synonymous with all branches of the sports world. Testimonials by great athletes such as Babe Ruth, Jack Dempsey, Red Grange, Bronco Nagurski, Otto Graham, Babe Didrikson, Patty Berg, Sam Snead, Ben Hogan, and George Mikan made Americans aware of the product.

The Wheaties Sports Federation

In 1956, General Mills sought a spokesperson to present the Wheaties story. From more than 500 candidates, two-time Olympic pole-vaulting champion Bob Richards, a well-known crusader for fitness, was chosen. The Wheaties Sports Federation was established with Richards as director. The organization worked closely with such groups as the U.S. Olympic Committee, the U.S. Junior Chamber of Commerce, and the President's Council on Youth Fitness to promote sports and athletic participation throughout the country. The Federation produced a large number of instructional and educational films, which were made available free to the public. It gave direct financial support to such activities as Olympic educational programs and the Jaycee Junior Champ track-and-field competition.

Bob Richards served as product spokesperson from 1956 until 1970. Beginning in 1977, Olympic decathlon champion Bruce Jenner took over as director of the Wheaties Sports Federation. Throughout the remainder of the 1970s, Wheaties' philosophy became one of promoting physically fit individuals rather than simply appealing to sports fans. Sports such as swimming, skiing, tennis, and golf were prominent on packages.

In 1983, Wheaties introduced its "Search for Champions" contest. Maintaining the decades-long tradition of Wheaties' sports association, the Search also featured the opportunity for amateur athletes to be nationally recognized on the covers of Wheaties packages. Donations of $1 per ballot were made to organizations sponsoring the top 50 candidates. More than 50,000 entries were received in the first year and the event has been repeated. Wheaties' Search for Champions was named one of the eight best programs of the decade by the editors of *Promote*.

Three years later, the brand initiated a sports award to recognize athletes for their sports accomplishments and their contributions off the field. Candidates were nominated by sports journalists and selected by a blue-ribbon judging panel. Chris Evert appeared on packages during 1987 as first recipient of the Wheaties Champions Award.

SUDS AND SPORTS

The link between the beer business and the sports world is so pervasive today that, in August 1988, *Sports Illustrated* ran a cover story on "Suds and Sports."

The magazine put it this way:

> Nothing loves suds like a sports fan loves suds. This is an indelible fact of contemporary American anthropology. It is a matter of demographic statistics. It is blessed chapter and verse in U.S. brewers' bibles of marketing

and advertising. It is the reason that almost every kind of sporting event—from a rinky-dink hometown road race to the Olympic Games—is played out, as often as not, in an environment of beer slogans, beer signs, beer songs and beer salesmanship.[2]

Sports has played a pivotal role in the ascendancy of both Miller Beer and Anheuser-Busch. Miller was the seventh-ranked beer when it was acquired by Philip Morris in 1970. With Philip Morris money and marketing know-how, Miller became deeply involved in TV sports and by the late 1970s was buying more than half of all beer commercial time on network sports programming. Miller Lite, with its funny, macho, over-the-hill-gang commercials, climbed to second place among all U.S. beer brands. In 1977, Anheuser-Busch got into the act in a major way, increasing its share of the national beer market from 22 to 40 percent. A-B marketing chief Mike Roarty said, "We think that came about largely because of our concentration on sports—plus, of course, the quality and consistency of our product."

In addition to football, baseball, basketball, motor sports, horse racing, boxing, tennis, golf, bowling, and track-and-field events on network TV, A-B sponsors "about a thousand individual events, competitions, and leagues" according to Roarty. They range from the Budweiser U.S. Pro Tour of Surfing and Body Boarding to the Bud Lite Ironman Triathlon World Championship in Hawaii to the Michelob Night Riders cycling circuit to the Carlsberg single-handed, round-the-world sailing race. The Triathalon was picked for Bud Lite when it was introduced in 1981 because it fit the desired image of a healthful low-calorie but macho product. The combination of swimming, cycling, and running, new at the time, fit the bill, and the Triathalon has moved from a novelty to a popular spectator and participant sport.

A-B is, of course, not alone in its sponsorship of all manner of sports events. Miller's largest commitment is to motor racing, but, according to *Sports Illustrated*, Miller also puts sponsorship money into a sports potpourri that includes tractor pulls, ski racing, and NBA All-Star balloting, and offers a million dollars to anyone on the pro bowlers' tour who wins a three-tournament parlay called the Lite Slam. Miller gains greater visibility for its NASCAR (National Association for Stock Car Auto Racing) sponsorship by displaying a duplicate of its car in shopping centers and other retail outlets, to attract crowds and interest in the race. Miller also sponsors "bathing beauty" contests in local bars to promote its pro beach volleyball tournaments. These tournaments are currently attracting average crowds of 25,000 at waterside sites all over the country and media coverage such as a *TIME* story, "Beach Volleyball Nets Big Bucks."

Coors underwrites softball, rodeos, and the Coors International Bicycle Classic; Old Style took over the Chicago marathon when the marathon's founding sponsor Beatrice Foods was taken over in an LBO; and other beer sports sponsorships continue to proliferate.

MCDONALD'S SPORTS MARKETING

McDonald's Corporation has become a major sports sponsor. The stated objective is to capitalize on sports and special-events opportunities to help build brand distinctiveness, brand presence, and brand preference for McDonald's on national and local levels. McDonald's sports-marketing activities encompass gymnastics, track, figure skating, golf, and basketball.

The company applies the following screens to evaluate a sports program:

- Does it enhance McDonald's leadership position?
- Does it deliver national TV presence?
- Can McDonald's own it?
- Does it help McDonald's stand out from the clutter?
- Does it provide local extensions?

Since its inception in 1977, nomination and selection to the McDonald's All-American High School Basketball Team has become one of the most prestigious honors for high school players. The team is composed of the top high-school-senior basketball players in the nation. It starts with the naming of the 1,500 most outstanding senior players, nominated by a committee of high school basketball coaches. From this group, the field is narrowed to 25 McDonald's All-Americans. Members of the "Dream Team" have included such greats as Michael Jordan, Ervin ("Magic") Johnson, Mark Aguirre, Ralph Sampson, Isaiah Thomas, and James Worthy. The McDonald's All-American High School Basketball game is the only event that brings together the best high school players from the East to compete against the best of the West. The proceeds from the game are donated to a local children's charity in the city where the game is played.

The event guarantees McDonald's network visibility and offers opportunities for local and regional publicity on sports pages and television sports broadcasts for all players nominated and selected for the team.

THE NASCAR WINSTON RACING SERIES

NASCAR is the largest motor-sports-sanctioning body in the world. People know NASCAR best because of the Winston Cup Series of championship stock car racing. The best drivers, teams, and cars compete all season long, in a total of 29 events in 16 cities, for the coveted Winston Cup. The event, the largest and most popular form of weekly racing, was described by CBS's "60 Minutes" as "the World Series and Super Bowl" of racing. Sponsors of the event position their product in front of 2.5 million fans in the grandstands and beam it to radio audiences (80 million) and television viewers (more than 175 million). In addition, every event is covered by the Associated Press, United Press International, and major newspapers, especially those in the southeast where NASCAR is king.

The December 1989 "60 Minutes" piece on veteran racer Richard Petty featured a parade of marketing executives not only from Petty's longtime sponsor STP, but such non-car-related products as Gatorade and Heinz Ketchup. All of them agreed that NASCAR sponsorship is one of the surest ways to move merchandise off the shelf. Racing fans are notoriously loyal to the brands that sponsor their heroes. Not only do they buy these products, but they advertise them on their hats, shirts, jackets, and T-shirts.

T. Wayne Robertson, senior vice president of RJR Nabisco's Sports Marketing Enterprises, Inc., says in NASCAR's flyer:

> R.J. Reynolds Tobacco USA's NASCAR sponsorship began in 1970, and we have been first-hand witnesses to stock car racing's dramatic growth into a major league sport. NASCAR Winston Cup events enjoy record crowds year after year, increasing our equity as a major sponsor. The Winston brand's association with NASCAR is almost universally recognized among racing fans and they acknowledge our sponsorship at the cigarette counter.

RJR has lots of good corporate company. Other major NASCAR sponsors include Anheuser-Busch, Piedmont Airlines, Sears, General Foods, Miller Brewing, Procter & Gamble, Eastman Kodak, PepsiCo, Quaker Oats, Coca-Cola, and Kraft, as well as automotive-related sponsors like STP, General Motors, Ford, Toyota, Mobil, AMOCO, Unocal 76, Goodyear Tire and Rubber Company, and Champion Spark Plug Company.

In its promotional piece to sponsors, NASCAR lists 17 "most popular methods of sponsorships":

○ Sponsorship of a car
○ Sponsorship of a driver
○ Car-and-driver combined sponsorship
○ Track sponsorship
○ Family-night sponsorship

- Series sponsorship
- Single-event sponsorship
- Lap sponsorship
- High-performance sponsorship
- Trackside-billboard advertising
- Program advertising
- Prize-money sponsorship
- Trophy-and-award sponsorship
- Corporate hospitality-area sponsorship
- VIP-suite sponsorship
- Grandstand-section sponsorship
- "Sponsorship of ironic occurrences"[3]

U.S. News & World Report sums up why these companies lap up these kinds of sponsorships: "Madison Avenue is recognizing what Detroit knew 30 years ago—stock-car racing sells products."

HOW MPR SUPPORTS TITLE SPONSORSHIPS

With the proliferation of competing television sports events and softening advertising support, the networks who once shied away from plugging an event's sponsor are now offering new opportunities for companies to own title to once untouchable big events. Buying title sponsorship helps advertisers avoid being part of the clutter of 30-second spots. During the college "Bowl" season of 1989–1990, viewers were able to enjoy such postseason classics as the John Hancock Sun Bowl, the Sunkist Fiesta Bowl, the Mazda Gator Bowl, the USF&G Sugar Bowl, the Federal Express Orange Bowl, the Mobil Cotton Bowl, and the Sea World Holiday Bowl.

The sun went down when John Hancock acquired title sponsorship by buying 25 percent of the commercial spots. As part of the deal, the company's logo faced the TV cameras on the 50-yard line. As part of its Sugar Bowl package, USF&G gained exposure at the event's festival via a regatta, an intramural flag-football competition, and a basketball tournament.

The print media have tended to look skeptically on the practice of title sponsorship linked to the TV ad buy and to drop the sponsor's name in their sports coverage unless the sponsor's name is inseparable from the event's name. That is why sophisticated users of MPR make certain that they capitalize on sponsorships by planning newsworthy activities around the event.

OLYMPIAN EXPOSURE

Every four years, corporations scramble to become official sponsors of the Olympic Games. Other companies have created astute public relations programs as an alternative to official sponsorship.

In 1984, AT&T outdistanced scores of sponsors who paid dearly to be called the official whatever of the Los Angeles Summer Games. The company sponsored a 9,100-mile, coast-to-coast, hand-to-hand, Olympic-torch relay that generated massive national and local exposure from May, when a special celebration launched the relay in New York, to August, when the torch was lit in a moving ceremony at the Olympic Stadium in Los Angeles.

The event occurred shortly after the breakup of the Bell system, and AT&T was, in effect, a "new company" to much of America. The Torch Relay helped establish the company's identity and new logo across the country.

The Wall Street Journal reported that research showed that every potential long-distance-phone-service customer was aware of the relay, that half were aware that AT&T had sponsored it, and that a strong correlation existed between those who recognized the company's sponsorship and those who would be inclined to choose it as their long-distance company. Clearly, the relay was "the right choice" for AT&T.

The relay turned out to be a public relations coup for the company, according to Charles L. Mitchell, Jr., PR director of AT&T Communications. He said that it "helped establish AT&T's new identity during a period of unprecedented competition and change in the industry."

"The Olympic torch relay for the first time gave corporate sponsors and individuals the opportunity to participate in the Olympics in a meaningful and emotionally involving way," according to Al Schreiber, director of event marketing at Burson-Marsteller, who managed the project.

Burson expects Olympics-related sponsorship activity to amount to 5 to 10 percent of its total worldwide fee income in 1992 when it will represent Ricöh Corporation, Coca-Cola Company, and the U.S. Postal Service as well as the U.S. Olympic Committee in Barcelona and Albertville, France, sites of the '92 summer and winter games.

Waste Management Cleans Up at Calgary

In order to finance the 1988 Winter Olympics at Calgary, Alberta, Canada, the Olympic Organizing Committee approached major American and Canadian firms and offered exclusive rights to use and market the Olympics in their industries as well as to obtain special on-site privileges at the games. Twenty-two companies, including such major players as General Motors, Kodak, Visa, IBM, and Coca-Cola became "official sponsors"; 26 others were "official suppliers" and 41 more were "official licensees."

Standing out from the crowd presented a major MPR challenge, particularly for one of the least glamorous suppliers. Cleaning up the mess of some 1.5 million spectators at a combination of indoor, outdoor, and mountain-top events at Calgary was the responsibility of Waste Management, Inc., the "official supplier of Waste Management Services for the XVth Olympic Winter Games." Waste Management wanted national and local print and broadcast publicity underscoring the company's ability to professionally manage trash tasks large and small.

Golin/Harris focused its efforts on publicizing John Lavender, who headed the company's garbage detail, and labeling him "Garbageman of the Olympics." The media received an irreverent, but informative, press kit including releases titled, "Trash Trivia," "Rules of Trash," and "When It's Thirty Below Zero, Taking Out the Trash Is an Olympic Task." The humorous approach to the company's clean-up assignment worked. Scores of features about Waste Management's sponsorship appeared in U.S. and Canadian newspapers and television sportscasts.

Seagram's Coolers Send the Families

The Seagram Beverage Company developed an alternative to official sponsorship of the 1988 Summer Olympics that won public approval and attracted widespread media attention to its Seagram's Coolers.

The Seagram's Coolers "Send the Families" program sent 550 family members, one for each athlete in 23 participating sports, to Seoul, Korea, for the 1988 Summer Games. The company described the program as "Seagram's Coolers' effort to reward the team behind the team—the families of U.S. Olympic athletes." A key public relations component was a giant greeting card that traveled 9,000 miles across the country, collecting 50,000 signatures and 200 million media impressions.

After the card's debut in New York, it traveled to 30 U.S. cities. In each city, it was the focus of special events hosted by members of the Seagram's Coolers' American Team Family Fund Advisory Board members, including company executives headed by House of Seagram president Edgar Bronfman, Jr., and former Olympic greats Wilma Rudolph, Carl Lewis, Rafer Johnson, and Bob Mathias. The combined MPR, "Send the Families" advertising, and sales promotion resulted in a 15 to 20 percent Seagram's Coolers sales increase over the previous year.

THAT'S ENTERTAINMENT

Barry Frank, senior corporate vice president of International Marketing Group (IMG), says, "In my experience client entertainment is one of the key reasons for and uses of event sponsorship. The ability to isolate and then entertain important clients in what is usually a desirable location, in an atmosphere of television cameras, sports writers, and glamour and to have these clients rub elbows with star athletes and sometimes compete with them in pro-ams is invaluable. Many firms actually choose events based on their site and the kind of customer turnout that site will attract."

Golf is the most popular and the biggest sponsorship in all of sports. Frank points out that every single event on the PGA tour and most of those on the LPGA tour have a complete title sponsor. A company may spend well over a million dollars to "buy the event" and like amount in television sponsorship. The client-entertainment factor was a key for Federal Express, who chose to sponsor the Orange Bowl because it is played in Miami, Florida.

NutraSweet paid a significant additional amount of money to have the "NutraSweet World Challenge of Champions," a major figure-skating event televised by ABC, held in Moscow in December 1989. NutraSweet wants to crack the Soviet Union with their product, and this event enabled them to illustrate to several key Soviet ministers and their guests the sincerity of their desire.

WOMEN'S SPORTS

Philip Morris became one of the earliest title sponsors when it committed Virginia Slims, its cigarette aimed specifically at the young, upscale woman, to sponsor the first women's professional tennis tour. Marketing public relations played a major role in making Virginia Slims synonymous with women's tennis. In those days, before Chris and Martina and Steffi were known to the multitudes, it was essential to introduce the players to the public and to develop excitement about women's tennis as a spectator sport.

The company's public relations firm, Ruder & Finn, designed a program to reach the media with stories and angles of interest that extended far beyond match results and sports pages. The publicity generated during the early years of the Virginia Slims circuit contributed greatly to the gain of popularity and attendance at women's tournaments. The Virginia Slims media guide, published annually and containing tournament results, earnings, and season and lifetime records of all the players, became the encyclopedia of women's tennis and served as an invaluable tool for sports media and the tennis establishment. A kick-off media luncheon was held every year in New York and a luncheon hosted by Philip Morris and honoring female athletes was held in each tournament city weeks before the local event. Charity tie-ins were arranged in each city to create publicity on newspaper pages other than sports pages and to identify the Virginia Slims tour with the local community.

The circuit brought widespread recognition to Virginia Slims entirely through nonadvertising channels. Despite the ban on cigarette advertising on television, the Virginia Slims Tournament was covered by network television. Virginia Slims became the pioneer in women's sports marketing, bringing the advertising slogan, "You've Come a Long Way, Baby," to life.

By 1987 the purses for women's tennis amounted to more than $18 million, and Virginia Slims was still the sport's largest sponsor, underwriting several individual events and the grand finale $1 million world-championship series each November. In return, "Virginia Slims gets worldwide publicity and an opportunity to sample adult audiences and to spin off retail promotions," according to Ellen Merlo, vice president of marketing promotion for Philip Morris USA. She says, "Sponsorship of the right sporting events will deliver the consumer groups you want in a place they choose to be."

Cigarette Sponsorship under Fire

Virginia Slims' sponsorship of women's professional tennis came under fire in 1990 when U.S. Secretary of Health and Human Services Dr. Louis Sullivan joined a coalition of health groups to protest the sponsorship. He said that cigarette sponsorship of sporting events like Slims' tennis implies that "smoking is compatible with good health." He called on tobacco companies to drop their sponsorships of all sports events and asked athletes not to participate in tobacco-backed events. Sullivan's pronouncement coincided with his attack on cigarette companies for targeting minorities, women, and young people. He specifically blasted R.J. Reynolds for its plan (leaked to the *Washington Post*) to market a cigarette called Dakota to working-class women.

A Philip Morris spokesman rejected the criticism, saying the company does not ask players to endorse smoking. He was supported by top-ranked tennis player Zina Garrison, who told AP, "Philip Morris has always been a classy organization, real good to us. They've done a lot for women's tennis and, as they say, women's tennis has come a long way, and they've been the reason." Billie Jean King says the company lifted women's tennis from stepchild status and helped bring it wealth, power, and prestige.

The New York Times pointed out that "the involvement of cigarettes and sports goes back so far that baseball may even owe part of its vocabulary to tobacco: 'bullpen,' some baseball historians say, derives from Bull Durham signs tacked on the outfield walls." According to the article, "Cigarette Wars Move to a New Arena," the interest of the cigarette companies became particularly intense after January 1, 1971, when the ban of televised tobacco advertising took effect. Both the Virginia Slims tournaments and R.J. Reynolds' Winston Cup began that year. Other sports sponsorships cited are Vantage Gold Scoreboard, Salem Pro-Sail Races, Lucky Strike bowling, the Winston Rodeo, Benson & Hedges on Ice, and Marlboro Cup horse racing.

The *Times* noted that cigarette signs and billboards are strategically placed at these televised events as well as at major league baseball games, and they are seen by large television audiences. For example, Reynolds' sponsorship of the 1986 World Cup in Mexico City enabled the company to post signs for its Camel brand near the field and in view of a worldwide TV audience of 650 million. Antismoking advocates believe that this kind of signage may violate the law banning TV cigarette advertising.

The battle lines are forming. Critics say that sports sponsorships identify sports with health and the tobacco companies defend their sponsorships as providing entertainment.

The L'eggs Mini Marathon

In 1978, L'eggs Products, Inc., became the sponsor of the original long-distance road race for women. Over the years, the L'eggs Mini Marathon has grown to be the world's most prestigious 10K running event for women. The finish line, with its highly visible L'eggs logo, is shown in Figure 15–1.

In 1972, the first Mini Marathon drew only 78 women runners to New York's Central Park; in 1989, over 9,000 women participated in the 18th running. Mary Gilbert, L'eggs PR manager, says, "The sport of women's road racing has taken great strides since the first Mini Marathon. It is no longer viewed as just a passing phase. Women now receive the respect and regard they deserve." She says that L'eggs sponsors running because it appeals to women at all levels of athletic proficiency from novices to the world's best.

It is now one part of a comprehensive L'eggs Running and Fitness Program that offers clinics and fitness events designed to help women achieve personal fitness goals and prepare for the L'eggs Mini Marathon. They include:

○ A New Runner/New Racer Clinic

○ Pregnancy and Fitness Clinic

○ The Annual Mother's Day 5K Tune-Up Run

○ The Little L'eggs Fun Run for girls ages 2–6

○ A L'eggs Master clinic for women over 40

○ A L'eggs Women's Running and Fitness Exposition

FIGURE 15–1 The L'eggs Mini Marathon has grown to be the world's most prestigious 10K running event for women. It is part of a comprehensive program designed by L'eggs Products to encourage women to take advantage of all the physical, social, and emotional benefits of running.

MPR plays a major role in the success of the program. It is used to keep up the status of the race and to reach sports fans who are pantyhose buyers across the country. The Mini creates excitement around the product, and newspaper sportswriters never seem to tire of turning a phrase around the fact that "our name is L'eggs and you use legs to run," Mary Gilbert says.

Publicity for the entire L'eggs Mini Marathon program in 1989 generated more than 215 million consumer impressions, according to Golin/Harris, who conducts the public relations program. The event was covered on ABC's "Wide World of Sports" and consumers were reached through a wide range of media outlets including sports, news, life-style, and women's health and fitness. A 1986 publicity coup found the Mini featured on the front page of the *Times* twice: A photo of the Little L'eggs Fun Run in May and another of the Mini itself appeared in June.

FIGURE SKATING SPONSORSHIPS

Campbell Soup and NutraSweet also concentrate their sports-marketing efforts on a single sport, figure skating.

Campbell believes that the sport provides a natural link with soup's warming properties and nutrition benefits. In 1982, the company became the first national sponsor of the U.S. Figure Skating Team. Campbell's goal has been to make amateur figure skating an accessible and enjoyable activity for participants as well as spectators. To reach this goal, Campbell has become involved in many areas of figure skating.

In 1984, the Campbell Kids, the company's famous advertising characters, ventured on the ice for the first time to show the company's support for the Winter Olympics at Saravejo, Yugoslavia, where Campbell's was the official soup. Since then, five-time U.S. Ice Dance Champions Jim and Judy Sladky frequently have performed wearing Campbell Kid costumes.

Campbell has sponsored Skate America, which has featured rising skating stars from all over the world, since its inception in 1982. Annually it stages "Campbell's Soup on Ice," to help the local press better understand figure skating and prepare for the upcoming National Championships. Favorite amateur skaters perform in a free exhibition while expert commentators explain the technical aspects of figure skating, scoring, and judging. This event not only helps the media do a better job in reporting the competition, but it affords Campbell the opportunity to gain pre-event TV, radio, and newspaper features. This includes interviews with Campbell-preferred athletes like Debi Thomas and Jill Trenary, who always discuss why nutritious soup is part of a skater's fitness diet. These preferred athletes also are featured in video news releases that are distributed nationally to news and sports programs.

The company is also the sponsor of the Campbell's Soup Tour of World Figure Skating Champions, a traveling exhibition featuring Olympic medalists and other world-class figure skaters. In 1989, the coast-to-coast tour visited 30 cities. In each, trade receptions were held where key customers and their families were entertained and had a chance to meet and get autographs from the skating stars. The 1989 World Tour was attended by more than 400,000 consumers, was aired on ABC's "Wide World of Sports" and generated excellent local media coverage in each of the 30 tour cities.

To enhance its brand awareness and help spectators better understand the sport, Campbell publishes a free "Campbell Soup's Spectator's Guide to Figure Skating" in conjunction with the United States Figure Skating Association. It ties its product with its skating sponsorships by conducting an annual Sports Medicine Seminar that provides skaters, parents, coaches, and the public with timely information on nutrition and other issues affecting the health of figure skaters. The company also publishes a monthly "Food for Thought" column dealing with diet and nutrition subjects in *Skating,* the official publication of the U.S. Figure Skating Association.

Another company that spends its sports budget on figure skating is the NutraSweet Company. Their TV sponsorship of the NutraSweet World Professional Figure Skating Championships and the NutraSweet World Challenge of Champions, plus the U.S. National Championships, has helped the company drive itself past rival artificial sweetener Sweet and Low despite a late start in the market.

To enhance its identification with skating, the company created NutraSweet Ice Skating Month in 1985. This family-oriented event is celebrated in every ice rink in the country. Rink owners are given a do-it-yourself kit that enables them to promote, publicize, and put on NutraSweet Skate Days in their rinks. On those days, NutraSweet offers free skate rental, time, lessons, and hot NutraSweet-sweetened cocoa.

GATORADE AND SPORTS PERFORMANCE

In the 1960s a team of researchers at the University of Florida developed a product that would rapidly replace fluids and loss of body salts brought about by physical exertion. The formula was tested on members of the university's football team. The University of Florida Gators enjoyed a winning season in 1965 and became known as a second-half team because of its endurance and efficiency. When the Gators defeated their opponents in the Orange Bowl, the losing coach said, "We didn't have Gatorade. That made the difference." The quote was picked up in *Sports Illustrated,* launching the phenomenal sales success of Gatorade and a quarter of a century of involvement with sports.

Media exposure continues to be integral to Gatorade sports sponsorships. The sight of their pro-football heroes drinking Gatorade from the familiar green cups during NFL telecasts reminds millions of fans of the product's benefits in achieving peak performance. H&K's Bob Dilenschneider recalls the agenda that was created to make Gatorade "a part of the game itself":

> If you want amateur athletes to buy Gatorade because it rehydrates you, show Heisman Trophy winners chugging it down when they have just finished an eighty-yard dash to the end zone. So, on the sidelines, we put huge chests of Gatorade with the trademark on the chest and added stacks of Gatorade cups. As television added more sideline reaction shots and personal coverage of the players, televised football became a continuous promotion for Gatorade. It was the teams themselves that launched the ritual of dousing winning coaches with Gatorade or ice water from the Gatorade chests.

In addition to the NFL, Gatorade is the official thirst quencher, or sports beverage, of the NBA, U.S. Swimming, PGA, LPGA, and NASCAR. Gatorade also has individual sponsorship agreements with nearly all NFL and NBA teams, which enable the brand to obtain exposure not only through signage but through local charity tie-ins and branded-item giveaways on special Gatorade days.

The PGA agreement includes sponsorship of 20 Gatorade Youth Golf Clinics prior to 20 PGA tour events every year. Gatorade's NASCAR sponsorship includes the Gatorade 200, held annually in Darlington, South Carolina. Other pro sponsorships include the LPGA/Gatorade Rookie of the Year award and the Gatorade Slam Dunk Championship held during NBA All-Star weekend.

Gatorade sponsorships also permeate the college and high school ranks. The company is an official sponsor of the NCAA, providing visual opportunities in all sports, and is the official sponsor of a number of high school athletic associations. The Gatorade Circle of Champions program, inaugurated in 1985, honors state, regional, and national winners in seven sports each year. Nearly 350 high school athletes were inducted into the Gatorade Circle of Champions during the 1989–1990 school year. The program, which is administered by *Scholastic Coach Magazine*, generates tremendous publicity nationally and in each of the markets where local athletes are honored.

Another key to Gatorade's commercially successful identification with sports is the leadership position it has taken in supporting the athletic training community at all levels. The link is important because athletic trainers are responsible for the treatment and prevention of athletic injuries, of which heat illness is the most common. As a result,

Gatorade is the official sponsor of the Professional Athletic Trainers Association, the National Basketball Trainers Association, the Professional Baseball Athletic Trainers Association, and the National Athletic Trainers Association. The company publishes media guides annually for the football, basketball, and baseball trainers, providing sports media with biographical information about the trainers of each league team.

The ultimate objective for nearly all of Gatorade's sports-marketing activities is to maintain and extend the product's sideline, courtside, and dugout visibility, according to Patti Jo Sinopoli, Gatorade's manager of sports communication. She points out that this has successfully aligned Gatorade with the product's target users, 12- to 43-year-old physically active males. How well is it working? Ms. Sinopoli points out that Gatorade has become Quaker Oats Company's number-one selling product.

AVOIDING SPORTS CLUTTER

Motor sports, golf, running, and tennis currently attract the greatest share of the sports sponsorship dollar. However, H. Kent ("Bud") Stanner, senior corporate vice president of International Management Group, believes that "the major professional sports and the recreational sports, like golf and tennis, will get their share of clutter, and smart marketers will move into leisure and life-style activities like bicycling and swimming."

ADWEEK says that it can be tough for corporate sponsors to find a sport that is not already "cluttered with logos and brand names":

> That's why so many marketing vice presidents have been sighted rummaging among the likes of triathlons for kids, polo circuits, steeplechases, volleyball championships, skydiving competitions, luge circuits, and ice-surfing tournaments. Even underwater hockey has been said to exert its soggy charm.[4]

Sponsorship opportunities in new-to-sponsorship sports like these enable companies to become identified with an affordable sport that appeals to target consumer groups. Sometimes the rationale is a stretch. NYNEX Corp. signed on as sponsor of the U.S. Luge Team because "luge is a new sport in the U.S. whose team is trying to make a name for itself on the international front. We saw that as an analogy of NYNEX," the company explained.

On-Premise Fun and Games

Newsweek ran a story on October 30, 1989, on corporate sponsorships of childhood games titled "Not Just Kid Stuff Anymore." "With the costs of backing big-time sports going through the roof, companies looking for a cheap marketing boost are putting grown-up money behind childhood games—everything from Wiffle ball and double dutch to 'finger-flick' football."

A color photo showed contestants participating in a Finger-Flick Football Tournament, sponsored by Southern Comfort, in bars around the country. Some 125,000 players vie annually for a trip to compete in the "Unbelieva Bowl" at New York's Downtown Athletic Club, site of that other prestigious football event, the Heisman Trophy awards ceremony. Unbelieva Bowl I was attended by Magic Johnson, assuring TV and other media coverage. The brand's share increased 8 percent during the promotion, according to Dan Edelman, whose firm conducted the program. Unbelieva Bowl II merited front page coverage in *The Wall Street Journal*. The *Journal* reported that "like any other bowl game—the Federal Express Orange Bowl or the Mobil Cotton Bowl—finger-flick football has not been able to escape the clutches of corporate sponsorship. Huge signs for Southern Comfort cover nearly every exploitable inch of the stadium. The sponsor must thank a handful of the employees at Edelman Sports, part of the Daniel J. Edelman worldwide public relations agency, for popularizing the sport for its client."[5] Southern Comfort has also successfully sponsored the national nerf basketball championships.

Another successful public relations engineered on-premise (beverage-industry talk for bars and restaurants, as opposed to supermarkets and liquor stores) program is the Canadian Mist Thumb Wrestling Tournament. It was created by the Edelman firm to build brand awareness through media attention, promote product trial, and strengthen the ties among manufacturer, distributor, and customer.

The PR firm set the rules for the 60-second match and added to the fun by creating the International Thumb Wrestling Federation, which sanctions the Canadian Mist Thumb Wrestling Tournament as its first and only tournament. More than 1,000 bars and restaurants ran tournaments. Each received an instructional videotape explaining how to run a tournament, posters, T-shirts, buttons, table tents touting the tournament's official drink, and the officially sanctioned wrestling arena. Male and female thumb wrestlers participated in regional playoffs and national finals, a media event complete with sports celebrities.

The event attracted print coverage in media as diverse as *The Wall Street Journal, The Sporting News,* and *The New Yorker* and was carried on "CBS Morning News" and on the network feeds of all three national networks—no mean trick considering the ban on alcoholic beverage TV advertising. The tournaments also provided an occasion for Canadian Mist tastings, a strategy that resulted in increased orders and in the opening of hundreds of new accounts.

Nintendo Crowns Video Wizards

A new fun-and-games World Championship was inaugurated in 1990 by the electronic game sensation, Nintendo. Nintendo of America said it anticipated that over one million players would participate in the Nintendo World Championships. That is not unrealistic, considering the fact that one out of every four U.S. homes now has a Nintendo system. The challenge includes competitions in three age groups from 11 years and under to adult. All entrants compete in three events: Super Mario Brothers, Road Racer, and Tetris.

Nintendo, a nearly $3 billion brand that reignited the video-game boom in the United States, believes the championship 30-city tour will keep the phenomenon going. *ADWEEK's Marketing Week* said that "with the Nintendo World Championship (NWC), Nintendo has turned a product into an event" and described the event as so big that five major-brand marketers have paid entry fees to associate with another brand's success. William White, Nintendo's director of advertising said:

> We've been struggling with how to harness the competitive energy of the Nintendo player base. The key is entertainment quality. We have to continue to excite the market and NWC is a way to do that.[6]

The Nintendo World Championships won *Promote* magazine's event-marketing grand prize for 1990. The magazine reported that more than 300,00 people attended the event, with another 378 million consumers exposed to Nintendo through the ensuing publicity.

Many press organizations treated the championships like an Olympic event. In Cleveland spots on the competition aired 27 times in three days. In New York City, 3 stations ran live remotes. Even the *New Yorker* magazine ran a piece on the Nintendo phenomenon. During the event, a special 900 number set up to provide information about the tour drew 10,000 calls per month.

The tour was credited with boosting first-half sales by 30 percent.

16

MPR, the Arts, and Entertainment

Public relations counselor Herbert Schmertz suggests that "corporate citizens have a responsibility to support and strengthen the society that permits us all to flourish . . . by supporting nonprofit institutions that enrich the quality of our lives."

In his book *Good-Bye to the Low Profile,* the former Mobil Corporation public relations chief and father of public-television sponsorship also suggests eight more directly self-serving reasons for corporations to be active in supporting the arts and culture.

First, cultural excellence generally suggests corporate excellence. Invariably, your support of first-rate programs in the arts and culture will significantly enhance the image of your company. If you undertake enough of these projects and you execute them well, you can, over time, convey the idea that your corporation is associated only with excellence.

Second, these discretionary projects offer the opportunity to present your top management not as narrow-minded experts, but rather as corporate statesmen whose concerns go beyond the bottom line. They will be seen as broad-based and far-reaching in their concerns and intellectually entitled to be listened to on vital public policy issues.

Third, arts and culture programs enhance the pride of your employees. Whenever a corporation is involved in a worthy project, its employees enjoy an added respect in their community and among their peers. As a result, whatever positive feelings they already have toward the company will be reinforced.

Fourth, your company's involvement in the arts provides an excellent opportunity for leadership in the community. It's no secret that those individuals who actively support civic activities usually find themselves in a position to play an influential role in the community's political affairs.

Fifth, the sponsorship of cultural events allows you to entertain important customers at openings, special tours, and similar events where you have the opportunity to introduce important people to other important people.

Sixth, because government leaders often have specific cultural interests and favorite projects, your sponsorship of similar projects and causes provides the opportunity to form useful alliances and valuable contacts.

Seventh, corporate sponsorship of the arts is good for recruiting. Many bright young people are eager to work in a company that clearly cares about community and cultural concerns.

Eighth, in an era when corporations are often criticized for their alleged lack of societal involvement, participation in cultural or arts programs can present excellent opportunities to be involved in constructive social action.

In addition to these principally corporate public relations advantages, arts sponsorships have proved to have equally important marketing benefits.[1]

Schmertz says that "after fifteen years of artistic and cultural activity, we now find that when we give certain publics a reason to identify with the projects and causes that we have chosen to support, they will translate that identification into a preference for doing business with us." He cites a 1982 Mobil public-opinion survey of upscale college graduates in the Boston area. Not only did the respondents identify Mobil with quality programming, but 31 percent of them said they bought Mobil most often, compared to far lower percentages for Exxon, Gulf, and Texaco.

Schmertz believes that support like Mobil's sponsorship of Masterpiece Theater builds brand loyalty, particularly among a growing number of consumers who are highly and deliberately resistant to product advertising. He says that the people in this group are upscale viewers with discretionary dollars to buy "for example, premium gasoline for all three of their cars."

He points out that it's not only these upscale viewers who consider much advertising infantile, shallow, and misleading. When they watch public TV, pay cable, or rent cassettes without advertising, "its more difficult than ever for them to sit through product advertising."

As conventional advertising runs up against a growing number of obstacles, corporations are quickly discovering that one alternative to the various problems of traditional advertising is "cause-related marketing"— also known as "affinity-of-purpose marketing"—which consists of identifying your company with a worthy cause that a high proportion of your target audience happens to believe in. As a result of that identification, consumers reward you by buying your product or otherwise helping your business. In other words, they are choosing to help a third party by doing business with a second party."[2]

EVOLUTION OF ARTS MARKETING

Schmertz equated "affinity-of-purpose" marketing with cause-related marketing, but a definite distinction emerged in the late 1980s. Cause-related programs, while public service in nature, are tied to a transaction; that is, the sponsoring company will donate a percentage of sales of its products to a recipient organization during a promotion period. The term was coined and trademarked by American Express but has come into generic use by all companies who link donations to sales transactions. Chapter 17 discusses this practice. This chapter describes the very prevalent marketing public relations practice of identifying companies and individual brands with arts and entertainment events of particular interest to target-market audiences.

These programs began with public-television underwriting, led by Mobil's sponsorship of Masterpiece Theater and corporate sponsorship of art exhibitions by companies like Philip Morris, IBM, Eastman Kodak, and Xerox.

As federal funding decreases, business is becoming a critical source of funding to the arts. The Business Committee for the Arts, Inc., a New York-based nonprofit organization, estimates that 10 to 12 percent of the average corporate philanthropic budget now goes to support of the arts and that business gave upward of $1 billion to the arts in 1989. That is 57 percent more funding than the National Endowment for the Arts and state arts agencies combined. Banks, financial services companies, HMOs, and insurance companies are among the most active new supporters of the arts. American Express donates $4.5 million annually to the arts. Among its most recent efforts to bring art to the people is an 18-city International Diamonds Are Forever fine arts exhibit on the subject of, not gems, but baseball. Pitching-great Tom Seaver is pitching for American Express as spokesperson, to maximize media coverage in the exhibit cities.

ADWEEK's Marketing Week quotes Richard C. Clark, president of Affiliate Artists, a New York nonprofit organization of performing artists, on the marriage of marketing and the arts:

> Arts institutions have come and asked us to repackage their sponsorship proposals to attract corporate marketing and PR dollars. We've layered onto these proposals parts of the marketing mix and suggested new

tactics for positioning the proposal which have helped these groups open new corporate doors.[3]

In an article called "Making the Most of Arts Sponsorships," *ADWEEK* quotes Tom Creighton, manager of advertising operations for Xerox Corporation:

> Sports is not the only thing our decision makers like. The arts broaden the breadth and scope of our promotions. It's a nice mixture.[4]

Trend forecasters John Naisbitt and Patricia Aberdeen agree. One of the "millennial megatrends" they predict in *Megatrends 2000* is a renaissance in the arts. They believe that during the 1990s, the arts will replace sports as society's primary leisure activity. They point out that companies will come to understand that while people spend more time and money on the arts, companies spend billions more sponsoring sports. Naisbitt and Aberdeen predict that companies will make up the time lag and that "corporate support of sports will plateau while arts sponsorship continues to grow in the next decade." Further, they forecast a "decidedly commercial cast" to corporate arts funding in the 1990s.

Traditionally, corporations have sponsored the arts as philanthropists. They doubtlessly continue to do so, but the new arts-funding push will focus on the marketing and public-relations value of the arts. Though some purists will find it distasteful, the new practical approach will enable corporations to justify greater arts expenditures when they know they will be getting more in return for their sponsorship.

Judith Jedlicka of the Business Committee for the Arts says, "We see a move away from the notion of pure philanthropy to a stance where you start from an alliance with the arts to help meet your business goals as well as help the arts."

Support of the arts is increasingly moving from corporate philanthrophy, a CPR function, to arts marketing, an MPR function. Arts marketing is coming of age as corporations learn how to get marketing mileage as well as gain corporate good will from its cultural sponsorships.

PHILIP MORRIS AND THE ARTS

David Finn, Chairman of Ruder & Finn, a pioneer in arts sponsorships, believes:

> . . . commitment, above all, is the key to the effectiveness of a public service program, whether it's corporate or product driven. Commitment

means being convinced that this is a sound policy for the product and the company, that it's worthwhile for the community, and that the PR and marketing mission is to stay with the project until the best way is found to achieve company benefits.

When Philip Morris began its sponsorship of the arts with what was then a leading-edge pop and op art exhibition, Finn says, it made little or no impact.

> But under the leadership of a management genuinely interested in the arts, the commitment was sustained and today Philip Morris is considered one of the handful of major corporate supporters of culture in our society. The program also has the full support of the firm's marketing executives who feel that it has been helpful in establishing a prestigious reputation not only for the company but for the brands as well.[5]

Philip Morris has contributed to close to 1,000 cultural organizations, programs, and activities since 1958. The company promotes newer emerging art forms as well as established institutions and minority cultural programs. Since "Pop and Op," its first museum exhibition in 1965, the company has sponsored such major shows as the landmark "The Vatican Collections: The Papacy and Art" (its $3 million gift to the Metropolitan Museum of Art was the largest corporate grant ever given to the arts); the much-heralded "Primitivism in 20th Century Art" (1984) and "Picasso and Braque: Pioneering Cubism" (1989) at the Museum of Modern Art; and "The Age of Sultan Suleman the Magnificent," organized by the National Gallery of Art, Washington, D.C. Philip Morris has also supported a number of Afro-American art and regional art exhibitions through the years. The company's World Headquarters Building in New York City even houses a branch of the Whitney Museum of American Art on its ground floor, which provides cultural enrichment to midtown audiences through both its permanent and changing exhibitions.

Performing Arts Support

Philip Morris has extended its support to the performing arts as well. Its sponsorships include the Joffrey Ballet (since 1982), the Brooklyn Academy of Music's internationally acclaimed avant-garde "Next Wave" Festival, and the extensive tours of the Alvin Ailey American Dance Theater, which brings America's indigenous jazz and blues music to many countries. The company is an active supporter of The Dance Theater of Harlem's Open House Series, which presents informal cultural programs to people living in New York's Harlem. A fund called The Theater Project provides operating support for theater groups of all sizes and was a model for three other funds: the Music Project, the Dance Project, and the Performance Centers Project.

In 1989, in honor of its 50th anniversary, Philip Morris gave the American Ballet Theater a grant of $750,000, its largest gift to any performing arts institution. The company also provided additional support for publicity and marketing, making it the largest corporate contribution that the American Ballet Theater has ever received.

In "Philip Morris and the Arts," an 84-page report of the company's first 25 years, the company described the role of publicity in extending the reach of its arts sponsorships.

> Through print and broadcast, many millions who did not attend the exhibitions and performances become participants, nonetheless, and share the stimulation and enjoyment. Key mass-circulation magazines devote major articles to our exhibitions. These are matched by extensive television and radio coverage, wire-service features, and newspaper editorials, special sections, and supplements. The Philip Morris art-film program extends the reach of these projects to millions more.

Company Self-Interest

Former Philip Morris Chairman George Weissman explained:

> Our company's commitment to change and innovation in our business affairs originally led us to support art as a great inspirational catalyst for all society, including its business sector. . . .
>
> Let's be clear about one thing. Our fundamental interest in the arts is self-interest. There are immediate and pragmatic benefits to be derived as business entities, and long-range benefits as responsible corporate citizens of our communities and country. They go together. This self-interest, endowed now with a more comprehensive definition, accounts for business's strong support and continuing commitment to the arts.
>
> How we at Philip Morris arrived at our definition perhaps may be constructive.
>
> In the early 1960s we were a small company doing three hundred million dollars a year in the tradition-bound cigarette industry. There were only six companies in the industry and we were at the bottom of the totem pole. We turned to the arts to provide us with the impulses for new ideas and innovative approaches. The fundamental decision to support the arts was not determined by the need or the state of the arts. We were out to beat the competition. We came to the conclusion that it was no longer possible for business to operate in the old time-tested and traditional manner, and still be successful.
>
> Because we are essentially an industry and a company of creative managers and creative marketers, we had to say to ourselves and to our people that we were open to new ideas, new approaches. At Philip Morris,

we began to deal with art, in our case primarily visual art, that would force us to look at everything in a completely new manner. For us, art was a restless, probing presence to help convert us into a creative mass-marketing organization.[6]

IBM AND THE ARTS

IBM has an even longer history of supporting the arts. The company has been involved with the arts since the 1930s, when IBM founder and chairman Thomas J. Watson, Sr., authorized the purchase of works of art from each of the 79 countries where IBM was doing business. Works from the IBM Collection were first shown at the 1939 New York World's Fair in an exhibition called "The IBM Gallery of Science and Art."

Today, IBM's support of the arts includes underwriting of major cultural projects in virtually every area of the visual and performing arts. Altogether, IBM supports nearly 2,500 cultural organizations.

IBM says it supports the arts because it makes good business sense and because the company wants to contribute to the quality of life in the communities where its employees and customers live and work. The company believes that business and art can contribute to each other's purposes.

In 1988, IBM contributed more than $14.2 million to support the arts worldwide through matched grants and direct grants to museums and other cultural organizations and institutions, performing arts companies, and public television.

IBM Gallery of Science and Art

A highly significant element of the company's association with the arts is the IBM Gallery of Science and Art in New York City. The gallery is free and has drawn more than 3 million visitors since opening in late 1983. It works in partnership with cultural institutions worldwide and brings high-quality science and art exhibitions to New York that otherwise might not be seen there.

An architectural exhibition drew 90,000 visitors to the gallery to see some 200 drawings, paintings, and models.

Scientific exhibitions have explored the nature of light and vision, microscopy, the planets as photographed by NASA satellites, and the contributions to physics of Sir Isaac Newton.

A major scientific exhibition, "Seeing the Light with the Exploratorium," featured 80 interactive exhibits and allowed visitors to investigate the concepts behind light, color, and perception. During its three-month showing, attendance was nearly 290,000, the highest for any IBM Gallery exhibition.

IBM Sponsorships

Since 1974, IBM has sponsored over 35 major art exhibitions at museums nationwide, including retrospectives of the works of Bonnard, Cézanne, Courbet, Degas, Eakins, Homer, Lawrence, Motherwell, Picasso, Pissarro, Raphael, Renoir, Rivera, Rodin, and Rothko. Other exhibitions have provided surveys of painting, decorative art, folk art, photography, design, and architecture. In addition, many other exhibitions have been sponsored by IBM organizations in other parts of the world.

In 1989, a retrospective of that exhibition, entitled "50 Years of Collecting: Art at IBM," was shown in the IBM Gallery in New York, with a broad selection of works from IBM locations around the world.

On public television, IBM has underwritten cultural and educational specials and series that have included documentaries, dramas, concerts, ballets, and children's educational programming. IBM provides free educational materials to teachers in conjunction with many of the television programs it sponsors.

In 1989, IBM and NYNEX Business Centers joined with the National Endowment for the Arts to donate advanced personal computers, software, and technical support to 50 arts organizations around the country, assuring the future of these organizations. The announcement was made at a press conference at the José Limon Foundation studio in New York where members of the Limon Troupe, one of the country's most celebrated modern dance companies and a recipient of the equipment, performed.

IBM heralds its sponsorships in its advertising. One ad showed posters for some of the many art exhibitions, musical events, and television specials it has supported over the years—"Which goes to show," according to the ad copy, "that a company known for its state-of-the-art technology can also be interested in the state of the arts."

AT&T: ON-STAGE

Although sponsorship of major art exhibitions has been taken up by many corporations, backing new theater has not attracted widespread support because the material is considered risky by many potential "angels."

Not so AT&T. The corporation got into supporting nonprofit theater in the mid-1980s and has supported 26 projects at 19 nonprofit theaters in 12 cities in its first 5 years. By 1990, AT&T had become the largest corporate contributor to nonprofit theater in the United States, according to the Theater Communications Group. Among its most notable successes was the Steppenwolf Theater's stage adaptation of *The Grapes of Wrath*, which received the 1990 Tony Award as best play of the year.

The New York Times reported that AT&T's money comes from two sources, the AT&T Foundation, which is the company's nonprofit philanthropic arm, and the company's corporate advertising and events marketing department. Ralph Zachary Manna, the department's director, told the *Times*, "My mandate is to provide a forum whereby AT&T is positioned in such a way that the people who attend our performances or exhibitions or whatever it is we sponsor will remember AT&T when they make a business decision."

In addition to "AT&T: On Stage," a trademarked series which the company supports with production and advertising monies, the company recently initiated "The AT&T New Plays for the 90's." For this project, the Foundation provides production grants that are matched by Manna's department for advertising support. This companion program specifically encourages new writing among women and minorities.

In return for its support of these theater programs, AT&T becomes sole sponsor, with its name credited above the title and mentioned on all promotional materials plus the right to host a gala theater party.

FROM CULTURAL SPONSORSHIP TO MUSIC MARKETING

While corporations like Mobil, AT&T, and IBM concentrate their efforts on sponsorships of the fine and performing arts, marketers of soft drinks, beer, and other consumer products are increasingly putting their marketing muscle behind sponsorships of popular music, often linking blockbuster concert tours with product commercials. Alan Pottasch, Pepsi-Cola senior vice president for advertising, says that "music is one of the three things that transcend cultural barriers—music, sex, and sports—and we think that sports has been somewhat overdone while music is 100 percent universal."

Jim Harris, who negotiated and implemented Anheuser-Busch's sponsorship of Genesis, Eric Clapton, and Steve Winwood, says, "Sports sponsorships were born out of the passion for participating in sports: seeking to tap into our other great leisure-time activity, broadly categorized as entertainment, was a natural progression."

"Done properly," he states, "entertainment marketing represents a win-win situation for the sponsor and the sponsored. The marketer strengthens its corporate image or brand imagery borrowed from the entertainer or event and the artist or event profits from the exposure and the direct fees from corporate underwriting."

Harris calls public relations a "critical element of a cost-effective entertainment marketing program," noting that "the beverage companies have been particularly adept at gaining media exposure, trumpeting their associations with entertainment events that reinforce the imagery central to positioning their lifestyle-oriented products."

Return of the Rock Legends

The publicity for music commercials and sponsorship of tours of the stars who appear in a company's commercials moves the event from advertising to news. *ADWEEK's Marketing Week* cites 1989 as the year of mega-marriages between rockers and marketers—Miller Beer's sponsorship of the Who tour, Visa's affiliation with the Paul McCartney tour, and Budweiser's sponsorship of the Rolling Stones tour "Steel Wheels." The Budweiser brand took the lead in the biggest merchandising campaign for a rock tour ever.

The sponsorship package included network TV support, major radio promotions, and ticket giveaways. Budweiser commercials advertised the tour and Bud's sponsorship, and incorporated clips of the Stones in performance. Budweiser was also able to cash in on a publicity bonanza: Mick Jagger was on the cover of *TIME* and *Vanity Fair* and, of course, *Rolling Stone*. The Stones tour was treated as a major news event in the 27 tour cities. As the tour neared its conclusion, "NBC Nightly News" reported:

> This is the show that is packing them in. The Stones are among rock-'n'-roll's most durable performers. A lot of people here started listening to them more than twenty-five years ago. Now their children are doing the same thing. And the Stones, once the bad boys of rock-'n'-roll, have become part of the establishment: a money-making machine. Three million tickets will be sold on this tour at an average price of twenty-eight dollars and fifty cents. That's a total box office of almost ninety million dollars. In addition to the ticket money, there's six million dollars from Budweiser, which has its name all over the place, and features the Stones in TV commercials.[7]

The news value of being a first-time sponsor of a rock superstar or other celebrity is in itself an important news hook that only happens once. Jay Coleman, president of Rockbill, the entertainment-marketing firm that was a pioneer in linking products with performers, says, "Getting a commercial virgin is very important. The first-time commercial affiliation has built-in publicity and awareness."

The 1990 return of Mick's fellow rock legend, ex-Beatle Paul McCartney, attracted headlines everywhere. *The Wall Street Journal* commented, "Old rock 'n' rollers don't fade away. Now they sign lucrative endorsement deals pegged to comeback tours."

Associated Press announced that "Rock music's Paul McCartney will be getting a little help from his friends at Visa USA during his comeback tour."

John H. Bennett, Visa's senior vice president for consumer marketing, said, "This fits in perfectly with our 'Everywhere you want to be' campaign. We're emphasizing the benefit of being able to use the card when and where you want to. We think of the McCartney tour as a major event, like the Super Bowl and Olympics."

The company sponsored the 12-city U.S. portion of the world tour. McCartney appeared in an $8.5 million TV campaign promoting the tour while not directly endorsing the product. The commercials—and the publicity about the tour—delivered the message that Visa was the only credit card that would be accepted for ticket sales and stadium souvenirs. Local newspaper ads announced that a limited number of select seats to "the hottest show in town" were reserved for Visa Gold cardholders. A special segment of CBS's "48 Hours" covered the tour, giving added exposure to Visa's sponsorship.

Reebok's Human Rights Now! Tour

Reebok International joined Amnesty International, one of the world's most influential human rights organizations, as the underwriter of the Human Rights Now! concert tour. The athletic shoe company sponsored the tour because it wanted to make a statement about Reebok and to differentiate itself from other sporting-goods manufacturers. Reebok spent $10 million to underwrite the tour, which featured rock superstars Bruce Springsteen, Sting, Peter Gabriel, and Tracy Chapman and played in 14 countries on 5 continents over 6 weeks in 1988. The company was careful to keep its identification subtle and tasteful. Its name appeared only on a hospitality tent and at the bottom of print ads and tour memorabilia, in a tag that read, "Made possible by a grant from Reebok."

C. Joseph LaBonte, Reebok president, told *The New York Times* that the Amnesty International tour reinforced in a way that was different, the positive image the company already has. "It's hard to say if we'll ever sell a pair of shoes with it, but you can't always equate a dollar spent with a dollar earned. It fit with our values and will live on with the young people who have made our company successful."

The Philip Morris Superband

Jazz appeals to a more elite audience than rock 'n' roll, but America's indigenous art form commands a growing audience that is truly worldwide. Andrew Whist, president of the Philip Morris Jazz Grant, says

"Properly presented, jazz has a near-magic grip on its devotees, emotionally and intellectually."

Philip Morris has presented jazz to international audiences since 1985. The series of Philip Morris Superbands have featured the greatest jazz artists in the world. The 1989 tour was the most ambitious of all. Philip Morris Superband XIX, shown in Figure 16–1, was truly a "dream band." The big band, led by pianist Gene Harris, was an all-star assemblage featuring legendary soloists and newer jazz voices. Supporting leader Harris were such all-time all-stars as bassist Ray Brown, guitarist Herb Ellis, sax stars James Moody and Frank Wess, trombonist Urbie Green, and trumpet-great Harry "Sweets" Edison. *Jazz Times* reported that "Never before—in 1989 or indeed in the annals of jazz—has so much money, marquee talent, and tender loving care been assembled under one tent."

Big bands are an expensive undertaking, but because of the Philip Morris Grant, international tours of big bands are back. The three-month tour, the longest ever by a jazz orchestra, covered 21 cities in 16 countries on 5 continents. After a premier concert at New York's Town Hall, the Superband took off for Morocco, then Hungary, Egypt, France, Turkey,

FIGURE 16–1 The Philip Morris Superband Series is a corporate communications project that reaches consumers and employees throughout the world. The 1989 tour featuring an all-star big jazz band led by pianist Gene Harris played in 16 countries from Morocco to Taiwan.

Russia, Switzerland, Poland, Italy, and both Germanys. After a ten-day break, the Pacific stage of the tour continued in Korea, the Philippines, Australia, and Taiwan.

Geoffrey C. Bible, president of Philip Morris International, said that the tour mirrored the international nature of the company's business. He explained:

> As an international corporation and a worldwide sponsor, Philip Morris has learned that art sponsorship is not impractical altruism but an enduring communications tool. It meets profound public needs among our customers and employees in all our markets. It has not merely been a form of entertainment but a valuable ambassador, working to bring about greater tolerance, understanding and harmony among people of varied cultures and ethnic backgrounds.[8]

A Philip Morris brand, Benson & Hedges cigarettes, combined tour sponsorship with cause-related marketing when it underwrote the 1988 20-city U.S. tour of the hottest keyboardists in jazz. Benson & Hedges Command Performances presented Herbie Hancock and the Headhunters II and the Chick Corea Elektric Band in concert. One dollar of each ticket sale was donated to benefit the homeless in each tour community.

17

MPR Public
Service Programs

One of the fastest growing areas of marketing public relations is sponsorship of public service programs that identify brands with the concerns of consumers as individuals and as members of society at large. Some of these programs bring people closer to products by relating the sponsor to issues that target consumers care about, and some are designed to build store traffic. Toys for Tots does both of these for Midas.

Midas International Corporation has tied in with the U.S. Marine Corps Reserve since 1982 as a corporate sponsor for Toys for Tots. More than 1,500 Midas shops in the United States have participated in the program, collecting toys for needy children in their areas. The program was designed to unite franchisees in a national community effort to promote a good-neighbor image of Midas, to increase shop traffic during the traditionally slow holiday business season, and to reinforce Midas's name awareness among car owners.

Other programs, like city cleanups, are more directly related to the specific benefit or use of the product. Glad Wraps and Glad Bags, in cooperation with local Keep America Beautiful affiliates, sponsors the Glad Bag-A-Thon, now being carried out in 50 cities. In every market, citizens are mobilized to clean up sections of their cities by collecting trash in Glad Bags. Ruder-Finn's public relations effort involves encouraging civic and community leaders to organize their constituencies to support the program. More than 6,000 tons of litter were collected by 250,000 participants in 1988.

S.C. Johnson's Raid Max Big Block Cleanup concentrated its efforts on some of New York City's dirtiest districts, as identified by We Care About New York, a nonprofit group dedicated to persuading citizens to clean up their streets. The sponsoring product, appropriately enough, is a new roach killer. We Care About New York sent out mailings to hundreds of community organizations to announce the program, and enclosed coupons for Raid. To motivate participation, consumers who signed up for Big Block cleanups were eligible for a sweepstakes that offered a top prize of $5,000 and seven $1,000 prizes to the block associations who did the best job. Raid provided branded trash bags, T-shirts, aprons, and painter's caps, and retailers were given trash baskets to place in front of their stores. The effort resulted in 12,000 New Yorkers participating in 700 cleanup events in the two-month promotion period. Black radio station WBLS, a cosponsor, broadcast shows from cleanup sites and contributed to 12 million media impressions.

THE KELLOGG CHOLESTEROL CHALLENGE

To increase consumers' awareness about blood cholesterol, Kellogg Company, in cooperation with the American Health Foundation, sponsored "The Kellogg Cholesterol Challenge." The program, which was conceived by Daniel J. Edelman, Inc., challenged residents of the capital cities of Lansing, Michigan, and Jackson, Mississippi, to a contest to see which city could lower its blood-cholesterol levels more. The program consisted of initial community screenings followed by a four-month health education effort and follow-up screenings.

The public relations program was kicked off at a New York press event; breakfasts in the two cities followed, to generate local support. The mayors of both cities and the governors of Michigan and Mississippi pledged their official support, and local media became cosponsors. The cities were selected because they had similar demographics and provided a good cross-section of the American population. The selection of a Northern capital city and a Southern capital city created a "battle of North versus South" that added to media interest and stimulated community participation. Publicity posters, flyers, and PSAs were used, to urge residents to take part in the challenge.

Initial screenings drew 21,000 participants, 14,000 from Jackson and 7,000 from Lansing, in February and March of 1988. Press conferences were held in both cities to convey the results of the initial screenings and to urge participants to have follow-up screenings. Program participants received a variety of information on the benefits of a low-fat, low-cholesterol diet. Local supermarkets, hospitals, and the media were involved in helping to keep the participants motivated. Nearly half returned for the follow-up tests.

Jackson won the Challenge and was rewarded by Kellogg with a $200,000 grant for future health programs focusing on teenagers. As a result of the program, Jackson reduced its average cholesterol levels from the borderline risk to below the national average. More important, pre- and post-surveys found an increase of awareness of good cholesterol levels in both cities.

The story of "The Kellogg Cholesterol Challenge" was covered extensively by the national and local media, strengthening Kellogg's identification with health and nutrition.

McDONALD'S "PLAN TO GET OUT ALIVE"

McDonald's "Plan to Get Out Alive" is a national fire-safety program designed to extend the proven effectiveness of school fire drills into the home. The program was developed by McDonald's Canada and introduced in the United States in partnership with the NBC television network and its affiliates, United States Fire Administration, First Alert, and other fire-prevention organizations.

In the first year, 1987, McDonald's restaurants distributed 22 million free step-by-step instruction pamphlets during National Fire Prevention Week. NBC aired a special fire-safety episode of "Valerie's Family" and helped announce the first national home fire drill on local newscasts. The next year, the company sponsored a 45-minute "Plan to Get Out Alive" video hosted by Dr. Frank Field, based on his 15-part WCBS-TV news series. Order coupons for the video were made available at participating McDonald's restaurants during National Fire Prevention Month. An educational guide was provided with the video to help teachers and parents share the lessons in the video with children. More than 34 million pamphlets and 20,000 home-safety videos were distributed in the first two years. The company and its franchisees and owner-operators were applauded by customers, fire departments, schools, community groups, and government agencies and were credited with saving lives.

During the third year, the program was extended by McDonald's when it hosted a nationally syndicated telecast of the home fire-safety video in the top 200 television markets. The company also provided copies of the video to each of the 1,000 Blockbuster Video stores nationwide in conjunction with Blockbuster's new Community Service Program, which offers free rental of public service videos to customers.

ADDRESSING ISSUES OF THE 1980s AND 1990s

Public service programs reflect the changing concerns of society. Among the most prominent of these concerns are substance abuse and education.

The extent of public concern is reflected in the rhetoric from Washington. Former First Lady Nancy Reagan made the "Just Say No" to drugs program her issue. President George Bush wants to be known as the "education president" and has declared a "war on drugs." First Lady Barbara Bush is a leader in the movement to combat illiteracy.

Pizza Hut's Book It! Reading Incentive Program

Companies like Pizza Hut and Jell-O have addressed the literacy issue through innovative public relations programs to encourage reading.

In 1983, the Library of Congress issued a report titled "Becoming a Nation of Readers," which identified reading as a major problem in U.S. schools and the nation. Pizza Hut saw this problem as an opportunity "to make a difference." The company consulted with the White House, the Department of Education, and educational organizations like the National Education Association, and developed a program they call Book It!

Here is how it works: Students sign up for the program on a classroom wallchart. Their teachers assign individual goals of a number of books to be read, according to each child's ability and learning level. The students read toward goals and are responsible for written or oral book reports. When they achieve their monthly goals, they receive immediate positive reinforcement in the form of Pizza Hut award certificates, redeemable at their local Pizza Hut for a free pizza and a Book It! button. Each award is treated as a mini-awards banquet. Students who achieve their goals for three consecutive months receive a teacher-merit-award bookmark. If all students reach their goal in four or five months, Pizza Hut throws a pizza party for the entire class.

The company sends parents a letter telling them how they can become involved in the program. Book It! also requires the support of franchisees who control nearly 2,300 Pizza Hut restaurants. They receive training manuals and are provided with a filmstrip to show all employees. They are cautioned against commercialism and are told that Book It! is a public service program and not a promotion.

In 1985–1986, more than 7 million children participated in the program. The average number of books read per student increased by 300 percent, reading levels improved by 53 percent, and reading enjoyment increased by 78 percent. Perhaps most important of all, student attitudes toward learning improved by 56 percent. The $50 million in free pizza was an investment in building Pizza Hut's customer base among its important youth audience. The results of the first year led to a continuing commitment by the company.

The Jell-O Reading Rocket

Another successful reading program, directed specifically to second, third, and fourth graders, was launched by Jell-O Desserts in 1988. Jell-O describes its program, the Jell-O Reading Rocket, as an intensive local-market effort with a national overlay, designed to inspire a love for reading among elementary school children. The program is based on a survey commissioned by Jell-O that found that 95 percent of parents consider reading to be the most important element in a child's education. It was developed to provide a "proprietary niche for the Jell-O trademark within the nation's elementary schools."

To establish credibility among educators, an advisory board of representatives from national educational organizations was formed. Children's Television Workshop, producers of "Sesame Street," created innovative, original program materials, which were tested in focus groups and in interviews with teachers, parents, and children. A 32-page, 4-color, interactive storybook called *The Great Space Chase* is given to participating children. It introduces them to reading through a space journey to the planets of mystery, humor, history, and poetry. Teachers are given a Teacher's Guide, a 4-color classroom poster, and a set of classroom activity sheets. Also included is a teacher pact to be signed by student and teacher in which they agree to commit to the Jell-O Reading Rocket program. Upon completion of the program, the child receives a special certificate. Under the program, the child and parent also sign a pact under which they agree to read together on a regular basis.

The Reading Rocket program was tested in three markets—Boston, Indianapolis, and Portland—in 1988. It was used by 1,380 teachers reaching 34,500 students and their parents. To assure brand identification, "blast-off launching parties" were held in every participating school; Jell-O pudding snacks were served and students received goody bags with Jell-O coupons and Jell-O recipe books, in addition to reading tips. Local television and print publicity was obtained through interviews with a children's author who spoke to students, teachers, and parents in each market and through a traveling Jell-O Reading Rocket Puppet Show.

The Kodak/Alan Page Challenge

Fourth grade is a critical year because many students, especially in large urban school districts where more students are at risk, begin to lose interest in school. This is the audience addressed by the Kodak/Alan Page Challenge.

In 1989, Eastman Kodak Company joined forces with Alan Page, former NFL All-Pro defensive tackle and now Assistant Attorney General of the State of Minnesota, in sponsoring an essay contest that encouraged students to think about why it is important to stay in school. They were asked to consider Page's basic message, "With an education, the future is yours," and to write a 150-word essay about what the statement meant to them.

A classroom poster distributed to 20,000 fourth-grade classrooms in 43 school districts that comprise the Council of the Great City Schools asked students to "write your own ticket to the 1990 NFL Pro Bowl in Hawaii and meet Alan Page in person." In addition to the top prize, 46 other students who wrote the best essays in their districts were each awarded a Kodak S100 35mm camera outfit and a $100 U.S. Savings Bond. Every student who entered the contest received an autographed poster of Page bearing the words, "Stay in school. You're too good to lose."

The contest and its accompanying motivational video are part of an ongoing program that takes Page to urban classrooms around the country under Kodak sponsorship to tell students that education is the key to their future. The video shows a variety of people, from astronauts and engineers to teachers and firefighters, in jobs that require an education, and it features Page on the field as a football player, at work as a lawyer, and in the classroom discussing the value of education with schoolchildren. Along with the video, Kodak provides a study guide and other materials to help teachers use the Challenge as a classroom project.

In announcing the Challenge program, Kay R. Whitmore, Kodak's president and executive officer, said it combines elements that appeal directly to fourth graders. "An exciting prize, combined with Alan's appeal as a star athlete, creates a powerful incentive to students who might otherwise be skeptical of thinking about what an education means." He was right. The company received more than 20,000 entries. The participation rate by the target audience of minority and disadvantaged students was outstanding, and the quality of the entries was so high that co-grand prize winners were selected by a panel of educators. They were all featured in *USA TODAY* with a by-line story by Alan Page and an interview with Whitmore on education that Kodak reprinted and mailed to business community and education leaders across the country. The success of the program convinced the company to repeat it during the 1990–1991 school year.

Keebler's "I Believe in Me"

When President Reagan called upon corporations, schools, and civic leaders to join forces in educating young people about the perils of drug and alcohol use, the Keebler Company was the first company to answer the president's call for private-sector initiative.

Experts had determined that peer pressure can lead to drug experimentation and use and that self-esteem is a deterrent to drug use. Keebler responded by developing a positive self-esteem program called "I Believe in Me" for fourth through sixth graders. The program is designed to prevent drug use before it starts by educating children, their parents, and teachers about the power of self-esteem in helping children resist negative peer pressure.

A mall show, media tour, feature film, teachers' guide, and parents' guide are used to extend the messages and programs to students, parents, and teachers. The mall show is a musical stage show featuring two puppets, Ernie the Keebler Elf and his mother, who interact with an actress. Through dialogue and song, the performers reaffirm that if children believe in themselves and perform their best, they will have the strength to succeed and will not need the false security of drugs. Children visiting the show in shopping malls receive "I Believe in Me" T-shirts, buttons, and self-esteem certificates. To assure media coverage, a consultant to the White House Drug Abuse Policy Office acts as spokesperson for the program and is interviewed by local media where the show appears.

The in-school element includes a 22-minute feature film that is distributed on a free-loan basis to teachers. The film explores the peer pressure that leads to drug abuse. The accompanying teachers' guide includes a classroom poster, classroom lesson plans, and take-home materials involving parents and family in self-esteem activities. The parents' guide is offered free to parents.

The program has successfully demonstrated Keebler Company's commitment to youth. Its company advertising spokesperson, Ernie the Keebler Elf, is used effectively in both the film and live show. The wise Ernie's "elfin magic" allows him to see the potential in every child.

The school program, supervised by Golin/Harris, has reached approximately a million students in 28,000 classrooms, far exceeding Keebler's goal. The success of "I Believe in Me" led to the development of another film on self-esteem, "Mirrors," which is the first major cooperative effort between the National Parent Teacher Association and a corporation.

A-B's Responsible Drinking Programs

Anheuser-Busch Company spends millions of dollars each year promoting what it calls its "responsible drinking" programs. In anticipation of college spring breaks, A-B runs ads listing "Pit Stops" where students can pull over and get a doughnut and a cup of coffee enroute to their destinations. The company has linked responsible drinking programs to its Budweiser, Bud Light, Michelob, and Michelob Light brands.

At sports events, the company beams messages from professional athletes on big-screen television and billboards reminding fans to be a "Good Sport" by not overindulging. Sports stars are also used to remind the public "When to Say When." This program also provides guidelines for bartenders, waiters, and waitresses. The company distributes to video stores nationwide a videotape titled "Your Alcohol IQ," featuring the stars of the popular TV show "LA Law."

A-B publishes *T.I.P.S.* (Training for Intervention Procedures by Servers of Alcohol), an instructional manual to teach retailers how to recognize and avoid troublesome situations involving alcohol. Its Buddy System tells college-age audiences how to establish a network of friends who will serve as designated drivers.

Collectively, Anheuser-Busch calls its program for fighting alcohol abuse "Operation ALERT," an acronym for Action and Leadership through Education, Responsibility, and Training. Vice president Stephen K. Lambright, who is the group executive responsible for the programs, describes them as a social commitment and says, "We hope to be part of the solution."

18

Cause-Related Marketing

The concept of cause-related marketing is deceptively simple: Buy a company's product and it will make a donation on your behalf to some worthy cause. Sometimes the donation is based on label and coupon redemption. Sometimes the purchase of a specific item or a service transaction results in a contribution.

These sponsorships not only raise money for good causes, but they also are good business. When consumers become aware of a company's involvement, sponsors believe the consumers will be more inclined to patronize its products and services.

CORPORATE TELETHON SPONSORSHIPS

The term *cause-related marketing* is new and it is hot, but the concept is not. McDonald's Corporation has practiced it successfully for more than 20 years. In 1967, at the recommendation of public relations counselor Al Golin, McDonald's became the first corporation to sponsor a national telethon, the Jerry Lewis Labor Day Telethon, which raises funds to fight muscular dystrophy. The company has contributed more than $25 million over the years to help "Jerry's Kids" by redirecting dimes and quarters from the sale of french fries, Cokes, and other menu items.

Dozens of corporate sponsors have followed McDonald's lead by making contributions based on sales generated by telethon promotions to help muscular dystrophy, Easter Seals, Children's Muscle Network, the United Negro College Fund, and others. Telethons give companies positive exposure in millions of homes. Jerry Lewis claims a total of 100 million viewers for the 21 1/2-hour Labor Day weekend telethon, and 17 million for any 45-minute segment. In 1989, the $42 million raised from viewers was supplemented by another $36.4 million raised with the help of companies and associations.

THE HOUSES THAT LOVE BUILT

Since the first Ronald McDonald House opened in 1974, local McDonald's restaurants have raised funds through special promotions to support these facilities where families of seriously ill children can stay for little or no cost while their children are treated at nearby hospitals.

Local McDonald's restaurants have served as a catalyst to raise funds for Ronald McDonald Houses. When the first house opened in Philadelphia, McDonald's restaurants there joined the Philadelphia Eagles in raising the $35,000 needed to purchase the Philadelphia house. There are now 125 Ronald McDonald Houses in the United States and 5 other countries. Local McDonald's restaurants run special promotions and donate part of the proceeds from the sale of McDonald's food or premium items to support the local Ronald McDonald House. These local promotions have raised tens of millions of dollars.

Each year, McDonald's develops nationally advertised fundraisers to support Ronald McDonald Children's Charities and Ronald McDonald Houses. Fundraisers have included Ronald McDonald wristwatches, gift certificates, and Muppet Babies plush dolls. Baby Kermit, Baby Fozzie, and Baby Miss Piggy dolls sold exclusively at McDonald's during the 1988 holiday season raised $10 million. The promotion was kicked off at a news conference featuring appearances by Kermit and the late Jim Henson, creator of the Muppets.

In recent years, McDonald's has attracted national corporate donors to help defray construction and operating costs. Since 1985, the Scott Paper Company has conducted an annual trade promotion among its grocery and supermarket outlets. For every Scott product purchased during the months of March and April, a percentage is donated to the Ronald McDonald House. The Scott effort, supported by television advertising and newspaper inserts each spring, raised over $5.5 million in the first five years. Local Scott and McDonald's representatives publicize the programs locally at each Ronald McDonald House.

Through the years, national publicity has played an important role in raising awareness of the unique and valuable service that the houses provide to the communities where they are located. The program has been the subject of features in major magazines like *Reader's Digest* ("The Houses That Love Builds"), *Better Homes & Gardens* ("Ronald McDonald Houses: The Spirit of Caring"), and *People* ("A Determined Family and a Lot of Hamburgers Create a Place Where Sick Kids and Their Parents Can Stay"). The houses have been the subject of special segments on all major television networks—half-time features during NFL football games, interviews with Joan Kroc, widow of McDonald's founder Ray Kroc, on "Good Morning America," and live coverage of the opening of the 100th Ronald McDonald House on the "Today Show." When Dr. Art Ulene asked "Today Show" viewers to support a new house in Galveston, Texas, their response included a $1.6 million grant from a Texas foundation and documented both the power of positive public relations to deliver results and the appeal of Ronald McDonald Houses.

CAMPBELL'S LABELS FOR EDUCATION

Campbell Soup Company's Labels for Education, introduced nationally in 1973, remains one of the nation's most successful cause-related promotions. In 1989, it was named by *Promote* magazine as one of the eight best programs of the decade. Designed primarily for elementary schools, it has been particularly effective because the school children who participate are able to see first-hand what they can accomplish for their school and themselves.

Here's how it works. Schools with any of grades K–12, preschools, and public libraries in the United States, its territories, and the District of Columbia are invited to collect product labels and other proofs-of-purchase from various Campbell's soups and other Campbell products such as tomato juice and beans, Franco-American pasta and gravy, V-8 juice, and Prego spaghetti sauce. These labels are redeemable for any of the more than 1,100 items of school equipment offered: audio-visual and athletic equipment, reference books and teaching devices, computers, and science, math, and reading aids.

The response from schools, as well as from parents and children, has made this annual event one of the food industry's most successful consumer promotions and the most notable collection effort ever developed by a company. With each succeeding year, more and more retailers have participated in their own areas by encouraging school participation through the use of in-store label collection centers. Creative merchandising support by local retailers makes Labels for Education a successful traffic builder.

In 1988, over 25,000 schools throughout the United States participated, and over 100,000 orders for free equipment were processed. Since the program began, more than 100,000 participating schools have ordered more than 400,000 items and collected more than 3 billion labels.

The Labels for Education Program has resulted in increased use of Campbell products, both nationally and regionally. It also enables retailers who feature Campbell products to enhance their image in the community by earning bonus label certificates to award to local schools.

ENTER AMERICAN EXPRESS

The term *cause-related marketing* was coined by the Travel Related Services subsidiary of American Express in 1981 and was subsequently trademarked. Louis V. Gerstner, Jr., then president of American Express (now CEO of RJR Nabisco), described it as a way to "move from checkbook philanthropy to find new and more creative ways to combine profit objectives with social commitments." Gerstner predicted:

> The new stage in this evolution will be an honest, straightforward marriage of corporate interests with worthy social and cultural programs. The net results will be a quantum increase in visibility and support for deserving programs because we will have circumvented the traditional and dismal zero-sum game in which every dollar going to support nonbusiness programs was a grudging subtraction from a corporation's near sacred bottom line.
>
> Since innovation in marketing has long been our forte, we instinctively focused on this route to fund-raising and decided to divert some marketing dollars to help not-for-profit organizations in communities where we do business. We did this despite the fact that American Express, like other organizations, has a foundation which makes grants annually to a wide spectrum of beneficiaries.[1]

As conceived by American Express, cause-related marketing ties philanthropy directly to the marketing of its travel-related services. The company selects causes that need visibility and marketing-and-management help in communities where American Express does business in the United States and throughout the world. Then it donates a small sum to the cause each time a customer uses the American Express card, purchases American Express Travelers Cheques, buys a travel package, or applies for and receives a new American Express card during a typical three-month promotional period. For each cause-related program, American Express creates ads and buys time and space to run them in local media. This support not only generates good will for American Express, but it generates media coverage that raises public awareness of the projects and their support by American Express. This editorial endorsement occurs in news stories and in print and TV editorials commending the company.

Since its cause-related marketing program began, American Express has provided funding for art and science museums, theater and ballet companies, symphony orchestras, operas, circuses and zoos, conservation programs, Olympic teams, and community outreach programs.

By far the best known American Express cause-related marketing program was the first that involved the entire United States. By donating a penny for every credit-card transaction and $1 for each new card issued, the company raised $1.7 million in 1983 to restore the Statue of Liberty and Ellis Island. Supported by a $4 million nationwide advertising campaign and massive publicity effort, the program alerted millions of Americans to the need for restoration at the time that fund-raising had just gotten underway. Credit-card transactions rose 30 percent, and the number of new cards issued increased by 15 percent during the promotion period.

The second nationwide program, Project Hometown America, launched in 1985, was designed to raise $3 million to help local groups fund over 200 programs that tackle human problems at the grassroots level.

The program has worked by benefiting the recipient organizations and by increasing business. On average, American Express cardmember charge volume has been 30 percent higher than normal during the period of its promotions than for the corresponding period of the previous year. Travelers Cheque sales, travel bookings, and new-card applications have also been stimulated by the program.

Gerstner says that cause-related marketing led American Express to redefine marketing success to include three criteria: superior business results, newsworthiness, and public service. These criteria underscore the importance of cause-related marketing as a marketing public relations concept, that is, identifying products with causes that customers and the media care about.

HANDS ACROSS AMERICA

On Sunday, May 25, 1986, six million Americans joined hands, forming a human chain that linked the country from New York to Los Angeles, to help the hungry and homeless. Supporting them were two principal corporate sponsors: the Coca-Cola Company and Citicorp.

Citicorp contributed $3 million and spent another $1 million on publicity. It contributed a penny for each purchase charged to its MasterCard or Visa card and $2 for each new MasterCard or Visa card approved during the Hands Across America promotion period. Citicorp, estimates that more than 7,000 print and broadcast media placements credited Citicorp and reinforced the bank's image as being socially conscious and committed to the betterment of its communities and customers.

TANG MARCH ACROSS AMERICA FOR MADD

One of the best examples of the role of marketing public relations in cause-related marketing is the Tang March Across America for MADD (Mothers Against Drunk Drivers). Tang, the orange breakfast drink, had been marketed by General Foods since 1959. In 1985, in an effort to boost declining sales, a new Sugar-Free Tang was introduced.

General Foods asked public relations firm, Richard Weiner Inc. (now part of Porter/Novelli) to design a program directed specifically to Tang's primary audience—mothers. This led to the creation of the Tang March Across America for MADD, the coast-to-coast walk for mothers. It linked Tang and MADD in a way that showed that the brands cared for the safety and well-being of the American family, raised awareness of Tang and Sugar-Free Tang through extensive media coverage, and became one of the most successful cause-related marketing programs of recent years.

The program was announced at New York's City Hall by Mayor Ed Koch, Governor Mario Cuomo of New York, and MADD's national president; their appearance assured that media coverage would continue throughout the March. The March itself was kicked off from the steps of Los Angeles's City Hall by Mayor Tom Bradley, wearing a "Tang for MADD" T-shirt. The 4,000-miles-plus March was carefully routed to pass through 15 of the top 40 ADI (area of dominant influence) markets, creating potential for national exposure. The March was publicized in several thousand newspaper and magazine articles and on local and network TV news programs including segments on the "Today Show" and "Good Morning America." The marketing support included a free-standing newspaper insert with a cents-off coupon offering a 10-cent donation to MADD for each coupon redeemed. Consumer purchases of Tang rose 13 percent during the 6-month march, when the company did no advertising or other promotions. Coupon redemptions made Tang MADD's largest corporate contributor ever.

CAUSE AND PRODUCT JOINT MARKETING

Cause-related marketing has been criticized by those who believe that the goals of the charitable organizations are compromised when it is used to sell products. Robert E. Hope, executive vice president of Burson-Marsteller, suggests that:

> There is a bridge that must be built between the product and the cause, and that bridge is more than a commercial tie-in. It's a bridge of compatible philosophies, strategies, and mutual benefit. . . .
>
> Cause-related marketing is a term that reflects the mission of the originators and was named from the marketer's viewpoint based on the benefits for marketing products. . . . a more accurate term might be "cause and product joint marketing" since the benefits must clearly flow both ways.

If cause-related marketing is to grow and help everyone involved in its efforts, nothing can replace the critical need of product marketers and causes in picking only the right things to do and then doing them right. . . . Let's try a new definition. Let's describe cause-related marketing as putting together a "cause and a product in a joint, mutually beneficial, marketing effort." . . . When it's all over, all the people in the company that manufactures and sells the product want to feel good about what they have done. In a way, this is the real proof of success . . . proof that there is real "heart" backing up the credit of being involved.[2]

19

Spokesperson MPR

In their book *High Visibility*, Rein, Kotler, and Stoller described the process by which executives, politicians, entertainers, athletes, and other professionals create, market, and achieve successful images. They pointed out the role of public relations in the process as "the voice of visibility":

> Today PR touches every facet of American life providing more than 70 percent of all information that is published as "news." As a result, news channels have become highly dependent on PR's output. On Monday, a thirteen-year-old baking wiz—representing the flour manufacturers—makes the rounds on local radio. On Tuesday, a research scientist—funded by a chemical company—describes how a certain mosquito repellent has more resistance power than its competitors. On Wednesday, a well-known actor speaks at the local drugstore chain for Fabergé, eats at a local restaurant, attends an art opening, and makes charming, off-the-cuff remarks to senior citizens. Thursday finds the attorney general's office releasing a study on gang crackdowns. As for Friday, Saturday, and Sunday, it is the usual potpourri of football interviews, film reviews, political and social commentary—all planted and skewed by PR.[1]

BUSINESS CELEBRITIES

It is significant that the first celebrity discussed in *High Visibility* is neither an entertainer nor a sports star, but that highly visible business celebrity Lee Iacocca, chairman of Chrysler Corporation. For Lee Iacocca, high visibility is a strategic tool and his transformation into a celebrity was "as deliberate as the manufacture of his cars—calculated to use his high visibility to bring buyers into the showroom. . . . As have Victor Kiam for shavers, Frank Perdue for chickens, and Frank Borman for plane tickets, Iacocca has become a celebrity in order to sell cars."

For these executives and latter-day business celebrities, public relations plays a vital role in linking the person with the product. Their celebrity rub-off is a marketing plus of immeasurable value. Their appearance at a news conference dramatizes the news, brings out the media, and assures maximum coverage. In my experience, the appearance of Lee Iacocca at the Allied Move to Freedom Exhibit (he was chairman of the Statue of Liberty-Ellis Island Centennial Commission), at the opening of the Diamond Star Motors plant (a joint venture of Chrysler and Mitsubishi) in Bloomington, Illinois, and at "Chrysler in the Nineties" exhibits made what were essentially local or regional stories into national news, covered extensively by print and broadcast media.

The business celebrity was virtually nonexistent thirty years ago when I wrote my master's thesis at the University of Chicago on "Celebrities as Popular Symbols." At that time, "idols of consumption" from the worlds of entertainment and sport had almost entirely displaced the "idols of production" as subjects of media coverage, and social critics were complaining about the lack of attention to successful business role models who had dominated the media in the first quarter of the century.

By 1989, business celebrities had become so pervasive that *Business Week* devoted a cover story to the subject, featuring such figures as Lee Iacocca, Steven Jobs, Donald Trump, T. Boone Pickens, Ted Turner, Peter Ueberroth, Malcolm Forbes, H. Ross Perot, and Michael Eiser.[2]

The article noted that Pickens made himself famous when he tried to take over Gulf Oil Corporation. Since that time, he has appeared on the covers of 20 magazines, on all the network news shows, and on "Lifestyles of the Rich and Famous." "Pickens now makes himself readily available to the press—after all, it is the media that creates celebrities. He accepts 100 speaking engagements a year, saying it's all just part of his job as chief of Mesa Petroleum Co.—and he makes it sound credible. 'It's very important that corporations are personalized.'"

Ted Turner, who owns his own television network, frequently appears on other networks and syndicated programs like "60 Minutes," "The Tonight Show," and "Donahue." His celebrity status serves a business purpose. "His Goodwill Games with the Soviet Union might never have gotten off the ground if a lesser light had tried to organize them."

Business Week commented that "Steve Jobs never made a commercial for Apple Computer Inc., but he was nearly synonymous with the company. 'People like symbols, and in looking for a symbol for Apple, many times they latched onto me,' he says. 'Other competitors were fairly impersonal, organizational entities, whereas Apple was in many ways like a person in formation, like somebody growing up.'"

Donald's Trump Card

Writing in *Advertising Age,* Jack Bernstein calls public relations Donald Trump's "trump card":

> Uncanny luck and a canny sense of public relations weigh heavily in Donald Trump's emergence of success. There's little he can do about luck except take advantage of it, which he does very effectively. But he recognizes the value of good PR and labors to achieve it. . . . Trump says he does not 'enjoy doing press' but understands that media exposure can be very helpful in making deals, so he's willing to talk about them. And does he ever! His appreciation of the value of PR enfuses virtually every move he makes, business and personal. . . . Trump is an aggressive advertiser but his comparison of the worth of advertising vs. that of editorial space should insure him a place of privilege in the PR pantheon.

Trump is quoted as saying, "If I take a full-page ad in *The New York Times* to publicize a project, it might cost $40,000 and, in any case, people tend to be skeptical about advertising, but if the *Times* writes even a moderately positive one-column story about one of my deals, it doesn't cost me anything, and it's worth a lot more than $40,000."[3]

It doesn't hurt that the Trump names appears on Donald's buildings, resorts, and airlines. His name made *Trump: The Art of the Deal* a runaway best-seller with 850,000 hardcover copies sold, and "Trump, The Game" one of the most popular board games of the late 1980s.

When the nation's news media were having a field day with Trump's marital problems in 1990, *Newsweek* reported that Donald was clearly enjoying the spotlight, commenting, "What he has missed most in recent months has been the glare of public attention. A friend said 'publicity is his cocaine' and any news was good.'

Trump told the magazine that the extramarital story had been "great for business and the blitz of publicity had sent curious people flocking to his various businesses"—the Trump Shuttle airline, the Trump Plaza and Trump Castle casinos in Atlantic City, and New York's Plaza Hotel. *Newsweek* said that, when Trump puts his name on his property, customers seem willing to pay a premium for the name, equating it with "glamour, affluence, and excitement."[4]

Trump opened the Trump Taj Mahal in Atlantic City, the biggest and most expensive casino resort ever built, with what *The New York Times* described as "industrial-strength hoopla." Some 1,800 reporters, photographers, and media types attended the lavish opening to ogle Trump and his 420-million-square-foot, billion-dollar "Eighth Wonder of the World." For the occasion, he brought his companion Marla Maples out of hiding for a "Prime Time" interview with Diane Sawyer and personally escorted millions of Americans through the Taj on network television.

The euphoria was short-lived. A month after the opening of the Trump Taj Mahal, *Forbes* ran a cover story on Donald Trump's cash flow problems. *The Wall Street Journal* followed with a front-page report on the impending collapse of the Trump empire. Trump's financial problems quickly became a hot news story in the mass media. Joining the "Stomp-the-Trump" media assault, *People* magazine ran a cover story called "Poor Donald," with a photo of "the Donald" in recent better days, holding $1 million in cash at the opening of the Taj Mahal.

Random House rushed release of *Trump: Surviving at the Top*. The publisher told *Advertising Age* that the book was "famous before it appeared." Random House planned for "a barrage of media during the first week" including an appearance on "20/20" with Barbara Walters and a two-part interview on NBC's "Today Show," and said it would "maximize free media exposure before committing to buy ad space" to promote the new book. The *Advertising Age* headline: "It's Hype, Hype Hooray for New Book by Trump."[5] The hype worked. *Surviving at the Top* reached the top of the *New York Times* best-seller list the week it was published.

Celebrity Backfires

Fame, fortune, and overexposure in the media has backfired for other business celebrities. The late Malcolm Forbes's lavish 70th birthday party was described in *Newsweek* as "a gift for the man who has everything: ink." Titled "Forbes' Publicity Machine," the story told how he flew "600 of his nearest and dearest" to Tangier, Morocco, for "the most conspicuous shindig since the Shah of Iran celebrated the 2,500th anniversary of the Peacock Throne."

The guest list included Walter Cronkite, Lee Iacocca, Henry Kissinger, Rupert Murdoch, Barbara Walters, and Forbes's companion Elizabeth Taylor, plus 300 chief executive officers (and spouses) of corporations that advertise in *Forbes*. According to *Newsweek*:

> Chairman Malcolm gets what he pays for. Over the years, the breathless coverage of his colorful enthusiasms has helped his magazine stand out from the pack. To that end, 100 reporters from around the world were flown free to the Tangier party, provided they wore black tie. The *New York Daily News*, for instance, allowed Forbes to pick up the tab for its two working gossip columnists, Liz Smith and William Norwich, as well as the publisher. The self-publicity machine is carefully built. "Forbes co-opts the press in a very sophisticated way," says Martha Sherrill of *The Washington Post*. "The attitude isn't 'We're glad you're covering it,' it's 'We're so glad you are here.' It's seductive" . . . the stories never seem to end. According to the NEXIS computer retrieval system, Forbes's name ran in 293 articles in 1989, before the accounts of the Tangier party began.[6]

While positive party press included a *Los Angeles Times* front-page story under the headline "Forbes Dazzles a Who's Who of Americans," the party "got a storm of bad publicity," according to *Jack O'Dwyer's Newsletter*. Some of the party-going press described the affair as a publicity stunt and felt they had been used, and uninvited press criticized the party as a tax write-off.

Forbes answered the critics by saying that the $2 million investment generated $100 million worth of publicity, and added, "We don't doubt the $100 million since every paper and TV station in America did something about the party." The pros and cons were even discussed by Ted Koppel's guests on an edition of ABC's "Nightline."

When Forbes died in 1990, *The New York Times* said that "through sumptuous parties like his Moroccan birthday celebration last summer, attended by heads of state, show business celebrities, journalists, and corporate chieftains, his balloon races and motorcycle escapades, Mr. Forbes drew wide attention to his magazine that undoubtedly converted into added advertising and circulation." The *Times* quoted magazine consultant James Kobak: "Malcolm with his games was the greatest public relations force in the world."

EXPERT SPOKESPERSONS

Not all companies are headed by such effective headline-makers. MPR programs often turn to company experts or outside authorities on either the product or the borrowed-interest subject used to bring attention to the product. When Kellogg Company and General Mills unveiled a new generation of breakfast cereals containing psyllium, a grain said to contain the highest level of soluble fiber of any natural grain, both companies launched their products at New York news conferences featuring doctors as endorsers.

Company experts are widely utilized in MPR programs. Auto manufacturers make both their divisions chief and their chief engineer available to the car-enthusiast publications at "long lead" press introductions of new models. Media outlets abound. In recent years, there has been a proliferation of marketing news on television, in major daily newspapers like *The New York Times, The Chicago Tribune,* and *The Los Angeles Times,* and in the newsweeklies. In addition, readership of business publications has increased. *The Wall Street Journal* now has a daily "Media and Marketing" section and *USA TODAY* features a "Money" section. These media frequently quote company marketing executives and market researchers. Pharmaceutical-company research directors are brought out to lend credibility to new-product introductions and to report on research studies verifying product efficacy. Company home economists frequently are quoted in women's magazines and newspaper food pages and appear on daytime TV talk shows demonstrating recipes and ways to serve their company's products.

Betty Crocker—The Greatest Spokesperson Who Never Lived

In addition to company executives, public relations programs have long been built around a company's advertising spokespersons, real or fictional. This tried-and-true practice predates the ubiquity of television.

Although Betty Crocker was never a real person, her name and identity have symbolized General Mills's continuing tradition of service for more than 65 years. Over the years, she has provided a link between the business of food development and the consumer.

In 1921, a promotion for Gold Medal flour attracted thousands of responses. Betty Crocker was created as a signature for responses to inquiries. In 1924, Betty acquired a voice for daytime radio's first food-service program. It was an immediate success and within months was expanded to 13 regional stations. Each station had its own Betty Crocker voice, reading scripts written at the Home Service Department in Minneapolis. Subsequently, the "Betty Crocker Cooking School of the Air" became a network program, continuing for 24 years with over one million listeners enrolled. By 1940, surveys showed that Betty Crocker's name was known to 9 out of 10 American homemakers.

Special services for schools, under Betty Crocker's name, began in 1956 and included filmstrips and student booklets on baking and meal planning, for classroom use. In 1957, Betty Crocker materials for visually impaired people were developed: "Talking Recipe Records" and a *Cooking with Betty Crocker Mixes* cookbook in large type, with braille and cassette-tape editions.

Betty Crocker's Picture Cookbook, first published in 1950, became a national best-seller and was followed by a series of cookbooks that today number more than 30.

Betty Crocker acquired a new look, her seventh, as well as a new book in 1986. The current Betty Crocker portrait was officially unveiled in connection with the introduction of the sixth edition of *Betty Crocker's Picture Cookbook.*

The new Betty Crocker, according to General Mills, portrays a professional woman, approachable and friendly, but also competent—in the kitchen as well as in the workplace.

The company recognizes that women of all ages, with or without careers, have active lives outside the home, but they are still concerned about meal preparation and nutrition. Many have grown up expecting advice from Betty Crocker. General Mills's goal is to provide an image that modern women can relate to, a reassuring reminder of Betty Crocker's promise of thoroughly tested products and up-to-date recipes.

THE TONI TWINS AND OTHER LIVING ADS

In 1988, Daniel J. Edelman, chairman of the public relations firm that bears his name, hosted a luncheon to celebrate the 40th anniversary of the first Toni Twins media tour.

In 1948 and 1949, two sets of twins, shown in Figure 19–1, traveled throughout Europe and 75 cities in the United States to bring to life the

FIGURE 19–1 Legendary broadcaster Arthur Godfrey welcomes the Toni Twins to his CBS program. The Toni Twin tours of 1948–1949 reinforced the famous "Which Twin Has the Toni?" campaign and introduced the media tour as a public relations vehicle.

now classic "Which Twin Has the Toni?" advertising campaign that challenged consumers to identify the twin with the home permanent (rather than the beauty-shop wave).

Twin Toni-Twin caravans, trailers painted to look like the Toni Home Permanent Box, carried sets of twins to cities in the East and West. They were greeted by mayors, made guest appearances in department stores, and were interviewed by fashion and beauty editors. They attracted national coverage, like a spread in *Parade* magazine called "The Toni Twins on Parade." When six sets of twins flew to Europe to introduce the home permanent, their arrival was covered by *LIFE* magazine, then the country's best-read weekly magazine.

An *ADWEEK* story on the anniversary said "Not only did they make headlines wherever they went, but their odyssey was the forerunner of the media tour, now an integral part of many a marketing strategy." Edelman told the magazine, "You can't just run ads. Whenever you can bring the story to the public on a one-on-one basis, or beyond one-on-one, in local newspapers, local television or radio, that's going to dramatize your story."

Following the success of the Toni Twins, the Edelman firm created "living ad" MPR programs for Kentucky Fried Chicken founder Colonel Harlan Sanders, 9-Lives Cat Food's advertising "spokescat" Morris, and popcorn maker Orville Redenbacher, among others.

Redenbacher was his company's chief public relations spokesperson long before he began to appear in commercials. When he began marketing his gourmet popping corn 15 years ago, major supermarket chains refused to carry it because of its higher price. A skillful MPR program was planned to reach the consumer directly. As a result of massive publicity, mostly featuring interviews with Redenbacher himself, thousands of consumers began demanding it and the stores responded by stocking it. The brand now holds a three-to-one lead over its closest competitor. Orville Redenbacher himself says that the primary factor in his success is public relations.

AD SPOKESPERSONS HIT THE PUBLIC RELATIONS TRAIL

Effective public relations campaigns can feature real spokespersons or invented ones like Morris the Cat, the California Raisins, or Mac Tonight.

In 1987, McDonald's introduced its "Mac Tonight" campaign to promote dinner business. The piano-playing, singing, half-moon character became an instant star when he made personal appearances in McDonald's restaurants. Customers flocked to McDonald's to meet him. Radio promotions invited listeners to call in with answers to moon-related trivia questions. In addition to news coverage of his local appearances, Mac showed up nationally on "Good Morning America," "Entertainment Tonight," and the pages of *USA TODAY*. So effective was McDonald's in making the moon into a star that he made a return appearance two years later in conjunction with a promotion called "Blast Back with Mac" that celebrated the 1950s when McDonald's was started.

Morris, the 9-Lives Cat

Morris the Cat was created by Leo Burnett Company, the advertising agency for 9-Lives Cat Food, and has been the focus of the public relations program for the brand, conducted since the early 1970s by Daniel J. Edelman, Inc.

In the early years, Edelman created a national Morris Look-Alike Contest, an attempt to find a cat with the same looks, charm, and finicky-ness as Morris. The contest was supported not only by publicity, but also by Morris Look-Alike entry blanks at the point of purchase in supermarkets. The contest was an enormous success; felines claiming a resemblance to Morris poured in from all over the country. A winner selected from each state was sent a year's supply of cat food and a sterling silver engraved feeding bowl. The winner and its owner were taken to Hollywood for the full star treatment—a suite at the Century Plaza, chauffeured limousine, special dinners, appearances, and press conferences resulting in widespread national publicity.

Another popular Morris contest was a "Win-A-Date-With-Morris" competition, launched through "purr-sonals" placed in major metropolitan newspapers. All entrants received a valentine, a paw-tographed picture, and a coupon for 9-Lives Cat Food. The winners from each state won heart-shaped sterling silver "My Heart Belongs to Morris" collar tags and cases of cat good. Morris flew to Indianapolis to personally escort the grand winner to a splashy hometown party.

Since Morris had been found in an animal shelter, he was offered to the American Humane Association as its spokescat for an "Adopt-A-Cat Month" to draw attention to the many cats and kittens needing to be adopted from shelters. Every adopting family received a special kit including cat-food coupons and an adoption certificate from Morris as a thank you for saving the life of a fellow cat. When Morris appeared at a New York news conference to launch "Adopt-A-Cat Month," the media responded not only with stories, but with adoption of a dozen cats from the local ASPCA. "Adopt-A-Cat Month" became an annual event; the publicity, promotion, and PSAs led to the adoption of hundreds of thousands of cats and kittens during the month.

"The Morris Award" was another public relations bonanza for the 9-Lives brand. In conjunction with the Cat Fanciers Association, a program was created to honor the best nonbreed cat of show. The prize, a bronzed statuette of Morris with his 9-Lives Bowl, is presented to winners of local cat shows throughout the country.

Morris went on to "author" books on cat care called *The Morris Method, The Morris Approach,* and his own story, *Morris, an Intimate Biography* (complete with nude centerfold), which became a nonfiction bestseller. He appeared in a television featurette, "The Morris Mystique."

When a 1987 Opinion Research Corporation poll showed that Morris was recognized by 70 percent of the public, more than other presidential candidates, he announced his candidacy for the nation's highest office. At a news conference at the National Press Club in Washington, his "campaign manager," Eleanor Mondale, daughter of the former Vice President, said that Morris would run as an Independent because of his finickyness. She released a "Pawlicy Statement" that included policies on the environment (Put a litter box on every corner), voting rights (One cat: one vote), politics (You rub my back and I'll scratch yours), population control (Neuter is neater), education (It all begins with good paper training), and Iran-Contra (Any cat would have smelled a rat).

The launch and campaign fly-around generated 600 million audience impressions in newsweeklies, television, and wire services, with comparable advertising value of $11 million. A national poll following the launch showed consumer awareness of the Morris campaign at nearly 60 percent.

Spuds McKenzie, the Original Party Animal

Another spokesanimal has made the transition from television star to national celebrity with the help of marketing public relations. Anheuser-Busch's longtime public relations firm, Fleishman-Hillard, designed a persona for Spuds McKenzie, "The Original Party Animal," and a national program to enhance, increase, and extend the value of the character for Bud Light in a way that advertising could not. They humanized and personified the character by creating "The Spuds Mystique." Spuds became an executive, hired by Bud Light to spread his "Philosophy of Fun" by writing and directing commercials and making personal appearances. He was given a title, "Senior Party Consultant/Bud Light," corporate letterhead and business cards, and an office and staff.

Spuds travels by limousine or private aircraft, appropriately attired and accompanied by his traveling entourage, "The Spudettes," who translate his facial expressions during his interviews, but he writes and signs his own letters to the media. Music videos, re-edited from Spuds commercials, are provided to television stations for use on newscasts.

To preserve the mystique, he makes few selected media appearances, making him more mysterious, less accessible, and, therefore, more appealing to the media. He appears only in grand fashion at major events that give him a legitimate reason to be in a market. He does human things like throwing out the first ball at a major league game, presenting a check to charity, or being the grand marshal of a Mardi Gras parade. Spuds is also featured in the company's responsible-consumption public relations programs, tying into this "Know When to Say When" commercial.

In one year, through extensive and controlled publicity and public exposure, the character became part of the American vernacular. Fleishman-Hillard points out that Spuds appears in only 20 percent of Bud Light's TV advertising. Spuds has become a celebrity whose name is dropped by comedians; he has been named to the best-dressed lists and is the recipient of daily mail and media calls. Writing in *New York Magazine*, Bernice Kanner said, "Although public relations man Bill Stolberg calls Spuds a 'social virtuoso who can play a crowded room like a Stradivarious,' it's really Stolberg who's playing the media. And so far the strategy has worked, generating millions of dollars of free publicity for Spuds and Bud Light."

It has paid off at the cash register. Since Spuds appeared, Bud Light has grown at four times the growth rate of the light beer category and is now one of the top five of all beer brands.

Those California Dancing Raisins

Since they were introduced in 1986, the California Dancing Raisins have become a pop-culture phenomenon rivaling Spuds McKenzie. Since the Claymation commercials developed by Foote, Cone & Belding and Will Vinton Productions went on the air, they have been among the most popular of all television commercials. However, media budgets were limited. The original 1986 campaign was supported by only $6 million for television advertising. To extend the success of the advertising campaign and maintain awareness and sales, the California Raisin Advisory Board's public relations firm, Ketchum Public Relations, brought the Dancing California Raisins to life.

The larger-than-life Dancing Raisins shown in Figure 19–2, provided an opportunity for them to meet their fans and media. In the first years Ketchum arranged for the Raisins to appear at a highly selective number of events that received national attention, such as the Macy's Thanksgiving Day Parade, a major celebrity tennis tournament, a nationally syndicated variety show, and the White House Easter egg roll and Christmas tree lighting.

By 1988 it was decided to invest in a national promotion, a tour of costumed characters on a typical American vacation in a motor home, to introduce the Raisins at the grassroots level and maximize their awareness

FIGURE 19–2 The California Dancing Raisins have been among the most popular television commercial stars. The costumed characters brought the commercials to life performing their "I Heard It Through the Grapevine" song in personal appearances across the country.

during the summer-long advertising hiatus. The vacation began in New York and ended 45 days and 10,000 miles later in Los Angeles. During the tour, the Dancing Raisins performed nearly every day. Local broadcast and print media in 27 cities covered the Raisins performing to the "I Heard It Through the Grapevine" music heard on the popular commercials. Twelve governors and mayors participated in the events, including Atlanta Mayor Andrew Young, whose picture appeared with the lead Raisin in *Newsweek*. Trade-out promotions were arranged with radio stations in each market. In exchange for licensed Raisin-product prize giveaways, DJs from the participating stations served as emcees at live events. The tour attracted crowds that averaged 2,000 per appearance (all of whom received raisin snack-packs), generated 110 million media impressions, and signed up 3,000 new members of the California Raisin Fan Club.

The Raisins visited and entertained at a children's hospital in each city and made stops at supermarkets. "Dinners with the Raisins" to which retail grocery trade representatives were invited were used to enhance sales relationships and to launch point-of-purchase promotions The last stop of the tour was Los Angeles, where the California Raisin Advisory Board sponsored a birthday benefit dinner honoring the star of a new commercial, Ray Charles, and his Claymation likeness, Raisin Ray. A press conference prior to the dinner featured a live performance of the life-size Raisins wearing tuxedos and top hats.

The effectiveness of the Vacation Across America program is attested to by the fact that raisin sales increased by 7 percent in July and 20 percent in August over the same periods of the previous year, despite the absence of advertising.

The next year, the newest commercial, "Michael Raisin," starring Michael Jackson as a California Raisin, was introduced in 5,700 theaters before going on network television. The whole idea of the spot, like all the California Dancing Raisin events, was "to be hip, be cool and have some fun with ourselves, our product and the audience," according to Robert Phinney, director of the California Raisin Advisory Board. Ketchum kept the news secret until a week before the movie premier, then mailed "hot off the press" news releases and Michael Raisin buttons to 30,000 members of the fan club and leaked the news to national gossip columnists. Because Michael Jackson was not available for a press conference or media interviews, a Claymation press conference was satellited to TV stations, allowing them to interview Michael Raisin instead. As a follow-up, a week after the commercial premiered the agency released a "Making of Michael Raisin" video feature with behind-the-scenes footage and interviews with Claymation creator Will Vinton.

CELEBRITY AND EXPERT ENDORSERS

Celebrities are often used to bring attention to products because they are certain to increase media coverage both nationally and in major markets where their appearance in a town or even by satellite is news. To be truly effective in interviews and credible to the consumer, the celebrity must have believable credentials. Otherwise he or she risks coming off like a "hired gun." Los Angeles Dodgers manager Tommy Lasorda, a self-styled restaurant expert, was effectively utilized in both advertising and MPR programs promoting Citicorp's CitiDining Card (before he became a spokesperson for Slim Fast, a weight reduction product). And days after leaving New York's City Hall, former Mayor Ed Koch weighed in during a press conference staged by Slim Fast to announce that he would join the roster of celebrity commercial spokespersons.

A celebrity need not be the advertising spokesperson to be used effectively as an endorser in MPR programs.

One of the reasons why Della Reese was, in the words of the president of Campbell USA, "one of the best salesmen we have ever had" is because she is an expert cook who had her own network cooking show before Campbell hired her as its spokesperson. Before taking her show on the road, Della insisted on working in the Campbell kitchens to develop recipes that she prepared on television and that were included in the "Della's Cooking with Campbell" recipe booklet she offered viewers. She told interviewers that she had worked too hard over the years to establish her credibility with her audience to jeopardize it by endorsing a product she did not use and believe in.

The importance of selecting believable celebrity spokespersons for MPR programs is underscored by the fact that more consumers are finding celebrity advertising unpersuasive. Many celebrities, recognizing that fame is fleeting, have lost credibility by unselectively appearing in too many commercials for too many products, when they have too little expertise. Examples of endorsers with no special product-expertise are Chicago Bears coach Mike Ditka, for Dristan, Midway Airlines, and a dozen other products; and former Speaker of the House Thomas P. ("Tip") O'Neill, who has endorsed American Express, Quality Inns, Miller Lite, Hush Puppies, Bank of New England, and the Trump Shuttle.

Video Storyboard Tests Inc. says that the number of consumers who find celebrity ads "less than credible" jumped from 38 percent in 1987 to 52 percent in 1988. The fastest loss of credibility was among younger viewers. "Consumers are more skeptical than ever of celebrities' motives for doing commercials," the testing company said.

20

Target Marketing Public Relations

The fragmentation of the mass market, the biggest marketing story of the 1980s, has been chronicled in a series of *Business Week* cover stories.

Big, bold headlines proclaimed:

"Marketing: The New Priority—The mass market has splintered so companies are targeting products" (November 21, 1983).

"Marketing's New Look—The selling of consumer products is changing dramatically as mass markets fragment" (January 26, 1987).

"Stalking the New Consumer—Call it micromarketing. In today's fractured world, companies are finding novel ways to reach the elusive consumer" (August 28, 1989).

The points made in these and dozens of other articles and books are:

○ The emergence of the fragmented consumer population has been coincidental with intense international competition, the impact of rapid technological change, the maturing or stagnation of certain markets, and deregulation, which has altered the shape of competition.

○ The companies that emerge successfully from this marketing morass will be those that understand the new consumer.

○ The brightest chances for success in the coming years will hinge on the development of innovative products aimed at specific consumer niches.

○ The U.S. market for many products is slowly breaking up along regional and demographic lines—an ethnic market here, a suburban market there, a yuppie market here, an elderly market there.

○ As national ad rates rise—particularly on TV—much of ad spending become inefficient. As a result, companies are turning to alternate and local media.

o Computerized sales data now make it clear that the marketplace is vastly more volatile than anyone had imagined.

o Traditional mass marketing has used national advertising to talk directly to consumers, creating customer "pull." As retailers gain access to sophisticated information through computers and bar codes on packages, the balance of power is shifting in their favor.

o Micromarketing is vastly more complicated than mass marketing. Rather than wagering big bucks in hopes of producing one boffo TV ad that will quickly boost sales, micromarketers spread their bets on lots of different efforts, each of which may pay off in small increments.

MPR AND MICROMARKETING

For marketing public relations, the belated recognition of market segmentation by marketers and the media is both no news and good news. It is no news because public relations programs have been directed to target markets for years. In the view of my colleague Kathy Rand, "Public relations has always specialized in micromarketing. We just never called it that. It's always been among our tactics to reach segmented target audiences. In some ways, we've probably been more effective reaching particular segments than we have reaching a mass audience."

It is good news because now that it is on the front burner, marketers will be required to consider the role PR should play in the micromarketing mix vis-à-vis promotion and advertising, traditional and nontraditional.

Public relations management consultant Al Croft believes:

> Many PR practitioners have been successfully communicating to smaller, precisely-defined audiences for some time. The disappearance of mass market magazines and the shrinkage in the number of major metropolitan newspapers, coupled with the appearance of a plethora of special-interest, limited-audience publications were early warnings that practitioners had better rethink the media and the approaches available to reach and influence audiences.
>
> As knowledge, sophistication and competence grew, practitioners learned that it was both possible and economically efficient to reach fractured, special interest audiences through a variety of new media and techniques. In addition, they found that "product positioning" was as practical as through mass advertising. Using PR—primarily publicity and special events—to reach micro markets and generate both product awareness and positioning has led to innovative approaches.[1]

The use of limited-audience, special-interest media to reach target audiences has become a valuable asset to public relations, but that is only part of the story. Companies and public relations firms have combined sophisticated use of demographic and psychographic research and a growing body of public relations knowledge to create programs that reach target-market consumers not only through the communications media but also through event marketing, created media, and person-to-person communication.

Localization and regionalization, long accepted as standard operating procedure by public relations practitioners, are accelerating as marketing management becomes sensitized to the value of reaching consumers where they live. Media tours are increasingly delivering more localized messages. Special events are held in popular high-traffic locations. Tie-in sponsorships are often made with local radio stations and newspapers. Participation in local festivals is on the rise. Company floats appear in local parades. Cause-related programs are designed to benefit local institutions and organizations. Local chapters of national public-service organizations often provide the arms and legs that assure the success of company-sponsored programs. Local franchisees speak for the company in their communities. Local customers are invited to and entertained at local appearances of company-sponsored sports and arts events.

MPR programs have been recast to support the decentralized marketing organizations of companies like Campbell Soup Company and Frito-Lay, which recently divided into four regional profit centers covering the Central, Northern, Southern, and Western sectors of the United States.

Public relations has for years created programs directed to discrete demographic as well as local audiences. Programs directed to schoolchildren in the classroom have long been used by companies to build brand awareness. The programs are often segmented precisely to fit the demographics of the brand's market. Jell-O's reading programs, for example, are created for second to fourth grade, Keebler's for fourth to sixth grade, and so on. Numerous programs are directed to high school students with discretionary income who buy things for themselves and share the responsibility of doing the grocery shopping for the family. Still others use college media or campus events to reach the hard-to-reach college market.

In recent years, greater attention has been focused on programs directed to senior citizens and minority markets. The rise of marketing consultants in these areas has been accompanied by the growth of public relations specialists in these markets. Some major corporations have employed internal marketing/community relations specialists. Several public relations firms specializing in minority markets have sprung up; major public relations firms have specialized black and Hispanic divisions.

It is quite impossible to document all of the public relations programs directed to all demographic, psychographic, geographic, and ethnic audiences, but it is certainly a safe bet to say that the majority of marketing public relations programs today are targeted to well-defined market segments and are strategically planned to reach those markets.

For purposes of simplification, the programs cited here were chosen as representative of hundreds of marketing public relations programs directed to audience markets of high current interest to marketers, that is, women, blacks, Hispanics, youth, and senior citizens.

CLAIROL'S PUBLIC SERVICE PROGRAMS

Clairol Division of Bristol Myers Corporation, a leader in hair care and hair coloring products for women, concentrates its public relations efforts on the professional women's market.

In 1974, it established the Clairol Loving Care Scholarship Program to support the educational pursuits of women who are at least 30 years old and who want to return to school to advance their careers. The financial aid provided by Clairol can be used for child care, transportation, books, and tuition fees. In 15 years, the program has distributed more than $775,000 in scholarship funds to 1,500 women.

The scholarship program is one of three programs, collectively called the Clairol Partnership with Women, that express the company's interest in their customers' lives and careers. The second element of the Partnership program is the Clairol Take Charge Awards. This program, started in 1986, recognizes the achievements of women who have overcome obstacles and taken charge of their lives after age 30. Twenty-five women are selected annually to be the recipients of the awards, which carry grants of $1,000.

The newest program created by Clairol and its public relations firm, Lobsenz-Stevens, is the Clairol Mentor Program, which encourages successful women to "adopt" an aspiring young woman in the same area of business and encourage her career development. To launch the program, Clairol asked young women in eleven career categories to submit 1,000-word essays explaining why they would benefit from a mentor relationship. The competition was publicized in national media, women's magazines, and business and trade media. More than 30,000 women entered the competition conducted by the National Women's Economic Alliance Foundation, and the winners were selected by the mentor in each category. They were announced by Clairol's president, who presented their awards along with actress Linda Evans, the chairperson for the Partnership program and a women's-issues activist.

Publicity about the program contrasted the Clairol mentor program to the "old-boy network" that has traditionally helped men advance their

business careers. Clairol believes that these programs form a partnership between the company and the customer by addressing issues that
arise at different stages in a woman's career and educational development and that "the bottom line is to help women achieve their full potential and meet the goals they set for themselves."

HISPANIC MARKET PUBLIC RELATIONS

Creating public relations programs specifically targeted to minorities is
still a relatively new marketing strategy for many U.S. corporations. As
the country's demographics dramatically change over the next decade,
with minorities expected to reach 25 percent of the total U.S. population
by the year 2010, the number of marketing and public relations programs
that are segment-minded will significantly increase.

Marketers spent $490 million in advertising to Hispanics in 1987,
according to *Hispanic Business Magazine.* They have very good reasons for
paying greater attention to the Hispanic market. Some 20 million Hispanics live in the United States today, representing slightly less than 10 percent of the total population and a buying power of $150 billion. The U.S.
Census Bureau reported in 1988 that the nation's Hispanic population
increased 34 percent since 1980, almost five times faster than the rest of
the population. With immigration and high birth rates continuing, Hispanics are expected to surpass blacks as the largest minority in the United
States in a few decades. *Promote* magazine says that "any company that
wants to grow in the future will have a hard time doing it without the
Hispanic market."

The Hispanic population represents a regional as well as an ethnic
market because two-thirds of the Hispanics in the United States live
in three states: California, Texas, and New York, and 90 percent live in
these states plus six others: Florida, Illinois, New Jersey, Arizona, New
Mexico, and Colorado. In the cities of Los Angeles and Miami, Hispanics
make up more than a quarter of the metropolitan population.

The largest Hispanic segment is Mexican (12.6 million), mostly concentrated in Texas and California; people of Central and South American
origin (2.5 million) largely live in California and New York; Puerto Ricans
(2.3 million) are mostly located in New York, and over 1 million Cubans
live in Florida.

Nine out of ten Hispanics speak Spanish, half of them as their first
language. In a recent survey, Nielsen Data Research found that 25.5 percent speak only Spanish; 18.6 percent speak mostly Spanish; 33.2 percent
speak Spanish and English; 12.5 percent speak mostly English; just over
10.2 percent speak only English.

Paul Alvarez, chairman of Ketchum Public Relations, insists there
is no universal Hispanic experience or culture. He says the "real common
thread tying the Mexican, Cuban, Puerto Rican, and Dominican people

together is their coexistence with, and assimilation into, the American mainstream." Alvarez points out that only 67 percent watch Spanish-language television, that only 21 percent read Spanish-language newspapers, and that younger and more affluent Hispanics prefer English.

Nevertheless, the increase of Hispanics has been accompanied by the rise of Spanish-language media. This includes between 400 and 500 newspapers and a Spanish-language Sunday supplement called *Vista* that has a one-million-plus circulation in 27 newspapers. In addition, there is a proliferation of Spanish television and radio stations. Radio is said to be the medium most commonly used among younger, bilingual Hispanics. Two Spanish-language TV networks, Telemundo and Univision, attract 5 percent of the total television audience during prime time. Telemundo, started in 1986, already reaches 75 percent of the U.S. Hispanic population. Every Saturday night, an audience of between 4 million and 8 million Hispanics tunes in to "Sabado Gigante," a 3 1/2-hour show featuring a popular host, Don Francisco, Latin stars, games, skits, and music. *Business Week* describes it as "a raucous Spanish-language extravaganza that is becoming as much of a family ritual for Hispanics as the 'Ed Sullivan Show' used to be for Middle America." The magazine says:

> The show is a marketer's dream: It's hard to tell where the ads leave off and the show begins. Brands such as Coca-Cola and Coors are openly pitched during the show, their names repeated dozens of times. The studio audience of 300, flown in from around the country at the program's expense, claps and sings in unison to jingles for Kinney's shoes, Ultra Pampers Plus and Tide Detergent.[2]

Hispanics are brand-conscious and brand-loyal. That is why virtually every consumer product company is trying to get a piece of the action. Many companies spend their money on event sponsorships. Strategy Research reports that 63.6 percent of Hispanics purchase products from companies that sponsor festivals or events. Calle Ocho, the Miami Carnival, is the best attended, attracting 1.5 million people and more than 100 corporate sponsors every year. Other big Hispanic events attracting 500,000 to 1 million people include the Puerto Rican Day and Hispanic Day parades in New York and Fiesta del Sol in Chicago.

Ana Bischoff, who heads Burson-Marsteller's Hispanic marketing efforts, counsels her clients to align themselves with causes that matter to Hispanics. She told *Relate* magazine,

> When it comes to the Hispanic market, the traditional four Ps are just not enough. You can have an excellent product and a good price, be in the right place in terms of the Hispanic market, and create an exciting promotion, but you need two additional Ps because the Hispanic market is becoming bombarded and the consumers are becoming jaded. You need power and participation.

P&G Plaza

Procter & Gamble has been among the most aggressive marketers to the Hispanic community. Soccer is the number-one sport among Hispanics, and P&G's sponsorship of "Classico Internacional" soccer matches reached the market and helped increase sales of Zest and other soap brands in Hispanic regions of the country. The games were held in San Antonio, Texas, and San Jose, California, where the American Olympic Team played a Mexican team. A local youth-all-star game preceded each match. Spectators were able to buy half-price tickets with P&G proof-of-purchase coupons. Supermarkets in Hispanic neighborhoods supported the matches with special store displays and local ads.

Cinco de Mayo (May 5) celebrates the victory by Mexico in its war with France. P&G chose the festival to test its national Car-Key promotion with the Hispanic market. The program offered purchasers of P&G products a chance to win one of 750 Chevrolet vehicles. A series of events, developed with Hill & Knowlton, included more than 100 pre- and post-Cinco de Mayo supermarket parking-lot festivals. Customers were attracted to participate in games related to P&G brands and receive free product samples. The vehicles to be given away in the national sweepstakes were displayed, and the contest was explained by bilingual interpreters. Two major celebrations were held on Cinco de Mayo weekend in parks in Santa Ana and in downtown Los Angeles. At each park, a "Plaza de Procter & Gamble" was set up to control sampling activities and coupon giveaways. A VIP reception for the retail trade was held at the Mexican Consulate overlooking P&G Plaza at Olvera Street in Los Angeles. The event received a Special Event Marketing Award from *ADWEEK* in 1987.

A P&G Plaza was also set up to break through the noise and to promote all of its brands at Miami's huge Calle Ocho and festivals in San Antonio and Houston in 1987. To attract people to the Pampers booth, Burson-Marsteller created "Bebe Pampers 1987," a beautiful-baby competition. At each, a photographer took instant pictures of moms and their babies. The winner received a $2,000 college scholarship and a six-month supply of P&G's new Ultra Pampers thin diapers. Nearly 6,000 babies and their parents or grandparents posed. Based on its first-year success, the program was extended into Los Angeles, El Paso, and Fresno in 1988. The event captured media interest and dozens of articles appeared with headlines like this one from the *Miami Herald:* "Contest Captures Thousands of Pampered Darlings." Another Burson-Marsteller program involved commissioning a popular muralist to direct over 100 children to paint an original mural depicting Hispanic family life at the Fiesta Y Cultura Children's Festival sponsored by Pampers.

Another Bebe Pampers MPR program, in conjunction with local hospitals at key Hispanic festivals, was Centro Pampers, sanitary diaper-changing centers, where women could join a mothers' club and receive product literature, coupons, and samples.

McDonald's Hispanic Heritage Art Contest

McDonald's also used the medium of art to enable young Hispanic students to explore and appreciate their Hispanic heritage through art. The program, which began in 1986 and is implemented by Golin/Harris, targets students in grades 1 through 9, particularly those who have the most difficult time adapting to the Anglo school system. The program encourages Hispanic pride among the students, their parents, and their teachers.

Art-contest brochures are distributed to 5,000 public and private elementary and junior high schools in the top 33 Hispanic ADIs in the United States and Puerto Rico. In the first year, over 2,000 children entered the contest; 28 semifinalists and 2 grand prize winners were selected. The grand prize winners and their parents and teachers were taken to Washington, DC, to attend Hispanic Heritage Week activities. All 30 award-winning drawings were displayed both at the Capitol Children's Museum, where Hispanic students from Washington schools viewed them, and at the Congressional Hispanic Caucus Banquet, where they were seen by more than 2,000 politicians and officials from the United States and Puerto Rico.

Following the Washington display, the art was exhibited in San Juan, Oklahoma City, Colorado Springs, Chicago, and Los Angeles. Creation of additional understanding of Hispanic heritage and of local publicity that would encourage entries in the second Hispanic Heritage Art Contest and Exhibit were the goals.

By 1988, the program had attracted twice the number of entries. The Rose Garden reception, at which President Reagan signed the Hispanic Heritage Week proclamation and the three grand prize winners presented their art to the President, was covered by network and local television, radio, and print media. The exhibit was hosted by eleven local markets and was widely covered by their Spanish-language and general media.

The 1988 contest, featured in a special five-minute segment on the Univision network's "Sabado Gigante," was aired in Mexico, Puerto Rico, and several other Central and South American countries. McDonald's and Raintree Publishers published the *McDonald's Hispanic Art Heritage Art Book*, using the grand-prize-winning artwork and semifinalist pieces from the first three contests.

Levi's Charro Competition

Levi Strauss & Co. is the creator of blue jeans, and Levi jeans have been a basic part of the cowboy's outfit since the days of the California gold rush. Sponsorship of the Mexican charro competition was a natural extension of the company's tradition. The contests are part of a Charro Federation–U.S.A. program to preserve and promote *charreadas,* the popular, exciting, Mexican-rodeo sport. The *charreada,* or *fiesta charra,* takes place in neighborhoods and at ranches located outside of major cities. In keeping with the culture and pageantry of the traditional *charreada,* the "Reina Charra," the queen of the *charreada,* leads a march into the arena before the charro competition begins.

Charros, men skilled in equestrian arts, compete for "Levi's Charreada Competition" team championship title by bronco busting, riding and roping bulls, and showcasing their rope techniques. All entrants are presented with traditional Mexican trophies and Levi's products, and the winners receive a charro-style Levi's denim outfit decorated by a Mexican designer. Following the competition, local retailers sponsor a Levi's Western Wear Fashion Show.

Levi's produces a bilingual brochure, "La Charreada Mexicana," to encourage people interested in participating in *charreadas* to join a charro group.

MPR AND THE AFRICAN-AMERICAN MARKET

While more companies are creating public relations programs like these to reach Hispanics of all ages and national origins, fewer companies are funding PR programs specifically directed to the nation's largest minority market, both in terms of size and spending power. African-Americans currently are 12 percent of the U.S. population. By 2000, according to estimates based on U.S. Census Bureau data, blacks will be the majority in 13 of the largest cities in the United States and will spend more than $400 billion annually on goods and services, or about twice the amount they spend now.

Since the late 1960s, creation of advertising that targets the black consumer market has been part of the marketing plans for many consumer-driven corporations like McDonald's, Coca-Cola U.S.A., and Ford Motor Company. Astute marketers at these and other companies have long understood the importance of developing segmented marketing strategies. It is not unusual, for example, for leading consumer brands to receive over 50 percent of their market share from sales to African-Americans, who are very brand-loyal consumers.

It has been estimated that as much as $700 million a year is being spent on advertising that targets this market. New media like Black Entertainment Television (BET), *Emerge* magazine, and several radio networks that include Sheridan Broadcasting and National Black Network have joined longtime leading publications like *Ebony, Jet, Essence,* and *Black Enterprise* to reach black audiences.

Still, too few companies have created MPR programs that target the market, and even fewer PR firms have the ability to reach them. *Relate* magazine points out:

> There are an estimated 18 million black adults in the United States, and like the Hispanics their spending power is increasing. Yet relatively few corporations have targeted these people, and even fewer PR agencies can boast expertise in reaching them. One reason for this may be that the black and white Americans are not divided by language differences. While language barriers emphasize the point that the Hispanic population has a distinct set of cultural characteristics, there may be an assumption that black Americans have assimilated more fully the characteristics of "the mainstream."

"Not so," says James Hill, president and CEO of Burrell Public Relations, the nation's largest minority-owned agency that specializes in segmented public relations targeting African-Americans and Hispanics. "African-American people have a culture that is different from that of whites," adds Hill. "Our life experiences are different; institutions important to us are often different from those of our white counterparts; the music we enjoy is sometimes not the same.

"As Tom Burrell, founder of Burrell Advertising, puts it, 'Black people are not dark-skinned white people.' The way you reach the African-American audience requires a sensitivity to and an appreciation for those differences which have to be considered when developing an effective targeted public relations program."

Canadian Mist's Fashions for Mist Behavin'

Hill cites a program his firm created for Canadian Mist. Since alcoholic-beverage advertising is prohibited from television and outdoor billboards in some states, reaching the African-American as well as the general market is a difficult task. PR can be especially important in positioning the product and reaching the African-American consumer in a meaningful way.

Burrell Public Relations did it through the creation of "Fashion for Mist Behavin'," a showcase of African-American fashion designers that celebrates the contributions African-Americans have made to the world of fashion. The show presents some of the hottest creations of both established designers and up-and-coming talents.

During the 1989–1990 season, "Fashion for Mist Behavin'" traveled to seven key markets and in each donated all the show's proceeds to organizations benefiting the African-American community. After three years, Canadian Mist contributions have totaled $200,000. The recipient organizations are profiled in the show's program brochure, which also highlights the designers, including the hometown talent of designers from cities on the tour.

Since the show is a benefit for local nonprofit organizations, public service announcements (PSAs) are used to promote the show on local television. Press kits are localized for each market, and local radio and television talk shows provide extensive coverage. It is estimated that the equivalent advertising dollars generated by the extensive broadcast and print media-relations campaign for the 1988–1989 tour was close to $400,000.

In addition to the coverage of the event, pre-publicity is gained in each market during the search for local models, which gives the show interesting local appeal.

McDonald's Celebrates Black History Month

Through the years, McDonald's Corporation has created a series of Black History Month programs. It has provided educational materials to schools on "Black History Through Art" and "Black History Through Music," as well as a film on the life of Dr. Martin Luther King. In 1988, the company created "McDonald's Black History Makers of Tomorrow," a program that honors outstanding black high school juniors who demonstrate leadership, character, exceptional scholarship, and "the potential to become black history makers of the future."

The program generates over 1,000 applications each year. From that number, 200 of the most outstanding applicants are selected and asked to write a 1,000-word essay on "The Making of Black History in the Future" and the role they personally will play in its development. From these 200 finalists, 10 national winners are selected. They are featured in television, radio, and magazine advertising in *Jet, Ebony, Crisis,* and *Black Enterprise* magazines during February, nationally celebrated as Black History Month.

"The students not only addressed problems facing black America, but developed viable solutions to meet these challenges head-on," said Ed Rensi, president, McDonald's U.S.A. "The essays were very insightful and . . . these students see themselves playing a very active and positive role in the growth of black America."

The highlight of the program for the 10 national black history makers is a 3-day leadership conference where they have the opportunity to meet some of the country's most outstanding leaders from business, civil rights, education, and politics.

Literary Achievement Awards. Another longtime program is McDonald's Literary Achievement Awards, started in 1978. This national competition honors insightful writing about the black experience in America. Awards given annually in poetry, fiction writing, and playwriting are named for three of the country's most esteemed black writers: the Nikki Giovanni Award for poetry, the Maya Angelou Award for fiction writing, and the Charles Fuller Award for playwriting. The program is presented in conjunction with the Negro Ensemble Company, one of the country's leading African-American theater organizations. Noted black writers and actors participate in a celebrity reading of the winners' works at an awards ceremony held in New York.

   McDonald's Dream Machine. McDonald's association with Jackie Joyner-Kersee is an extension of its commitment to young people through sports. In 1990, McDonald's announced that it had teamed up with Joiner-Kersee, winner of two Olympic gold medals and one of the world's greatest female athletes, on a new program called "McDonald's Dream Machine." The "McDonald's Dream Machine" message is simple: "Believe in your dreams and they can come true." The program emphasizes staying in school, staying away from drugs, and setting and achieving goals. Jackie Joyner-Kersee, who grew up in a poor, drug- and crime-ridden neighborhood in East St. Louis, Illinois, delivers her message to young people in school assemblies and neighborhood centers. She and her husband and coach Bob Kersee also conduct track-and-field clinics for young athletes as part of the "McDonald's Dream Machine" program. They conduct media interviews nationally, as well as in each local "Dream Machine" market, and they appear at local McDonald's restaurants to sign autographs.

Black Backlash: Uptown Goes Down

Positive outreach public relations programs cannot compensate for marketing campaigns for products that are perceived by blacks to provide a poor value or to be harmful to the consumer.

   As cigarette consumption declines in the United States, cigarette companies have increasingly targeted their messages to specific heavier-user groups, including blacks. More than 44 percent of black adults smoke, compared to 37 percent of other adults. In 1990, R.J. Reynolds announced its plans to test-market the first cigarette brand especially created for African-Americans. "Uptown" was carefully researched; its graphics, packaging, advertising, and name were designed to appeal to blacks. When the news broke that the product was to be test-marketed in Philadelphia, the city's medical and black communities took their protests to the media and found a powerful ally in U.S. Health and Human Services Secretary Louis W. Sullivan.

   In a speech at the University of Pennsylvania, the nation's top health official, himself black, denounced Reynolds for its "slick and sinister advertising" and declared "Uptown's message is more disease, more suffering, and more death for a group already bearing more than its share of smoking-related illness and mortality." He wrote a letter to Reynolds's president urging him to drop the product. Three weeks before the planned Philadelphia introduction, the company abruptly canceled the product, stating that because of the publicity it would be "unable to receive an accurate test-market reading on Uptown."

The company's marketing vice president issued a statement shifting blame to "the anti-smoking lobby." He said that Reynolds':

> sole purpose, plainly and simply, was to test-market a cigarette among smokers who currently buy competitive products. . . . We regret that a small coalition of anti-smoking zealots apparently believe that black smokers are somehow different from the others who choose to smoke and must not be allowed to exercise the same freedom of choice available to all other smokers. This represents a loss of choice for black smokers and a further erosion of the free enterprise system.[3]

The company told *The New York Times* that the only thing unusual about marketing to blacks was saying so and argued that a larger percentage of blacks prefer menthol cigarettes than other smokers. A spokesperson told *Time* that if Sears were to develop a line of clothing for blacks, it would go unnoticed.

The Uptown experience illustrates the increasing role of publicity in the marketplace, and, in the words of marketing consultant Al Reis, "The enormous power that consumer public opinion can have."

THE ASIAN-AMERICAN MARKET: MPR OPPORTUNITY

While marketers have targeted Hispanics and blacks for special attention, only a few have directed programs to the Asian-American market. Yet, as *The Wall Street Journal* has pointed out, "Its population is younger, more affluent, and more quality conscious than the U.S. as a whole, and it is one of the fastest-growing minorities in percentage terms."

According to the *Journal*, marketers have been reluctant to go after this market for a number of reasons. "Many say Asians will see and respond to ads in regular publications or on television. Some companies say they haven't yet researched the market, or think it's too small to bother with. Still others cite the diversity among Asian-Americans."

According to the U.S. Census Bureau, in 1988, there were 6.5 million Asians living in the United States, a dramatic increase from 3.8 million in 1980. The rise is largely due to immigration from the Philippines, China, South Korea, and India. Japanese-Americans were the largest Asian group for many years but in 1988 ranked fifth, making up 12.3 percent of the Asian population in this country, according to the Population Reference Bureau. Filipino-Americans are the single largest group (21.5 percent), followed by the Chinese (19.3 percent), Vietnamese (13.2 percent), Koreans (12.5 percent), and Japanese.

In his book *Futurescope*, Joe Cappo predicts that while Asians still make up less than 2 percent of the total U.S. population, their total numbers will double in the next 20 years and, by the middle of the 21st century, Asian-Americans will have as large a share of our population as Hispanics have today.

Asian-Americans present marketers with an ethnically diverse and highly regionalized market. About 35 percent of all Asian-Americans live in California, and another 40 percent are concentrated in four other states: Hawaii, New York, Illinois, and Washington.

The market also shares some other demographic traits. Impact Resources Inc., a Columbus, Ohio, market research firm, conducted a national survey of Asian consumers that revealed that they tend to live in larger households than the general market. Two-thirds of them live in dual-income households, as compared to 53 percent of the general market. The report stated that Asians share a strong family orientation, value security, and often place quality over price when shopping. The median family income of Asians exceeds that of other groups. So does the number of Asian-Americans who classify themselves as professionals.

This emerging market presents both advertising and MPR opportunities. The number of magazines, newspapers, and television and radio stations directed to Asian-Americans is expected to grow, providing marketers with new niched advertising media and publicity outlets. Sponsorship of Asian-American events such as the annual Chinese New Year Parade in San Francisco provides other promotional possibilities. The parade attracts 300,000 people as it snakes through Chinatown to the city's financial district, and it is telecast in San Francisco, Los Angeles, and Honolulu on Chinese-language television, offering sponsors of floats and commercial spots an opportunity to reach an even larger audience.

MPR GOES TO SCHOOL

Whittle Communications' announcement of "Channel One," a plan to beam a daily TV teen-news program with commercials to high school classrooms, ignited a new debate on the subject of commercialism in the classroom. The show's use of flashy graphics, quick-paced style, and youthful hosts appealed to students and those educators who see it as a way to involve students in the world at a time when schools lack funding for up-to-date learning materials. Other teachers, parents, and state legislators were concerned that two minutes of commercials in each twelve-minute show created a commercial intrusion in the classroom.

Newsweek described chairman Chris Whittle's $200-million investment in Channel One as "A Golden Boy's Toughest Sell," but Whittle hoped to beam his newscasts into 320,000 high school classrooms by the end of 1990. As an inducement, he offered $50,000 worth of free video equipment to schools that take the show. Whittle's competition is "CNN

Newsroom," which is commercial-free and available to schools on VCR. The program was estimated to be in 8,000 schools in 1990.

The teen-news-show medium may be new, but the advent of commercial exposure in schools is not. A *U.S. News and World Report* cover story reported that:

> Budget-bludgeoned schools are discovering they have a hidden gold mine: their appeal to marketers. . . . As a community service and good corporate public relations, companies have always cranked out reams of free instructional materials as supplementary aids for teachers on every subject from automobiles to zoology. Educators Progress Service of Randolph, Wisconsin, puts out catalogs listing thousands of pamphlets, booklets, filmstrips, and videotapes. In the last few years savvy educational marketers like Lifetime Learning Systems and Scholastic have developed this dull art form into an amazingly effective education and targeted-marketing tool. The two goals are not necessarily contradictory. The marketing value of these teacher kits depends on their educational value, on the degree which teachers find them useful in arousing students' interest in a given subject.[4]

The magazine cites "Quality Comes in Writing," a Lifetime Learning Systems kit sponsored by Bic pens and used by 1.2 million students. The kit includes work sheets on how to write a letter, a ballad, a diary, an advertisement, and a newspaper story. The story pointed out that "the sponsor's logo appears liberally throughout the work sheets and on an accompanying poster."

Other examples cited by the article include a program on "Being a Pet Parent," sponsored by Ralston Purina, and a program called "Bringing Kids and Books Together," in which Mott's Apple Juice rewards book readers with apple stickers. Other in-school reading programs like the "Jell-O Reading Rocket" and "Pizza Hut Book It!" programs are described earlier in this book.

Consumer Reports found that more than 20 million students a year use corporate-sponsored teaching tools.

McDonald's All-American High School Marching Band

McDonald's All-American High School Marching Band has provided outstanding young musicians with All-American status for over two decades. In its first 22 years, more than 70,000 young musicians have been nominated by their high school band directors and the Band itself has over 2,000 alumni.

In the spring, high school band directors nationwide take part in the annual search by nominating two of their best musicians. The thousands of nominations are reviewed by a selection committee composed of music educators. Final selection is based on the nominating band director's recommendation, the student's honors, and a taped audition.

Selection as an All-American offers each member special travel and performance opportunities. The McDonald's All American High School Marching Band appears annually in the Macy's Thanksgiving Day Parade in New York City and has marched in the Fiesta Bowl Parade in Phoenix and the Tournament of Roses Parade in Pasadena, California. In 1989, the All-American Marching Band performed on McDonald's World's Largest Concert simulcast on PBS. The Band's appearance with Willard Scott on NBC's "Today Show" on the day before Thanksgiving has become an annual tradition. The Jazz Band appears each year on the Jerry Lewis Labor Day Telethon to benefit the Muscular Dystrophy Association.

The top jazz players from the McDonald's All-American High School Marching Band are selected for the McDonald's All-American High School Jazz Band. It has also performed on the Lou Rawls's Parade of Stars Telethon to benefit the United Negro College Fund and at holiday concerts at New York's Carnegie Hall with jazz stars like Lionel Hampton and Maynard Ferguson.

The Band program gets national coverage through network exposure and print publicity and is publicized extensively on the grassroots level— from the nominations, through the selection process, to the band's performances. Local McDonald's operators announce and present certificates to all local nominees and honor those selected in publicized ceremonies. The local musician's appearances in national parades are celebrated in local newspapers and on radio and TV.

Levi's College Program

The public relations effort for Levi's 501 Jeans, the world's original blue jeans, has been directed to college students, an important and tough-to-reach segment within the brand's 16-to-24-year-old target market. The program was designed by Golin/Harris to make a 135-year-old product relevant to the lifestyle of today's youth and to make 501s competitive with new, fashionable jean designs from other companies. The program promotes Levi's 501 Jeans as a fashion necessity for today's college students. Product-specific activities include the Levi's 501 Report and The Levi's Campus Public Relations Challenge.

The Levi's 501 Report is a survey of 1,000 college students on 25 college campuses. The Roper organization conducts the poll through personal interviews with survey respondents. Students are asked to describe their tastes in fashion and lifestyles. Results every year since the poll began in 1985 reveal that students consider Levi's 501 Jeans the most essential item in a college wardrobe, enabling the firm to position its jeans as the pants of choice among today's college students and to establish Levi Strauss & Co. as an expert on youth culture. Most results are released to fashion and lifestyle media to coincide with Levi's peak back-to-school selling season. Other results are held for release at specific times throughout the year, to maximize media opportunities.

The poll receives extensive media coverage. Television coverage has included a four-minute "Today Show" segment on the poll, incorporating a video history of 501 Jeans that shows them being worn by President Reagan and Bruce Springsteen, and a fall campus fashion show modeled by college students. In addition to national coverage, the poll is localized in key sales markets where survey results are broken out by geographic region. As a result of the poll, media coverage of 501 Jeans as a fashion item increased by 27 percent. The report is conducted annually and many fashion and lifestyle editors now use the survey results every year in their fall back-to-school fashion sections.

The Levi's Campus Public Relations Challenge, created in 1984, is an annual competition sponsored in cooperation with the Public Relations Student Society of America (PRSSA). The program gives students the opportunity to promote Levi's 501 Jeans on their campuses and in their college communities, with the guidance and direction of the Golin/ Harris Levi's account team. PRSSA chapters nationwide are invited to "pitch" the Levi's 501 Jeans account by developing an 8-week publicity proposal for the product. The 25 chapters selected to compete are provided with guidelines, a budget, and product and promotional material and are asked to create and run fashion shows and other special events and to secure editorial coverage of the product in college and local media. Each chapter is required to submit a final report at its program's conclusion, reviewing activities, expenditures, and media results. A panel of professionals evaluates the programs for their creativity, writing skills, media relations, and the quality of their special events. The top chapter in each category wins cash prizes, and the overall winning chapter is awarded a trip to San Francisco to present its program to Levi Strauss & Co. management. In addition to student participation in campus events and coverage by campus and local media, cooperating retailers report significant sales increases during the competition period.

MPR AND THE POST-YOUTH CONSUMER

In a special report on "Marketing in the Year 2000" in *ADWEEK's Marketing Week*, Ken Dychtwald, author of the book *Age Wave* and a leading authority on marketing to older consumers, reminds marketers that the 76 million baby boomers born from 1946 to 1964 are now becoming middle-aged and by the year 2000 will be crossing the 50-year threshold:

> As they do, the spotlight of American culture will age with them. . . . For the past 40 years, we have been a youth-focused nation. Now as the result of elevating life expectancies, decreasing fertility and the middle-aging of

the baby-boom generation, the American marketplace is becoming increasingly middle-aged and mature. An era dominated by youth is ending. What we eat; what we wear; where, how and when we travel; what we buy and why we buy it, all will change as vast numbers of consumers face the opportunities and milestones of their journey beyond youth.[5]

Another expert on the 50 + population, Jeff Ostroff, says:

> For marketers, an understanding of today's older consumer is essential to both short- and long-term propriety. Not only are these consumers many and diverse, but their needs and wants are enormous. With a growing percentage of America's purchasing power in their hands, mature adults are showing an increasing willingness to spend for goods and services. This market offers a myriad of opportunities that will only magnify as our society continues to age.[6]

He describes the 50 + population as possessing nearly half of all discretionary income held by American consumers and accounting for 30 percent or more of all dollars spent for such things as ranges and refrigerators, floor coverings, new cars, grocery purchases, and jewelry.

Marketers are taking note of the healthier, wealthier, retirement-age group often called the "young old," especially since *Modern Maturity,* with 20.3 million subscribers, overtook *TV Guide* as the nation's most widely read publication in 1988. *Reader's Digest*'s *New Choices for the Best Years,* formerly *50 Plus,* has a circulation of more than 550,000. In 1989, Whittle Communications announced that it was planning a variation of its *Special Reports* specifically for adults 50 and older.

United Airlines Silver Wings Plus

The "greying of America" and its impact on consumer marketing was addressed at the 1989 PRSSA Conference by Camille Keith, Southwest Airlines' vice president of special marketing. She pointed out that 1 in 9 Americans is now over 60, that in 20 years the ratio would be 1 in 4, and that these mature Americans are more affluent than ever before. She said, "The impact on the way we all do business will be phenomenal. . . ."

Airlines have been among the first industries to identify the maturing of America as an opportunity. In 1986, United Airlines directed its attention to this fast-growing population when its market research showed that more than 5 million people over the age of 65 travel by air and control a larger amount of discretionary income than ever before.

United responded by creating Silver Wings Plus, a travel club for people 60 and over. United was not alone in recognizing the potential of the market. In 1986, American Airlines, TWA, Delta, and Eastern all introduced travel clubs with similar benefits. United's challenge was to set its club apart from the others by positioning itself as having the most concern for older travelers. To complement the marketing effort, United and Hill & Knowlton designed a strategic public relations program to increase revenue of the club and generate revenue for the company.

Focus groups with senior citizens revealed that seniors have special needs quite different from those of business travelers and that they are wary of the difficulties of travel. As a result, United selected as its Silver Wings Plus spokesperson a senior citizen who was knowledgeable about the ins and outs of travel. Betty Lowry, a 67-year-old former United chief stewardess and an employee of the airline for 37 years, was asked to come out of retirement to serve as "president" of Silver Wings Plus. She was booked on media in markets that were serviced by United and had a high concentration of citizens over 60.

On her tours, Betty Lowry offers a free book, *Senior Travel, No Better Time*, produced by United to clear up the confusion of travel for seniors. The book details airline services relevant to seniors' needs, such as wheel-chair availability, baggage assistance, and special needs, as well as basic tips of how to plan and pack for a vacation. Advertising expenditures were minimal and United credits the public relations program for helping Silver Wings Plus exceed its membership goals, generating millions in revenue for United.

Choice Time for Seniors

In 1987, Aetna Life & Casualty Company and its public relations counsel, Ketchum Public Relations, launched a public education program to help seniors understand and plan ahead to meet the potentially devastating costs of health care. Surveys indicated that up to 80 percent of older Americans erroneously believed that Medicare covers extended stays in nursing homes. In 1985, Aetna introduced long-term care (LTC) insurance to cover nursing home expenses. A communications program called "Choice Time: Thinking Ahead on Long-Term Care" was developed as a public service to sensitize seniors to the need for LTC insurance and to enhance Aetna's image as a concerned and knowledgeable provider of LTC insurance to people over 65.

Esther Peterson, respected consumer advisor to three presidents and herself a senior citizen, was invited to represent Choice Time, adding credibility and appeal to the program. She wrote and offered a free booklet that explained costs and sources of LTC insurance and guided readers in shopping carefully for protection.

Benchmark and follow-up research revealed that the Choice Time program increased awareness of Medicare's inability to meet nursing care costs, increased awareness of LTC insurance, and increased awareness of the Aetna product. The program also increased the visibility of Aetna sales managers in their communities and excited agents about the senior market.

21

The Future of Marketing
Public Relations

Harold Burson, CEO of Burson-Marsteller and one of the most influential
figures in expanding the boundaries of public relations, has said that there
will continue to be a "growing demand for what public relations does even
though it may not always be called public relations." He told the Public
Relations Society of America's Counselors Academy in 1989 that:

> Business will continue to face intense competition; business will be
> pressured to reduce costs; business must continue to develop new markets,
> to find new niches for its products and services, . . . business will con-
> tinue to be regulated by governments, business will continue to satisfy
> the voracious appetites of consumers for information. In other words, busi-
> ness will continue to face problems whose solution is attitude-based and
> communications-driven. The discipline of public relations is best equipped
> to deal with problems of that kind.[1]

PUBLIC RELATIONS IN THE AGE OF MARKETING

In order to forecast where marketing public relations is going in the 1990s
and beyond, it is instructive to look at how public relations has both
reflected and supported the marketing milestones of the age of marketing
that began in the post-World War II era.

At the American Marketing Association World Conference, on May
27, 1987, Philip Kotler identified the most significant marketing concepts
to emerge in the past four decades.[2] Virtually all of these milestones can
be said to have influenced or been influenced by public relations. So
closely do the two functions parallel one another that Professor Sidney
Levy, Chairman of the Marketing Department at the prestigious Kellogg
School of Management at Northwestern University, has commented that

public relations is really a better description of what "we marketers do than marketing." He laments the fact that the public relations people got to the label first.

In the following sections, the milestones of each decade listed by Kotler are described. The concepts have been adapted and enhanced over the years, but they encompass a compendium of contemporary marketing thinking.

Marketing Concepts of the 1950s

○ **The Marketing Mix**. The combination of elements used by companies to market their products to consumers. As we have seen, the marketing mix for an increasing number of consumer products now includes marketing public relations along with advertising, promotion, and sales.

○ **Product Life Cycle**. The stages from product introduction through growth, maturity, and decline of sales. This concept has undergone many refinements and variations, but whatever the nomenclature, MPR has played an important role in all stages by communicating new news and identifying products with newsworthy associations.

○ **Brand Image**. How consumers feel about products and the companies that make them. Introduced in 1955, this idea is, according to Kotler, "especially beloved by advertisers and public relations people."

○ **Market Segmentation**. The partitioning of the market into meaningful segments, to focus marketing efforts more precisely. MPR has been especially effective in targeting specific "publics" and developing programs to reach them.

○ **The Marketing Concept**. Making what will sell, as defined by the consumer, rather than selling what is made. Public relations supports this concept by communicating messages about how products answer consumer needs and make life easier, happier, and better.

○ **The Marketing Audit**. Monitoring marketing strategies, structures, and systems to keep them attuned to changing market conditions. The public relations audit, which arose simultaneously, monitors a company's relationships with its publics. The marketing public relations audit concentrates on analyzing the company's marketing communications to vital audiences, including but not limited to the ultimate consumer, and, importantly, communications to those who influence consumer attitudes and purchasing decisions.

The Soaring 1960s

○ **The Four Ps Classification of the Marketing Mix**. Product, price, place, and promotion. Public relations fits in the promotion P. Some public relations practitioners believe that a fifth P may be most important of all. That P is perception, since people's brand preferences and buying behavior are largely the result of how they perceive products and the companies that market them.

○ **Marketing Myopia**. Companies fail when they focus on the product and not the consumer. Since editors act as gatekeepers of the news, marketing public relations must focus on disseminating information of value to the consumer, that is, reader, listener, and viewer, in order to gain the implied editorial endorsement of the media.

○ **Lifestyles**. The psychographic definition of consumer audiences and appeals. MPR is more and more grounding programs in life-style research and shaping product messages and event sponsorships on their appeal to psychographically defined audiences.

○ **The Broadened Concept of Marketing**. Advanced by Kotler and Levy, the application of marketing not only to products and services, but also to organizations, persons, places, and ideas. MPR programs are used to market nonprofit organizations, business leaders, and celebrities of all sorts, as well as companies and brands. It has been shown how a corporation's positions on various issues of concern to consumers affect their patronage.

The Turbulent 1970s

○ **Social Marketing**. Calling attention to the role that marketing can play in affecting social causes. Public relations is arguably the most effective marketing method for achieving social change. It is used by consumer activists and by proactive companies and trade groups to advance their positions.

○ **Positioning**. How brands are ranked against the competition in customers' minds. Introduced by Al Reis and Jack Trout, positioning has been applied by Kenneth Lightcap and others to public relations strategies that identify brands with consumer-service programs, that set the stage for positive reception of product advertising.

○ **Strategic Marketing**. Pursuing marketing strategies, sharply distinguished from marketing tactics; an offshoot of the corporate strategic-planning concept promulgated by the Boston consulting group in the early 1970s. Public relations plans of the past focused almost exclusively on tactics—the trick was to come up with a Big Idea that would generate headlines. Today, MPR tactics are more likely to grow out of strategies that work with the other elements of the marketing mix to meet marketing objectives. MPR programs are evaluated on how well ideas/tactics support marketing strategies.

○ **Societal Marketing**. Calling upon business to factor into its decisions the long-term interests of consumers and society. Public relations plays a unique role as "the conscience of the company" in counseling marketing management on changes in the social environment to which they must adapt and in identifying opportunities to take actions that will win consumer approval and trust.

○ **Macromarketing.** Examining the aggregate effects of business activity on consumer welfare and values. Macromarketing combines the disciplines of marketing public relations (MPR) and the specialized area of corporate public relations (CPR) known as issues management.

○ **Service Marketing.** Regarding the marketing of services as having needs that are separate from product marketing. MPR programs have proliferated in recent years in supporting such services as management consulting and financial services and, more recently, medical services (hospitals and HMOs) and law and accounting firms. These programs build positive awareness of the institution's distinctive competence and tend less to market "product" benefits.

The Uncertain 1980s

○ **Marketing Warfare.** Promoting product benefits and positioning brand benefits directly against the marketing strategies of competing brands. Public relations has played a key role and often provided the competitive edge in the cola wars, the beer wars, the burger wars, and the athletic shoe wars, among others.

○ **Internal Marketing.** Establishing a marketing culture in a company. Public relations plays a unique role in broadly communicating the company's new marketing orientation to both external and internal audiences in an organized pragmatic way.

○ **Global Marketing.** Developing more uniform product and communications plans around the world. Theodore Levitt proposed global marketing in 1983, on the theory that too much adaptation to local markets results in a loss of economies of scale. This theory has been adopted by some multinational advertising agencies and public relations firms through simultaneous worldwide product introductions and sponsorships.

○ **Local Marketing.** Marketing efforts tailored to the local market environment. Simultaneous with global marketing, a trend led by the Campbell Soup Company, Nabisco, General Foods, and others, which says that marketing—from product variations to benefits to local advertising and promotion—starts at the local level. MPR programs have long been adapted to the needs, wants, and life-styles of consumers, city by city, region by region, or country by country.

○ **Direct Marketing**. Reaching the individual consumer with a product or message. Direct marketing has gone beyond door-to-door selling to party selling, telemarketing, TV home shopping, and shopping by personal computer. All of these methods gain credibility when the product or selling company has first earned consumer trust and confidence by gaining endorsement from media and other third-party endorsers reached by MPR.

○ **Relationship Marketing**. Building interactions with consumers. The term came into usage in the mid-1980s and holds that relationships, more than transactions, better capture the spirit of marketing. This is, of course, the ultimate public relations oriented definition of marketing, because building relationships with "publics" is what public relations is all about.

○ **Megamarketing**. Harnessing political and public relations skills to overcome marketing barriers. In Kotler's words, megamarketing addresses "the problem of breaking into protected and blocked markets." This book defines the approval of society's gatekeepers as a "pass" strategy that must be considered by today's marketers, in addition to the traditional trade "push" and consumer "pull" strategies.

MPR IN THE 1990s AND BEYOND

Marketing public relations has played an integral role in supporting each step in the evolution of the marketing concept and is certain to continue to do so in the future.

The CEOs of the two largest U.S.-based PR firms see the 1990s as a period of unprecedented growth, provided PR is up to the challenge. H&K's Bob Dilenschneider says that the world of business will be "shouting for what PR professionals can do in the 1990s." Among the reasons, he cites:

○ Companies now know that they need public consent to do business.

○ Technology has created the need for instant, and often global, information.

○ Media and government control are more incisive and resourceful than ever before.

○ Society all over the world is swamped in a flood of public policy initiatives.

○ With the gradual decline of advertising, marketers want powerful weapons—public relations weapons—in their mix of tactics.[3]

Burson-Marsteller's Jim Dowling predicts that PR will gain recognition in the 1990s. "The real challenge will be to keep up with the demands made on us in an increasingly complex and global world, a world in which the PRF (Public Relations Factor) may well spell the difference between success and failure." Dowling believes that "the deregulation and less government interference of the eighties have sowed the seeds for a revival of activism and increased demand on business to solve a much broader array of social problems in the nineties." The role of public relations will increase as activists accelerate their demands on business, placing more products at risk.

The specific direction of MPR in the 1990s and beyond will be shaped by the clarification, if not the resolution, of a number of distinctions and dichotomies.

MPR versus CPR

Some public relations counselors have begun to advocate patterning PR firms like law firms. Herbert Corbin, managing partner of KCS&A Public Relations says the law-firm-type structure engenders continuity of service and holds partners accountable not only to clients but to other partners of the firm. He cites product litigation, handling tender offers, and crisis management as the kind of sophisticated communications problems requiring partner involvement. This kind of organization is most applicable to the CPR firm that counsels top management on matters involving the company's vital interests with government and the financial community.

Marketing public relations serves a parallel purpose for advertising and promotion, and the firm specializing in MPR is organized similarly to advertising and sales-promotion firms. The management level of the MPR firm devises strategies and is responsible for developing creative tactics that support those strategies. The implementation of tactics is the responsibility of an account-management team, usually headed by a supervisor who keeps the program on course, on schedule, and on budget. The next level on the MPR table of organization is the account executive, who is responsible for the day-to-day implementation of the program.

This functional difference supports the contention of this book that MPR and CPR should be recognized as separate, self-sufficient disciplines and that corporations and PR firms should reorganize to take best advantage of the particular expertise and skills of each.

The two are closely interrelated when marketing decisions affect or are affected by corporate philosophies and actions. But the role of MPR should be focused on helping the corporation achieve its marketing objectives, while the role of CPR should be to counsel management on corporate positions and actions as they relate to the achievement of corporate goals. CPR then acts in an advisory staff function, while MPR is a line function whose role is to support the successful marketing of the company's goods and services.

Local versus Global

CPR programs have traditionally included community relations programs in plant and headquarters locations, support of local philanthropies, and events designed for employees and their families, such as open houses and outings. Likewise, MPR has long had a local focus. Most "national" programs are locally driven and require the development of angles that will attract local media and involve local consumers. A water purifier company recently conducted a media tour that linked the need for its product with a report on the condition of local drinking water compared to other cities. Campbell Soup localized the National Soup Month story by announcing the most popular soups by city.

Peter Gummer, chairman and chief executive of Shandwick PLC, contends that "public relations is essentially a local activity." He told *The New York Times*, "It is about changing attitudes and ideas about products and services in a local market. That means getting hold of people who influence opinions—journalists, politicians—and changing their attitudes on a local basis." For that reason, the PR firms acquired by Shandwick throughout the world continue to operate under their former names rather than the Shandwick brand. Gummer feels it is a competitive advantage to keep names of PR firms that are well-known and respected locally. He believes that the emphasis on local markets works because "PR is a terribly personal business."[4]

On the other hand, the other two PR giants, Burson-Marsteller and Hill & Knowlton emphasize their ability to provide worldwide "seamless" service to their clients. In a 1989 story called "The Image Polishers Go Global," *The New York Times* reported that B-M and H&K "are marching across the globe, opening offices in places that once seemed barely worth a business trip." B-M's Jim Dowling told the *Times*, "We start our own offices because its cheaper and because we want all of our people steeped in the Burson culture," adding, "you have to be an effective national organization in all of your locations before you become an effective international company."

The move toward worldwide coverage is certain to accelerate in the 1990s and beyond, stimulated by the emergence of more multinational client companies, the burgeoning markets in the Asia/Pacific world region, the effects of the breakdown of European trade barriers in 1992, the emergence of free-market economies in the countries of Eastern Europe, and the expansion of markets in the Soviet Union and even in China. As noted earlier in the book, one of the largest Golin/Harris assignments of 1989–90 was the opening of McDonald's largest restaurant, in Moscow.

Jim Arnold, president of Chester Burger Company, a management consulting company specializing in public relations, says of the increasing, worldwide expansion of public relations firms, "It's turning into a global shootout. Even when the profits aren't there, no one wants to be seen as pulling back. Instead, everyone is advancing the flag, and growth is the name of the game."

The globalization of public relations can be seen in the ownership of PR counseling firms. A decade ago, all of the world's top five public relations firms were American owned. Today, Burson-Marsteller is the only one.

Generalist versus Specialist

H&K's Bob Dilenschneider believes that public relations is in the process of dividing into small "boutique" firms and global agencies. He points out that "specialization is often a factor in this transformation, with consultants possessing not only communications skills, but a knowledge of a particular industry."

Steve Lesnik says these boutique firms will not be unimportant. "The boutique scenario will offer small, competent shops of yesteryear a chance for survival. The boutique scenario will offer narrow services in a speciality in which it truly excels. Or it will be a firm which has deep roots, special understanding and relationships, or great power in a particular geographic location."

The emergence of public relations mega-agencies is not likely to entirely replace the small and midsize public relations firm. There are many clients who prefer to be a larger fish in a small pond. Bruce K. Berger, director of worldwide human-health public relations for Upjohn Company, says, "Generally small to midsized agencies for whom we represent the significant account seem to work harder and more cost-effectively for us."

The 1980s saw great growth of new public relations firms specializing in high technology and healthcare. Firms specializing in the entertainment business, like Rogers & Cowan, and in the retail business, like Margie Korshak, continued to grow, as did specialists in food, fashion, and travel.

The largest specialty agency and one of the fastest growing of all public relations firms is Regis McKenna Inc., the Palo Alto-based company that prefers to be known as a "marketing company." McKenna has helped some of America's leading hi-tech companies, including Apple Computer, map out and implement their total marketing programs, not just their marketing communications.

In the 1990s, environmental public relations is certain to impact marketing and become the dominant growth area for public relations firms and corporate public relations departments.

Independence versus Advertising Ownership

Relate magazine has referred to the ownership of public relations firms by advertising agencies as "a marriage of inconvenience." While acquired PR firms have picked up some business from the advertising clients of the parent company and tapped the parent for capital to expand, the jury is still out on the workability of the integrated services concept. Many clients seek counsel independent of advertising control. Bob Dilenschneider says, "An advertising executive once told one of our people that it would be bad for client relations to challenge the client with different ideas. The client looks at it very differently. Bill Lemoth, CEO of Kellogg, told me he didn't care how the budget was divided up as long as it sold cereal. That's what our main focus should be."

Recent experience has shown that when push comes to shove advertising decisions will (and, from a dollars-and-cents point of view, *must*) prevail. Martin Sorrell, head of WPP Group, ordered its Hill & Knowlton public relations subsidiary to stop working for the head of Louis Vuitton because of a conflict with the Hennessy Cognac and Chandon Champagne advertising account, which was controlled by a rival for the Moet-Hennessy-Louis Vuitton empire. London's *Sunday Times* reported that when the client reminded Sorrell that H&K's work could jeopardize millions of pounds' worth of cognac and champagne advertising, he intervened and gave 30-days' notice to H&K's client that he was removing the PR firm from the battle.

The split of Golin/Harris from its parent advertising firm, FCB Communications, an otherwise harmonious and productive relationship, was caused because of the threat of a client conflict. When FCB decided to pursue the $200-million Burger King advertising account, a conflict of interest was created with its public relations subsidiary. Golin/Harris had represented industry leader McDonald's Corporation for more than 30 years, and it was the firm's largest and best-known client. Something had to give, and it was the relationship with FCB. The conflict set the wheels in motion for the sale of Golin/Harris to Shandwick PLC. Ironically, the management of both Burger King and its parent company, Pillsbury, changed during the advertising solicitation as a result of the company's takeover by Grand Metropolitan P.L.C., and all bets were off. FCB did not get the Burger King business, and the conflict might have been averted.

In a speech to the American Association of Advertising Agencies (4As) shortly after this episode, I said that "my advertising colleagues over the years accept as an article of faith that advertising, especially television advertising, is the universal solution to all marketing problems" and that "no matter how sincere ad-agency management may be in their dedication to total communications, it hasn't trickled down. The manager of an advertising profit center is evaluated on his bottom line, and this is far more motivational than contributing to corporate goals like the total communications concept."[5]

The 4As, recognizing the need for member advertising agencies, particularly those with PR units, to understand public relations better, has sponsored a public relations seminar annually for the past several years. In 1989, the 4As published a booklet called "What Every Account Executive Should Know About Public Relations."

Integration versus Specialization

While some marketers agree in principle with the notion of one-stop shopping for marketing communications services, there have been problems in execution, organization, fixing of responsibility, and delivery of uniform-quality service across the board.

Ogilvy Group recently reorganized its operations in an attempt to get more of its clients to use more of its services. Under the new organization, a senior executive on an account, known as a "client service director," is responsible for all client contact and for coordinating the work of all of the agency's services. The system is too new to evaluate, but questions have been raised about the ability of the "client service director" to function as an all-purpose marketing communicator and to understand the various disciplines well enough to orchestrate them. A further complication is the fact that the client "contacts" for advertising, sales promotion, and public relations are often different people in different, unrelated company departments with different reporting structures. J. Raymond Lewis, senior vice president of marketing at Holiday Inns, Inc., says:

> I don't think there is anything inherently beneficial in having all the services under one roof. In my experience, advertising agencies have enough difficulty coordinating all the functions they already have—creative, media, account management—without worrying about bringing public relations into the mix. Furthermore, it doesn't fit our structure. Our advertising agency reports to the vice president of consumer marketing, our PR firm reports to the director of PR. Although both of them report to me, they are autonomous in their own areas.[6]

While some clients may prefer one-stop shopping, an opposite number of clients look to a variety of sources for marketing input and want to be exposed to more options and alternatives rather than a neatly integrated, advertising-centered plan. Susan Henderson, marketing/PR manager at Miller Brewing Company, says, "It's not the name on the door that's important, it's the talent in the room."[7]

This much is clear: Marketing plans must integrate all elements of the mix. Greater knowledge and understanding of MPR are called for, as well as advertising and promotion on the part of the marketing "client" and greater interaction among the communications firms or departments that conceive and execute the plan. The client must inevitably be the coordinator of integrated marketing communications services. It remains to be seen whether the advertising agency will become the principal provider of all of these services.

Regulation versus Business as Usual

The growth of marketing public relations has benefited not only from the increasing costs and decreasing efficiency of advertising, but from government restrictions and regulations imposed on advertising of certain products and categories. Both the federal government and the states' attorneys general have formed coalitions to prevent marketers from making claims about the health benefits and efficacy of their products. As a result, many marketers have turned to public relations to carry their message to the consumer.

Despite the fact that this product information has passed editorial muster and is edited and transmitted as news by the media, some critics argue that the public relations message needs to be scrutinized and regulated in the same way as advertising.

The increased use of video news releases (VNRs) by TV stations—a result of the downsizing of news departments, the desire for visually interesting stories, and the interest of viewers in business news—has created particular concern that VNRs are advertising masked as news and thus are subject to regulation. The FDA is studying whether the use of VNRs, news conferences, and paid "spokesdoctors" and patients by pharmaceutical companies constitutes promotion rather than an exchange of information.

The war against smoking has resulted in pressure from the U.S. Secretary of Health and Human Services, among others, on cigarette companies to drop their sponsorships of sports events, especially those televised events where cigarette logos are shown on signs, banners, clothing, and vehicles. Further tobacco and beverage regulation will raise First Amendment questions about the rights of companies to market their products and of consumers to choose to use products that are legally sold, questions that could be implied from a current Philip Morris corporate-advertising campaign celebrating the bicentennial of the U.S. Bill of Rights.

Blind Faith versus Measurement

The need for improved ways to measure MPR results is greater than ever. The subject is not new. Companies like AT&T and Procter & Gamble, and PR firms like Burson-Marsteller, Ketchum, and Porter/Novelli, have developed their own systems to evaluate PR programs, but there are no universally accepted and applied research systems that measure outcomes of MPR programs and compare results with industry norms. With more numbers oriented product managers making PR decisions, the need to quantify results has never been greater. Most product managers, by both training and experience, are focused on advertising and accept its predominance in the marketing mix as an article of faith. Philip Kotler says that ad people can hide behind recall scores, but there is more pressure on PR people to work harder at tracking success stories.

While it is often difficult to separate out the effect on sales of MPR and other elements in the market mix, measures can be perfected to evaluate the trust factor that underlies consumer receptivity to many MPR programs.

MPR AND THE MAKER'S MARK

Laurel Cutler, futurist, marketing guru, and simultaneously vice chairman of FCB Leber/Katz and vice president of Chrysler Corporation, examined the future of the mass brand and the mass consumer at the 1989 meeting of the American Association of Advertising Agencies. Her analysis of marketing trends of the future bodes very well, indeed, for MPR. She suggests that marketers "pursue the mass corporate brand in the 90's by exploiting the 'Maker's Mark.'"

She says that the 1990s will not see the introduction of many new high-risk brands because they are too expensive and receive too much resistance from the trade. Instead, smart marketers will concentrate on revitalizing the basics by "putting new wine in old bottles," that is, taking the old brand into new adjacent categories.

In 1989, two thirds of the packaged goods introduced to the marketplace were improved formulations, new sizes, or new packages for existing brands, according to Marketing Intelligence Service Ltd., a new products reporting firm. Among these products labeled "Sequels for the Shelf" by *Newsweek* were Life Savers Holes, Son of Snickers candy bars, and Arm & Hammer Super Carpet Deodorizer and Oven Cleaner.

Cutler contends that the "Maker's Mark" is the overarching identity for a portfolio of products that can hold them together while separating them from competition. The "Maker's Mark" will become increasingly important in the future, because "as brand choices expand beyond our ability to cope, consumers will seek out the company behind the brand to simplify decision making."

For that reason, the customer link or bond will increasingly extend from the current customer-to-brand bond to an added customer-to-company bond that offers long-term bonding, an equity with both a past heritage and presumably a long-term future. The "Maker's Mark" provides long-term commitment, adds value to existing brands offering an extra point of difference and reassurance, and creates credibility for new brands, providing familiarity to the unfamiliar.

Herb Baum, president of the North American Division of Campbell Soup Company and one of the country's leading marketers, agrees:

> People who respond to our research say that they automatically know that our products will taste good, that they're safe and that they can count on us because over the years Campbell has had such a strong quality image. What that means is that when a new product carries the Campbell name, consumers will try it because they know they won't be disappointed. Our brand image gives us a leg up on the competition. Consumers trust our brands. That doesn't mean we're not going to spend money marketing our products, but brand images stretch your marketing firepower.[8]

Cutler further contends that "the 'Maker's Mark' will bring to the corporate portfolio integrity, standards, an ethical contract with the consumer, the good character of the company, a filter for overwhelming product multiplicity, and what could be the critical difference in a sea of sameness." Her proof? "The recovery of Tylenol after two knockout punches because the company behind the brand behaved superbly and retained America's trust."

If Cutler, Baum, and other marketing authorities championing the customer-to-company bond are correct, MPR is strategically positioned to assume a role of far greater importance than ever before in marketing of the future. After all, the stock-in-trade of marketing public relations is to build bonds, links, and bridges between companies and consumers. Public relations holds that consumers like to do business with companies that they know and trust. MPR programs exist to "relate" companies and their products with consumers and their wants.

The new-product news of the future will build on new products under highly recognized, respected brand names. Companies will direct marketing efforts to repeating the success of Diet Coke, the brand of the decade. Marketing public relations is the made-to-order medium for maintaining brand franchises whether it is by providing information and service to the consumer, identifying the brand with causes that consumers care about, or sponsoring high-visibility events that excite consumers.

Credibility is the key, and MPR is uniquely able to add the dimension of credibility to companies and their products.

References

Acknowledgments

1. Ronald Alsop and Bill Abrams, *The Wall Street Journal on Marketing*. New York: Dow Jones–Irwin/New American Library, 1987.

Chapter 1

1. Alice Gautsch, "Conversation with a Marketer," *Food & Beverage Marketplace* (Spring 1989), p. 12.
2. Philip Kotler, "Public Relations versus Marketing: Dividing the Conceptual Domain and Operational Turf." Position paper prepared for the Public Relations Colloquium 1989, San Diego, January 24, 1989.
3. Robert Dilenschneider, "A Strategy for Integrated Marketing Communications." Speech to the International Association of Business Communicators, Chicago, October 3, 1988.
4. Tom Duncan, "A Study of How Manufacturers and Service Companies Perceive and Use Marketing Public Relations," December 1985.
5. Shandwick PLC, "The Public Relations Consultancy Market Worldwide" (Autumn 1989); study published by company.
6. Art Kleiner, "The Public Relations Coup," *ADWEEK's Marketing Week* (January 16, 1989).
7. Scott M. Cutlip, Allen H. Center, and Glen M. Broom, *Effective Public Relations*, 6th ed. (Englewood Cliffs, NJ: Prentice-Hall, 1985), p. 4.
8. James H. Dowling, "No Definition Needed," *PR Week* (November 14–20, 1988) p. 10.
9. Kotler. "Public Relations versus Marketing," *op. cit.*
10. Kotler, *ibid.*
11. Isadore Barmash, *Always Live Better Than Your Clients*. New York: Dodd, Mead & Co., 1983, pp. 80–82.
12. Chester Burger, "Credibility: When Public Relations Works," *The Quarterly Review of Public Relations* (Winter 1967) 7(1).

Chapter 2

1. "Faster—The 1980's: When Information Accelerated," editorial, *The New York Times* (December 31, 1989).
2. Robert Dilenschneider, "A Strategy for Integrated Marketing Communications." Speech to the International Association of Business Communicators, Chicago, October 3, 1988.
3. Steven H. Lesnik, untitled speech to 1989 Medill Corporate Associates Conference, Northwestern University, November 21, 1989.
4. Joanne Lipman, "Spending Forecast Augurs Ho-Hum 1990," *The Wall Street Journal* (December 12, 1989).

5. Scott Hume, "Most Consumers Ignore Contests, Adore Coupons," *Advertising Age* (September 11, 1989).
6. Randall Rothenberg, "An Iconoclast Takes a Look at the Future," *The New York Times* (August 1, 1989).
7. Joanne Lipman, "Television Ads Ring Up No Sale in Study," *The Wall Street Journal* (February 1, 1989).
8. John O'Toole, "Simplify Life, Reduce Expense—And Lose Market Share," *The Newsletter of the American Association of Advertising Agencies* (Fall 1989).
9. Lesnik, untitled speech, *op. cit.*
10. Robert Dilenschneider, "A Strategy for Integrated Marketing Communications," *op. cit.*
11. "Stalking the New Consumer," *Business Week* (August 28, 1989) p. 54.
12. Joanne Lipman, "Back to Basics: As Network TV Fades, Many Advertisers Try Age Old Promotions; They Switch to Direct Mail, Coupons and PR Ploys," *The Wall Street Journal* (August 26, 1986).
13. "Free plugs supply ad power," *Advertising Age* (January 29, 1990).

Chapter 3

1. Patrick Jackson, "Reconciling the Specific Sphere of Marketing with the Universal Need for Relationships." Position paper prepared for the Public Relations Colloquium 1989, San Diego, January 24, 1989.
2. Glen M. Broom, "An Essential Double Helix," *Public Relations Journal* (November, 1989) p. 40.
3. Robert Dilenschneider, "A Strategy for Integrated Marketing Communications." Speech to the International Association of Business Communicators, Chicago, October 3, 1988.
4. Philip Kotler, "Public Relations versus Marketing: Dividing the Conceptual Domain and Operational Turf." Position paper prepared for the Public Relations Colloquium 1989, San Diego, January 24, 1989.
5. Scott M. Cutlip, Allen H. Center, and Glen M. Broom, *Effective Public Relations*, 6th ed. Englewood Cliffs, NJ: Prentice-Hall, 1985, p. 89.
6. Philip Kotler and William Mindak, "Marketing and Public Relations," *Journal of Marketing* (October 1978).
7. Philip Kotler, "Megamarketing," *Harvard Business Review* (March–April 1986).

Chapter 4

1. Daniel J. Edelman, Noel Griffiths Lecture, Sydney, Australia, February 16, 1989.
2. Chester Burger, "Credibility: When Public Relations Works," *The Quarterly Review of Public Relations* (Winter 1967) 7(1).
3. David Ogilvy, *Ogilvy on Advertising.* New York: Crown Publishers, 1983, p. 90.
4. James Arnold, "A Failure to Communicate," *Relate* (March 27, 1989) p. 18.
5. Horace Schwerin and Henry Newell, *Persuasion in Marketing.* New York: John Wiley & Sons, 1981, p. 153.
6. Philip Kotler, *Marketing Management,* 6th ed. Englewood Cliffs, NJ: Prentice-Hall, 1988, p. 612.
7. The Council on Economic Priorities, *Shopping for a Better World: A Quick and Easy Guide to Socially Responsible Supermarket Shopping,* 1988.

Chapter 5

1. Daniel J. Edelman, Noel Griffiths Lecture, Sydney, Australia, February 16, 1989.
2. Roger Cohen, "What Publishers Will Do for a Place on the Right List," *The New York Times* (August 2, 1990).

Chapter 6

1. Don E. Schulz, Dennis Martin, and William P. Brown, *Strategic Advertising Campaigns.* Lincolnwood, IL: NTC Business Books, 1988, p. 12.
2. Scott M. Cutlip, Allen H. Center, and Glen M. Broom, *Effective Public Relations*, 6th ed. Englewood Cliffs, NJ: Prentice-Hall, 1985, p. 4.
3. Walter Lindenmann, "Beyond the Clipbook," *Public Relations Journal* (December 1988).

Chapter 7

1. Michael J. McCarthy, "New Pop Art Museum Promotes Coke," *The New York Times* (August 2, 1990).
2. "Talk About Placements . . . ," *Newsweek* (July 31, 1989) p. 50.
3. "Iacocca's Back as a Pitchman," *Chicago Tribune* (February 22, 1990).
4. John von Rhein, "The CSO in Flux," *Chicago Tribune* (September 25, 1988).

Chapter 8

1. Randall Rothenberg, "Commercials Become News and the Air Time is Free," *The New York Times* (January 8, 1990).
2. Scott Hume, "Free Association; More marketers seek out media exposure to enhance their traditional paid campaigns," *Advertising Age* (October 23, 1989).
3. Rothenberg, "Commercials Become News . . . ," *op. cit.*
4. Thomas R. King, "Berlin Wall Lands Leading Role in Three U.S. Television Spots," *The Wall Street Journal* (December 5, 1989).
5. Jeffrey K. McElnea, "Event Promotions that Impact Retail," *Marketing Communications* (November 1987).

Chapter 9

1. Davis Young, "We Are in the Business of Enhancing Trust," *Public Relations Journal* (January 1986).
2. John F. Love, *McDonald's: Behind the Arches.* New York: Bantam Books, 1986, p. 212.
3. Alvin Golin, "Community Relations." In Bill Cantor, *Experts in Action: Inside Public Relations.* New York: Longman, Inc., 1984, pp. 111–122.
4. Charles Rubner, "Allies in Megamarketing." Presentation to joint meeting of the American Marketing Association and Public Relations Society of America, Chicago, May 5, 1988.
5. "McDonald's Deserves Praise," editorial, *Philadelphia Inquirer* (July 28, 1984).
6. Kenneth Lightcap, "Marketing Support." In Bill Cantor, *Experts in Action: Inside Public Relations.* New York: Longman, Inc., 1984, chap. 8.

Chapter 10

1. Lee Iacocca with William Novak, *Iacocca: A Biography.* New York: Bantam Books, 1984, pp. 66–67. Reprinted with permission.

2. Iacocca, *ibid.* pp. 71–73.
3. James R. Healy, "New Escort's Debut Doesn't Match Hoopla," *USA TODAY* (April 2, 1987) p. 1.
4. "Into the Wild Blue Yonder," *TIME* (April 13, 1987).
5. Mark Lewyn and John Hillkirk, "IBM Drops a Bomb on Competitors," *USA TODAY* (April 2, 1987) p. 1.
6. Andrew Pollack, "The Return of a Computer Star," *The New York Times* (October 12, 1988).
7. "Gillette Nicks Critics with Sensor Sales," *USA TODAY* (August 12, 1990).
8. Stan Bratskier, "The Miracle of Perrier," unpublished article, 1980.
9. "Perrier Recalls Entire Inventory of Bottled Water from U.S. Market," *The New York Times* (February 10, 1990) p. 1.
10. Janet Key, "Rivals Flow In to Fill Perrier Gap," *Chicago Tribune* (February 13, 1990).
11. Dan Koeppel, "With Simplesse OK'd Can Nutrasweet Market Its Own Ice Cream?" *ADWEEK's Marketing Week* (February 26, 1990) p. 5.
12. Patricia Gallagher, "Cabbage Patch Is Blooming Again," *USA TODAY* (December 21, 1989) p. 6B.
13. Carol Lawson, "When Magic Meets Money: Show and Sell at Toy Fair," *The New York Times* (February 15, 1990) p. B1.
14. "Batmania," *Newsweek* (June 26, 1989).
15. "Boffo Box Office Boost to Biz," *Newsweek* (July 31, 1989) pp. 60–61.
16. Caryn James, "Batman, Champion of Truth, Justice and PR," *The New York Times* (November 19, 1989) p. H31.
17. "You're Under Arrest! Hollywood Goes Florida at Disney–MGM Park," *TIME* (May 8, 1989) p. 102.

Chapter 11

1. "Miracle Drug," *Business Week* (August 29, 1988).
2. Thomas L. Harris, "Marketing Communications." In Bill Cantor, *Experts in Action: Inside Public Relations,* 2d ed. New York: Longman, Inc., 1989, chapter 5.

Chapter 12

1. "All in a Day," reported by Rob Wilson. Canadian Broadcasting Company news coverage of McDonald's opening in Moscow, February 12, 1990.
2. "Kids Show It's a Small World at Big Bash for Mickey's 60th," Associated Press/*Chicago Tribune,* (November 19, 1988).
3. Thomas L. Harris, "Marketing Communications." In Bill Cantor, *Experts in Action: Inside Public Relations,* 2d ed. New York: Longman, Inc., 1989, chapter 5.

Chapter 13

1. Rinker Buck, "Editor's Note," *ADWEEK's Marketing Week* (January 29, 1990) p. 16.
2. "The Tylenol Comeback," Johnson & Johnson Special Report, undated, p. 8.
3. "Kraft Is Big Loser In Botched Contest," *O'Dwyer's PR Services Report* (August 1989) p. 6.
4. "Rogers—A Good Man in a Crisis," *PR Today* (October 23, 1989).

5. Hodding Carter, Jr., "Alar Scare: Case Study in Media's Skewed Reality," *The Wall Street Journal* (April 20, 1989).
6. Natalie Angier, "Heart Association Cancels Its Program to Rate Foods," *The New York Times* (April 3, 1990) p. 1.
7. "Environmentalism: The New Crusade," *FORTUNE* (February 12, 1990).

Chapter 14

1. Art Stevens, "Brandstanding: Long-Lived Production Promotion," *Harvard Business Review* (May–June 1981) pp. 54–58.
2. Steven Morris, "Corporate Sponsorship Becomes Life of the Party," *Chicago Tribune* (March 27, 1988).
3. Bud Frankel, "Event Marketing: Panacea or Problems?" *Marketing News* (December 5, 1988) p. 12.
4. Don E. Schultz, "Add Value to the Product and the Brand," *Marketing News* (October 23, 1989) p. 13.

Chapter 15

1. "Nothing Sells Like Sports," *Business Week* (August 30, 1987).
2. William Oscar Johnson, "Sports and Suds," *Sports Illustrated* (August 8, 1988).
3. "The Art of Moving Products at 200 MPH," NASCAR Inc., promotional flyer.
4. Nancy Medlin, "Finding the Hot Sports for Sponsorships," *ADWEEK* (June 17, 1986) p. 27.
5. Mark Robichaux, "This Is It: A Season of Football, Coming Down to One Game—and May the Best Finger Win," *The Wall Street Journal* (January 17, 1990) p. 1.
6. Matthew Grimm, "Nintendo and Its Groupies," *ADWEEK's Marketing Week* (March 12, 1990) p. 31.

Chapter 16

1. Herb Schmertz with William Novak, *Good-Bye to the Low Profile.* Boston: Little, Brown & Co., 1986, pp. 210–212. Reprinted with permission.
2. Schmertz, *ibid.,* p. 218.
3. "The Art of the Mix," *ADWEEK's Marketing Week* (September 18, 1989).
4. Jack Feuer, "Making the Most of Arts Sponsorships," *ADWEEK* (November 17, 1987).
5. David Finn, "Tie Public Relations to Public Good," *Marketing News* (September 12, 1988).
6. George Weissman, untitled speech to the first symposium, Mayor's Committee on the Arts and Business Committee for the Arts, Denver, September 1980.
7. "NBC Nightly News" with Tom Brokaw, reported by Tom Brokaw and Mike Jensen, 1989.
8. "Philip Morris Presents Gene Harris and the Philip Morris Superband 1989," program foreword.

Chapter 18

1. Louis V. Gerstner, Jr., "Value in Cause Related Marketing," *Financier* (May 1985).

2. Robert E. Hope, "Cause Related Marketing." Speech to the Public Affairs Council, Philadelphia, May 24, 1988.

Chapter 19

1. Irving Rein, Philip Kotler, and Martin Stoller, *High Visibility.* New York: Dodd, Mead & Co., 1987, p. 278.
2. "Business Celebrities," cover story, *Business Week* (June 23, 1986).
3. Jack Bernstein, "Donald's Trump Card," *Advertising Age* (March 7, 1988).
4. "Divorce Isn't His Only Worry." *Newsweek* (March 5, 1990) pp. 32–33.
5. Jennifer Laurence, "It's Hype, Hype Hooray for New Book by Trump," *Advertising Age* (August 6, 1990).
6. "Forbes Publicity Machine," *Newsweek* (August 28, 1989).

Chapter 20

1. Al Croft, "PR and the New Consumer," *Relate* (October 30, 1989).
2. "Fast Times on Avenida Madison," *Business Week* (June 6, 1988).
3. Anthony Ramirez, "Reynolds, After Protest, Cancels Cigarette Aimed at Black Smokers," *The New York Times* (January 20, 1990) pp. 1, 11.
4. "The Selling of Our Schools," *U.S. News & World Report* (November 6, 1989).
5. Ken Dychtwald, "Get Ready for the Post-Youth Consumer." In *ADWEEK'S Marketing Week* special report, "Marketing to the Year 2000," September 11, 1989.
6. Jeff Ostroff, "Reaching the 50+ Consumer," *ADWEEK's Marketing Week* (July 31, 1989).

Chapter 21

1. Harold Burson, "The Practice of Public Relations: Where It's Been, Where It's Going." Speech to the Counselors Academy of the Public Relations Society of America, April 5, 1989.
2. "Marketing Milestones of Four Decades," *Marketing News* (July 31, 1987).
3. Robert Dilenschneider, "Make-or-Break Decade," *Public Relations Journal* (January, 1990).
4. Randall Rothenberg, "Shandwick Promotes Smallness," *The New York Times* (May 31, 1989).
5. Thomas L. Harris, "The Advertising–Public Relations Partnership." Speech to the 1989 AAAA Public Relations Seminar, Ritz Carlton Hotel, Chicago, March 22, 1989.
6. "A Marriage of Inconvenience, Part 2," *Relate* (June 26, 1989) p. 24.
7. *Ibid.*
8. Herb Baum, interview in *Sense 91,* special publication of Lippincott & Margulies, Inc., 1989.

Bibliography

Barhdt, James D. *The Complete Book of Product Publicity*. New York: AMACOM, 1987.

Barmash, Isadore. *Always Live Better Than Your Clients*. New York: Dodd, Mead & Co., 1983.

Cantor, Bill. *Experts in Action: Inside Public Relations*, 2d ed. White Plains, NY: Longman, Inc., 1989.

Cappo, Joe. *Futurescope*. Chicago: Longman Financial Services Publishing, 1990.

Cutlip, Scott M., Allen H. Center, and Glen M. Broom. *Effective Public Relations*, 6th ed. Englewood Cliffs, NJ: Prentice-Hall, 1985.

Degen, Clara. *Communicators' Guide to Marketing*. White Plains, NY: Longman, Inc., 1987.

Dilenschneider, Robert L., and Dan J. Forrestal. *Public Relations Handbook*. Chicago: The Dartnell Corporation, 1987.

Dilenschneider, Robert L. *Power and Influence*. New York: Prentice-Hall Press, 1990.

Goldman, Jordan. *Public Relations in the Marketing Mix*. Lincolnwood, IL: NTC Business Books, 1984.

Iacocca, Lee, with William Novak. *Iacocca: An Autobiography*. New York: Bantam Books, 1984.

Kaatz, Ron. *Advertising & Marketing Checklists*. Lincolnwood, IL: NTC Business Books, 1989.

Kotler, Philip. *Marketing Management*, 6th ed. Englewood Cliffs, NJ: Prentice-Hall, 1988.

Love, John F. *McDonald's: Behind the Arches*. New York: Bantam Books, 1986.

Nager, Norman R., and Richard H. Truitt. *Strategic Public Relations Counseling*. White Plains, NY: Longman, Inc., 1987.

Naisbitt, John. *Megatrends*. New York: Warner Books, 1982.

Naisbitt, John, and Patricia Aberdene. *Megatrends 2000*. New York: William Morrow & Co., 1990.

Ogilvy, David. *Ogilvy on Advertising*. New York: Crown Publishers, 1983.

Rein, Irving, Philip Kotler, and Martin Stoller. *High Visibility*. New York: Dodd, Mead & Co., 1987.

Sauerhaft, Stan, and Chris Atkins. *Image Wars*. New York: John Wiley & Sons, 1989.

Schmertz, Herb, with William Novak. *Good-Bye to the Low Profile*. Boston: Little, Brown & Co., 1986.

Schultz, Don E., Dennis Martin, and William P. Brown. *Strategic Advertising Campaigns*. Lincolnwood, IL: NTC Business Books, 1988.

Schwerin, Horace S., and Henry H. Newell. *Persuasion in Marketing.* New York: John Wiley & Sons, 1981.

Seitel, Fraser P. *The Practice of Public Relations,* 4th ed. Columbus, OH: Merrill Publishing Co., 1989.

Stevens, Art. *The Persuasion Explosion.* Washington, DC: Acropolis Books, Ltd., 1985.

Weiner, Richard. *Webster's New World Dictionary of Media and Communications.* New York: Simon & Schuster, Inc., 1990.

Wood, Robert J. *Confessions of a PR Man.* New York: NAL Books, 1988.

Index